AMOROUS
FIAMMETTA

AMOROUS FIAMMETTA

BY

GIOVANNI BOCCACCIO

AUTHOR OF "THE DECAMERON"

REVISED FROM THE ONLY ENGLISH TRANSLATION
WITH AN INTRODUCTION

BY

EDWARD HUTTON

WILDSIDE PRESS

CONTENTS

THE FIRST BOOK

THE SECOND BOOK

CONTENTS

THE SECOND BOOK—*continued*

THE THIRD BOOK

CONTENTS

THE FOURTH BOOK

CONTENTS

THE FOURTH BOOK—*continued*

THE FIFTH BOOK

CONTENTS

THE FIFTH BOOK—*continued*

e

CONTENTS

THE SIXTH BOOK

THE SEVENTH BOOK

CONTENTS

THE SEVENTH BOOK—*continued*

The end of the Table

Il fait bon fin qui meurt pour bien aymer

Il decimo l'Anno terzo d'Aprile 1587

THE
FIRST BOOK OF BOCCACE
HIS FIAMMETTA

IN the time when the revested earth doth show itself more pleasant and fair than in any other season of the year : born of most noble parents, and received here of bountiful and favourable Fortune, I came into this World.

Accursed be that day, and hated of me more than any other, in the which I first enjoyed this common light. How happy had I been (alas) if I *The men born that were sown of Cadmus' teeth lived but a day* had never been born, or if I had at the time of my unfortunate birth been carried to my grave, or had not breathed any longer time than the teeth sown of Cadmus : or else, if Lachesis, at one and selfsame hour, had begun and cut in two her vital thread : because then, in that small time of life, these infinite woes, which are now a sorrowful occasion to put my pen to Paper, should with the same have been concluded. But what doth it now avail for these causes to lament : for here I am nevertheless by the general decrees and pleasures of the Gods.

Being received then (as I have said) in most high delights, and nourished only amongst them,

and in my young and tender years brought up
under a reverend and sage Matron, I early learned
every good quality, which was most convenient and
commendable for any young and noble Woman.
And as my personage did with passed years increase,
so were my beauties also multiplied, which were the
only and especial occasions of all my sorrows and
infinite griefs. Alas (although I was yet but a little
one) how greatly did I glory with myself, in hearing
my commendations in everyone's mouth, and did
therefore with art and industry daily study to make
them more perfect and curious.

But arrived now from my childhood, to a more
full and riper age, and conceiving, by the instincts
Beauty of nature, with what burning desires
hurtful to amorous young Gentlewomen may en-
her that
hath it tice young and wanton youths, I perceived
that my surpassing beauty (a miserable gift to her
who loves to lead a virtuous life) did not only incend
most of all those young Gentlemen, who lived at
the time in flourishing youth like myself, but many
other noblemen, with a fervent and amorous fire :
who infinite times with divers drifts, many means,
and sundry flights (unknown to me as then), did
attempt to kindle me with that fire wherewith they
themselves did burn, and that it should not then
only scorch me, but in process of time, in long and
lingering flames, utterly consume me. And of many
with earnest suit, as well to my Parents, as especially

2

to me, I was requested in marriage. But after that one among all the rest (a most absolute (in my opinion) and perfect Gentleman) had won that prize, for which they strived all, the importunous and troublesome rout of wooers (being now past all hope) did cease to solicit me any more with their cunning and daily pursuits. Wherefore remaining in just content with my loving Husband, I lived a most happy and joyful Woman, until furious Love with a secret kind of unknown fire, and never felt of me before, entered into my tender and young breast. Alas there was not anything, that might satisfy either my desire, or any Woman's else, which presently I had not for my pleasure and contentation. I was the only joy and singular felicity of my young Husband, and as he was truly beloved of me, so did he equally and greatly love me again.

O how happy might I have thought myself above all other Women, if this new love had for ever continued inviolated in my heart? Living therefore in great happiness, and spending my youthful years in daily sports, and joyful feasts, false Fortune, the sudden changer of worldly things, and most envious of the selfsame goods that she had erst bestowed on me, purposing now to withdraw her hand, and not knowing by what means to spit forth her venom, with subtle and Sophistical arguments made an adverse way (leading to the Dungeon of sorrow) open to mine eyes. And truly by no other means,

3

but by those by which fond Love entered into my
heart she could entrap me, or use her force at all,
but the Gods favourable to me, and careful of my
affairs, perceiving her covert and malicious guiles, did
intend to arm my yielding heart and feeble breast
with weapons, if I had been so wise to have taken
and used them for my defence, because I might come
forewarned and not unarmed to the battle in the which
I should inevitably have fallen. Wherefore with a
manifest vision in my dreams, the very night before
the day (that dismal day I say) did come, which was
the sorrowful beginning of my endless pains, and
loss of liberty, they did clearly admonish me of
future accidents in this sort.

Methought lying in a fair broad bed, with every
part of my body resolved into deep sleep, I saw the
Dreams fairest and brightest day that might be,
sometimes and myself (I know not how) more jocant
foretell
things to and merry than ever I had been before.
come And joying all alone in this kind of mirth,
I did imagine that I sat in a sweet Meadow, upon the
green grass, and amongst many golden and pleasant
flowers, defended from the heat of the Sun, and
from his parching beams, with many cool shadows
of divers Trees, newly apparelled with thick and
green leaves. And having gathered many flowers in
the same, wherewith all that place was most bravely
depainted, with my little white hands I did separate
one from another as they lay confused and mingled

4

in my lap, and with the finest that I could pick out I
made a fair and little Garland, wherewith I did adorn
my stately head. Beautified thus, and rising up (as
Proserpina did, when Pluto did ravish her from her
mother), I went singing up and down in this pleasant
and trim Meadow, rejoicing at the entrance of merry
Springtide. And afterwards, feeling myself somewhat weary, I laid me down amongst the thickest
and freshest grass to rest myself a little. But like as
that little hidden Viper did prick Euridice's tender
foot, even so a lurking and creeping Serpent did
likewise appear to my sight, as I lay along upon
the soft and thick grass, the which (methought) did
with her cruel tongue sting me under the left pap,
which venomous biting, at the first entrance of her
sharp teeth, did seem to burn me like a scalding and
fiery flame. And then being almost assured, and past
fear of the worst, methought I put the cold Serpent
into my burning bosom, imagining that, with the
benefit of her cold skin, she should a little ease me,
and be more favourable unto me for this gentle deed.
But emboldened rather by the same, and now become
more fierce than before, to the foresaid sting she
rejoined her cruel mouth, and having after a good
while sucked a great quantity of my vital blood, methought, that merely going out from my wounded
bosom (though I did strive to the contrary), she
went also away with my fainting soul. At the departing of which, the golden day obscured, and (like

a shadow driven by the Sun coming behind me) did cover me all over, after which followed a foggy and misty darkness, accompanied with multitudes of black and thick clouds, which, hanging upon it, did seem to be drawn after, and like a confused and deformed Chaos to follow. And not long after (as a little white stone cast into a deep and clear water, doth by little and little vanish away from the sight of them that do behold it), even so was the brightness of this Sunshine day taken away from my dimmed sight. Then might I perceive the Heavens to be overcome with darkness, and the gladsome Sun retired back, and obscure night approaching, made me call to mind, that this sudden alteration was not unlike unto that which happened to the Grecians,

Atreus his fault was, that he made the Father, which was his brother, to eat his own Son, whereupon the Sun retired back again, because it would not see so wicked a mess and table when the Sun did hide his face, because he would not for shame behold the enormity of Atreus his foul fault. The fearful lightnings piecemeal glanced up and down in the air, and cracking thunders made the earth, but me most of all, afraid. And the wound, which until this time had but only stung me (methought) by reason of the late biting, remaining now full of viperous venom, overran and occupied all my body with most filthy and loathsome swellings, no secrets of physic being able to cure the same. Whereupon feeling myself at the first without any spirit, and afterwards the force of the

6

poison by more subtle entrances searching every **vein** of my heart, I tumbled and tossed myself up and down the green grass, expecting always when death would assail me. And now the final hour (to my thinking) being come, terrified also with the horror of the time, and with the extreme grief of my infected heart, attending the mortal stroke of death, made me to think and start on a sudden in such sort that it caused my deadly sleeping body to shake again, and so break me out of that horrible and ghastly dream.

After the which (as it was very sudden), and not a little afraid also of those things which (methought) I had seen, with my right hand I made great speed to my bitten left side, seeking that presently there, which was afterwards prepared for me in time to come. But yet when I found no wound, nor any sign thereof, passing merry again, and careless, I began to deride, and laugh at the foolishness of dreams, and so accounted the labour of the Gods herein but vain. But wretch that I am, how justly (though then I scorned them) have I afterwards to my great grief of mind believed, and found them most true, and planted them without any fruit, being no less grieved at the Gods, who declare their secrets to uncapable minds with so great obscurity, the which no sooner showed, but incontinently they happen. Being therefore thoroughly awaked, I lifted up my head, and by a little crevice in the door did see Titan forsake Aurora's Chamber, and enter into

mine. Wherefore casting all such fond conceits aside,
I rose up.

That was a high and festival day almost to all
the world, in the which everyone, to honour the solemnity of it, attired themselves with their best and
bravest robes : wherefore, apparelling myself most
curiously with garments woven with shining Gold, and
with cunning and skilful hand setting everything in
every part about me in the finest order, and adorned
like to the fairest of those three Goddesses which
Paris saw in the Valleys of Ida, I prepared myself to
go to this solemn and high feast. And while I was
beholding myself on every side, not otherwise than
the Peacock doth her gay Feathers, and imagining
as well to please others, as myself, one of my flowers
(broken from my crown by the Curtain of the bed,
or else perhaps plucked from my head by some
celestial and invisible hand) fell from my head to
the ground. But I taking no regard of the secret
operations of the Gods, and esteeming it as nothing,
took it up, and put it in his former place again, and
so passed it slightly over.

Alas what more manifest sign could the Gods give
me of that, which afterwards did happen, than this.
Truly none at all. This had been sufficient enough
to declare unto me, that my soul, that day so free,
and mistress of itself, laying down her sweet signory,
should be made servile and bond, as it happened indeed. Oh, if my mind had been sound, how had I not

8

then foreknown the day (that blackest day), that afterwards happened unto me, and had safely over-passed it without going once out of my doors. But the Gods although they lend them (with whom they are angry) certain signs and tokens of their welfare, yet do they nevertheless deprive them of the due knowledge of the same. And so in one hour seem to do their willing devoyre, and to fulfil their wrathful minds. My hard destinies therefore did (as it were) drive me on forwards like a vain and careless Woman, and being accompanied with many Gentlewomen, that served on my train, with a soft and stately pace, I went to the holy Temple, in which the solemn and divine office, due for that day, was celebrated. The antiquity of my generous predecessors, and my nobility also, had reserved a high place for me, amongst other most excellent and worthy Ladies there, in the which, after that I was set, observing my old custom, which was in suddenly casting mine eyes round about, I saw the Church equally full of Men and Women, in divers companies, diversely to employ themselves. But no sooner was I espied in the Temple, though in the midst of sacred service time, but (as it was a common thing many times before so then did it also fall out) that not Men only, but every woman did turn their eyes towards me, to behold me : and wondering at me, as if Venus or Minerva (never seen of them before) had been verily come down from Heaven amongst them.

THE FIRST BOOK

Oh, how many times did I smile with myself, feeling such content to tickle me, and glorying in myself no less than a Goddess, being not a little proud of all these most happy favours. All the company therefore of young Gentlemen, leaving off (at sight of me) to gaze upon other Gentlewomen (of which there was no small number of rare and passing *A fine* beauty), and placing themselves about *description of a trim* me, did in manner of a Crown compass *woman* me round about. And everyone, after his own fancy, speaking and diversely discoursing of my beauty, but all concurring and concluding in one sentence, did highly extol and commend it. But I, who with mine eyes turned another way made a semblance to busy my mind in devotions, but giving attentive care to their talk, did conceive and feel in myself a certain kind of desired pleasure and content. Wherefore thinking, and showing myself greatly beholding unto them, with a gracious eye and pleasant regard, I did sometimes requite them again. Whereupon I might many times perceive, that many of them, fondly conceiving and gathering a little vain hope thereof, did greatly glory, and foolishly rejoice with their companions for the same supposed favours.

Whilst I remained thus, looking but a little on a few, and beheld greatly of many, and thinking that my beauty should captivate others, it chanced that another's most unfortunately entrapped me. And

10

being now near to that dolorous passage, which of most certain death, or else of such a kind of life, that should be full of anguish and sorrow, might have been a sorrowful and sinister occasion, I knew not with what spirit moved, but with a seemly grace lifting up mine eyes, with an earnest and sharp view I sped their beams amidst the multitude of young Gentlemen, that did environ me round about. And *Fiametta is* beyond them all I espied a proper young *enamoured* Gentleman, leaning upon a Marble pillar, *in the* *Temple* as directly object to my sight as might be. And instigated by my pursuing destinies, I began to mark his personage, and his behaviour, which of any other before, I had never to do so much. I say therefore, that (according to my slender judgment, which was not yet very ripe about love matters) in his countenance he was passing fair and amiable, in his actions sweet and pleasant, and in his attire decent and comely. And the little golden and crisped wool which began to appear on his lovely cheeks did give a manifest sign of his young and flourishing age. Who being no less pitiful (as it seemed) than wise, omitted not, between Man and Man, to requite me with loving looks again. And though I had sometimes the power to withdraw mine eyes a little while from beholding him, yet no accident whatsoever, no, not myself (though striving to the contrary) could make me leave off to traverse many strange and uncouth thoughts in my mind. And so lively was his very

11

counterfeit, and sweet Idea imprinted in my heart, that with what secret delight I did contemplate the same, I am not able to express. And with many arguments did affirm with myself all these things, which did appear in him, to be most true. Wherefore being most contented in mind, and wishing that he would eye me again, I cast sometimes a glance aside, to mark if he did look upon me.

But amongst many other times that I beheld him (unable to defend myself from the secret snares of love), fixing mine eyes at one time somewhat longer upon his than I was wont to do, and the piercing beams of his fair eyes encountering with mine, methought that with a pitiful and sweet countenance he seemed to speak these words: "O Lady, thou art mine only joy and singular felicity." Truly if I should say, that these words did not work an extraordinary delight in me, I should flatly lie: the supposition of which did so highly please me, that from the centre of my heart they drew forth a sweet and profound sigh, which came accompanied with these words: "And thou art mine." But that remembering myself, I took them from my mouth. But what did it avail? That which was not expressed and uttered forth, my heart did conceive and imagine with itself, retaining that in it, which if it had gone forth, perhaps I should have yet been free. Then from that time forward, making my foolish eyes the whole arbiters of that, the good whereof they were so greedy to enjoy, I did (methought) in so doing greatly content and please them. And certes if the Gods, who deduct all things to some known and certain end, had not taken away my understanding, and bereaved me of my due knowledge, I might have still been mine own woman. But all such considerations laid aside, I followed my sensual appetite, and quickly persuaded myself to yield to love. Because no otherwise than the elementary coruscations shooting themselves from one part of the air to another, a shining light issuing from out his clear eyes, and running by a most subtle and fine beam, did meet and hit directly against mine, which contending to pass farther, by what secret ways (I know not) suddenly went penetrating to my very heart, which fearing their violent entrance, and calling to it all her exterior forces, left me altogether pale and cold. But their abode was not so long there, but the greatest fear was past, and then were they welcomed with a hot and burning passion : whereupon the foresaid forces returning to their places again, brought with them a certain heat, which driving all paleness quite away, painted my face like the vermilion Rose, and made me burn as hot as fire. And yet, beholding from whence all this did proceed, I could not but breathe out a sorrowful sigh. And from that hour forward, my thoughts were occupied in nothing else, but meditating of his brave

13

personage, and apparent virtues, and especially in imagining how to please him.

In all these intercourses, without changing of place or countenance, he did most privily steal now and then a look at me again. And peradventure as one who had been a tried Soldier in other amorous battles, and knowing with what Engines his wished prey might best be taken, with arguments of greater humility, continually he showed himself more pitiful, and full of amorous desires. Alas how much deceit was hidden under the veil of that pity, which (according as the present effects do testify) being now mortified in his heart, where it never remained again), bear only but an outward show and visard of love. And because I may prosecute every thing and action in particular, whereof there was not any which was not fraught with rare fraud and cunning guile, whether it was he that voluntarily did work it, or my unlucky stars that would have it so, thus it fell out, that (wanting the due skill exactly to show you how) I found myself entangled with sudden and unlooked for love, as at this present I am not free from the same.

This therefore was he (most pitiful Ladies) whom my conquered heart with a foolish conceit, amongst *Naples* so many noble, beautiful and valiant young Gentlemen, that were not only there present, but also in all my Parthenope, did choose to be the first, the only, and last Lord, and master of my

14

life. This was he whom I loved, and do love still more than anyone in all the world besides. This was he who was the beginning and principal occasion of all my woes, and shall be (as I hope) the final cause of my tragical death at last. This was that day in the which, first of a most free and happy Lady, I became a most miserable and unhappy captive. This was that day, in the which I did first apprehend the miserable effects of foolish love, never known of me before. This was that day, wherein venereous venoms contaminated first my pure and chaste beauty. Alas, poor wretch, how many sorrows, and what misery came this day into the world to thee, by thine own default. How far (alas) should annoy and grief have been from me, if this day had been turned into darkness : and how great an enemy was this day to my unstained honour.

But evil things (alas) which are committed and past may be easier reprehended than amended. I was therefore taken (as I have said), and *All things which are done, may be sooner controlled than remedied* whether it was some infernal fury, or envious fortune, which did so emulate my chaste felicity, laying snares to entrap me, may this day with hope of infallible victory triumph and rejoice in my miserable fall. Being therefore possessed, nay rather oppressed with new kinds of passions, as one astonied and like a defenceless Woman I sat amongst the other Ladies and Gentlewomen. And troubled thus in mind, I

15

did neglect the sacred and divine service, which as
I did scarcely hear, so did I not understand it at all :
and thought the sundry speeches and discourses of
Gentlewomen, that sat round about me, but a kind
of buzzing and murmuring in my troubled ears. And
so this new and unexpected love did take sudden
possession of my tender heart, so that either with
mine eyes or with my thoughts I was ever contem-
plating on my beloved young Gentleman. And yet
my simplicity was such, that I did not almost then
know what end I might wish or desire of such a
strange and fervent passion. How many times
(alas) coveting to have seen him approach near
unto me, did I blame his staying behind all the rest
of the Gentlemen, thinking with myself that that
was but a cold kind of affection in him, which he
did perhaps craftily use, and for a policy, to make me
more desirous to look on him, and in looking to love
him more.

And moreover, the company of lusty youths,
that stood before him, did greatly hinder my sight,
of whom, whilst that I busied mine eyes in looking
sometimes amongst them, there were not a few that
(thinking, that for their sakes I looked so much towards them) did vainly perhaps believe that I did it
for love of them. But while my thoughts and senses
were occupied in these fancies, the solemn service
was finished : and the Ladies and the rest of my companions were risen up to depart, when I, recalling

16

my wits together, which went wandering about the sweet imagination and figure of their only object, at the last I beheld my lovely young Gentleman again. And now myself risen up with the other Gentlewomen ready to be gone, and turning mine eyes towards him, I perceived that by his pitiful looks (which I had thought to have prevented by mine) that his departure, and mine did greatly grieve him. But notwithstanding, after certain secret sighs, and yet ignorant of what parentage, estate and condition he was, I went away.

Alas (gentle Ladies) who would believe it possible that one's heart in a moment and point of time should alter and change so much? Who would say that a man never seen before might be so extremely loved at the first sight? And who would think that the desire of seeing should be so fervently kindled in one's breast, as the very sight itself, and being deprived of that, to feel the greatest pain in the world, for desire to see the same thing again? Who would imagine that all those things that have been so joyful and delightful to us before, in respect of a new thing come *How love is* in place, should not yield any more pleasure *engendered* at all? Not anyone truly, unless he had *in divers* proved and felt them, as I do now. Alas *parts* *of the body* that love is not only content to use such *successively* a strange, and too severe kind of cruelty towards me, but in subduing me to his might, to prescribe new Laws, clean variant from others. I have

B   17 oftentimes heard that love in others at his first entrance is but light, but by nourished thoughts augmenting his force is made greater. But so it fared with me : for he entered into my heart with that same force, wherewith he continued ever afterwards, as one who at the very first assault had most entire and free possession of me. And like as the green wood, which is hardly at the first set on fire, and doth lie a long time before it receiveth flames, but after it is once kindled, with greater heat doth conserve the fire longer, even so it happened unto me, who with this kind of pleasing passion, never overcome of any before (though attempted of many) and at the last conquered of one, have burned and kept (as yet I do more sensibly) these new flames, that have taken more hold of me, than ever they did of any other, who before have assayed the like. But leaving aside many thoughts, which with divers accidents that morning turmoiled my troubled mind, and besides these, which now I have told, I say, that being incended with a new fury, with my captivated and bond soul I returned again thither, from whence (not long since) I had brought it free.

Where afterwards, that I was now come into my Chamber all alone, kindled with variety of burning desires surcharged with new thoughts, and pricked with a thousand stinging cares, terminating every end of them in the imagined apprehension of my young Gentleman, I thought, that if I could not

wean myself from this new love, at the least, in my
secret and sorrowful breast, wisely to have nourished
and governed the same, and warily to have brought it
to some good effect. Which things, how difficult they
are to perform, none can tell unless they prove them,
undoubtedly believing, that they do no less harm than
love itself. Wherefore, confirmed as it were in this
opinion, I said thus to myself: "Alas thou art in love,
poor soul, and yet thou dost not know with whom."

What kinds of cruel thoughts, and how many
careful cogitations were engendered of this love, it
should be too tedious for you dainty Ladies to hear,
and too grievous for me to tell. But yet (though
forcing myself thereunto) to obtain the more pity
at your hands, and some comfort thereby, I mean
to unfold some of them unto you. I say therefore,
that careless of all other things, to spend the time in
thinking of my beloved and amiable young Gentleman, was only most dear and pleasant unto me. And
imagining with myself, that persevering in this, that
which I did intend to conceal might perhaps have
easily been presumed, I oftentimes found fault with
myself for it. But what did it help ? My own reprehensions gave place to my desires, and like words of
light worth passed away with the air. I chiefly desired, many days together, to know what my beloved
youth was, to the understanding of which thing,
new thoughts made me an open way, by means of
which most warily and privily I knew it, and whereof

I remained not a little contented. By goodly ornaments likewise, which (as one that little need them)
were not before this time so much in request with
me, began now to be greatly liked of me, thinking
that being adorned with them, I might please the
more. Wherefore I esteemed now more of gorgeous
apparel, gold, pearls, and other precious stones, and
gems, than ever I did before. And I, who until this
time had frequented the holy Temples, Feasts, Sea
banks, and pleasant Gardens, without any further
intent or desire than to keep other Gentlewomen
and Ladies company, began (altered now in mind)
for new purposes to resort more often to the foresaid
places, thinking, that there I might with pleasure
not only behold, but with delight and desire be seen
again But the great affiance (truly) which I was
wont to have in my beauty forsook me now quite,
wherefore I never went out of my Chamber without the infallible counsel of my trusty Glass. And
my cunning hands (I know not by what curious
instructor newly taught) finding every day more
brave and rare ornaments, conjoining artificial with
natural beauty, did make me (like Venus star) shine
amongst other Ladies. The great honours moreover,
courtesies, and obeisance, which other Ladies and
Gentlewomen of their mere good wills and duties did
unto me, although indeed they were incident to my
nobility, I now began to accept and expect as services
duly and worthily belonging to my high estate,

thinking that I should please my lover most of all, when by these means he did perceive, that I was of noble birth and lineage. And that common covetousness, which is naturally born and engrafted in all Women, did work in me (eschewing the same) no other effects, than to esteem all my riches, land and treasure, as if they had not been mine own : whereby I became not only liberal, but feeling also a certain seemly boldness to increase in me, made me devoid of all womanly and suspicious fear, accounting but one thing only dearer to me now than before. And besides all this, my eyes, which until this time had been but simple, and unexpert in amorous regards, changed their former fashions, and grew marvellous skilful in performing their parts. And I discovered moreover in me divers other mutations, all which, by one and one, I care not to set down, because, first, it would be too long a labour, and secondly, because I believe that you (fair Ladies), enamoured perhaps like myself, are not ignorant how great and many those are, which accompany lovers in like causes.

The young Gentleman was most wary and wise, as many times by experience I was sufficiently thereof ascertained. He came but seldom times, and that in most honest and seemly sort, where I was, and having (as it seemed) purposed the selfsame thing that I had done, which was to conceal altogether these amorous flames, did yet, with many privy and stealing looks, not a few times pitifully behold me. He did therefore make those kindled flames in me more fervent and lively, and revived those again (if any they were) that were spent and quite consumed in me. But the beginning of all this love was not so joyful and happy, but the sequel and end of it was more sorrowful and unfortunate, at what time I remained deprived of his sight, because these eyes being denied their wished joy did minister a grievous occasion to my poor heart of grief, whereupon my sighs both in quantity and quality were greatly augmented. And hot desire, occupying *Divers acci-* almost every least sense of mine, did make *dents of love,* me live as one besides myself, as if I had *especially in a weak* not been there where I was, made many *mind* that saw me to wonder oftentimes at me, attributing afterwards infinite and feigned occasions (taught me only of love) to such strange and uncouth accidents. And besides all this, taking from me many times my sweet rest in the night-time, and appetite in the day, did drive me sometimes to certain sudden and furious kinds of actions, and transported my tongue into strange and fond speeches. Behold how my unaccustomed gorgeous apparel, my prodigal attire, my scalding and new sighs, my unwonted gesture, frantic fits, the loss of my rest, quietness and health, and many other things, which this new love brought with it, amongst many other Servants and familiars in my house, made a Nurse of mine especially to marvel much,

22

who as she was burdened with many years, so in ripe wisdom and good experience she was not young at all. And who having sometimes known and tried the heat of Cupid's flames, and making semblance to the contrary, did oftentimes reprehend me, and my suspected follies. But finding me on a day laid upon my bed, and oppressed with deep melancholy and sadness, and perceiving by my face that I was overcharged with burdens of heavy thoughts, and seeing no company with me but herself, began thus to say unto me:

"O Daughter, dearer to me than mine own heart strings, what cares do molest thee thus of late? Now *The Nurse* thou spendest not one hour (whom some- *her speech to* times I was wont to see merry and free *Fiammetta* from all pensiveness) without infinite cares, and burning sighs."

Then after a great sigh, and often changing of my colour, turning me now this way, now that way, my tongue being scarce able to form and fashion one word aright, I answered her again:

"O dear Nurse, no new thing doth annoy me, neither do I feel any more grief than I was wont to do, these natural courses only excepted, and influences, which, never keeping us in one stay and estate of life, make me at this present (more than they were wont) both painful and pensive."

"Thou verily dost deceive me, Daughter" (answered the old Nurse again), "nor dost conceive how great a matter it is, to make temperate and

23

advised persons believe one thing in words, and to show the contrary by demonstration. Thou needest not to keep that hidden from me, which many days since I did know to be in thee."

Alas when I heard her say so, surprised with great marvel and grief, knowing myself to be touched to the quick, with an angry countenance I said to her:

"Then if thou dost know, why dost thou ask? Wherefore I request no more at thy hands, but to conceal and keep that close which thou knowest."

"I will not, believe me," (said she again) "disclose that which is neither lawful nor reasonable to acquaint others withal, earnestly beseeching the Gods, that before I manifest (during the well-nigh finished course of my poor life) anything which (much or little) may turn to thy shame, or that may in any one jot prejudicate thy honour, honesty and virtuous name, the earth may open and swallow me alive. It is a good while since, my Daughter, that I learned to keep secrecy in matters (perhaps) of as great importance as this. And therefore live secure of this, admonishing thee to take diligent heed, and to be very careful, lest others know that by thy indirect dealings, and unadvised practices, which without report either of thyself, or of any other but thy outward countenance only, and mere behaviour, I have perceived. But if this kind of mad folly, into which (I know thou art rashly fallen) were beseeming a Woman of thy estate, if thou wert as wise now,

24

as of late thou wert, I would leave it to thine own
consideration, being certain that my counsel herein
should take no place, as a thing needless. But because this cruel Tyrant (to whom like a young and
ignorant Woman, not taking any heed of him, and
of his poisoned baits, thou hast simply subjected thyself) hath, together with thy sweet liberty, bereaved
thee also of thy sound understanding, I think it not
amiss to put thee friendly in remembrance, and
humbly to entreat thee, that from thy impotent and
chaste breast thou wouldst banish all wicked things,
and naughty thoughts, and by oblivion consume
these unhonest flames, and not to suffer thyself become a handmaid and bondslave to most filthy hope.
And now it is time to resist with force and courage,

He that re-
sisteth love because whosoever doth stoutly resist, and
in the begin- oppose himself in the beginning, he may
ning doth easily drive out this villainous and envious
overcome it love, and like a worthy and wise Con-
in the end queror may safely triumph over him. But
whosoever with continued thoughts and flattering
imaginations doth continue and maintain it, may
hardly, and too late, cast off his yoke, into the which
voluntarily he did put his neck."

"Alas," (said I then) "how easy is it to talk of
those things, and how difficult a matter to remedy
them."

"Although " (said she again) "that they are very
hard to be done, yet are they possible enough to be

25

reformed, and ought to be performed. Thou seest, or (at the least if thou wilt) mayst see, that in following thine own fancies, thou hast (as it were) a certain kind of desire to ruinate the highness of thy birth, to obscure the great and shining fame of thy manifold virtues, to lose the flower of thy beauty, to blemish thy honour in this present world, and to discredit all those other good parts in thee besides, which ought of all Women to be kept holy and unstained, and especially of such as thou art, whose virtues (as in nobility thou art above the rest) should also shine above the rest. And besides all this, to hazard the loss of the gracious favour of thy noble Husband, whom thou hast so long (and yet dost) loved so well, and who entirely loveth thee again. Thou shouldest not truly have so much as a thought of idle love, neither do I think (if like a wise Woman thou dost but take sound counsel of thyself) that thou wilt, nor canst busy thy wits about it. But these old breasts of mine with many years worn out (of the which thou didst first suck out thy nourishing milk and living sustenance) even by these, most humbly I pray thee, that thou wouldst in these timorous occurrents succour thyself, and be careful both for thy health and honour, and in these thy perplexities not to reject my weak and willing comforts. And think moreover that an earnest will and desire to be made whole again is not the smallest part, and no little help to recover thy former health."

Then I began thus to reply : " O dear Nurse, well do I know that these things which thou tellest me are most true, but frantic fury compelleth me to follow that which is my bane, and my guilty mind, over-rash in her desires, attempts in vain to put thy counsel in practice, because that which reason willeth me to do is overcome by unruly will, which most mightily doth dominate in me. Love with his deity doth possess my heart, and there, with his mighty signory overruleth my subject mind. And how hard a matter it is for a feeble woman to resist his forces (ah, Nurse) thou knowest well enough."

A will to be healed is part of health in anyone that is sick

And having so said, overcome by the force of my grievous passion, and fainting, I fell between her arms. But she, troubled in mind more than before, with an austere countenance, and sharper speeches, began to discipline me thus : " You wilful company of amorous and wanton young Gentlewomen, kindled with burning desires, and fiery lust, which spurring you forwards to impious idolatry, have fondly found out Love to be a God, who more justly deserveth the title and name of frantic fury, and call him the Son of Venus, saying that he deriveth his omnipotent power from the third Heaven, as though you would excuse your follies with a needless kind of necessity. O deceived souls, and utterly devoid of all reason, and most ignorant of that which you say. Sent from the infernal furies, with a sudden and swift flight he

27

visiteth all the world, bringing to him that doth entertain him, not deity but despair, not friendly

Wanton felicity, but fiendly folly, alighting on those
love re- whom he doth know to abound in super-
proved fluity of worldly goods, and to enjoy them with a vain and prodigal mind, and on him whom he thinketh fittest and most forward to make him place. And this is here most manifest by thee. Why, do we not see holy Venus to dwell often-times in little cottages, both profitable and necessary for our procreation? Yes, truly. But this, who by frenzy is called Love, coveting ever dissolute things, lodgeth in no other place but where happy Fortune doth smile, and where her gifts abound. This dainty one, disdaining no less sufficient food to satisfy nature, than necessary clothing, doth frame all his persuasions to delicate fare, and sumptuous attire, and so intermingling his secret and sweet poison with them, doth deceive and destroy unwary and ignorant souls. This, more willingly and often seen in high and princely Palaces, is seldom or never seen in poor and Country cottages. Because it is a certain precise pestilence, which doth choose out only brave and stately lodgings, as most agreeable in the end to his wicked practices. We see in poor and simple people, effects of good and quiet consequence, but in the rich, wallowing in pleasure, and shining in their abundance of gold (insatiable as well in this as in all things else) that he is (more than is requisite) for

the most part found : and that which he cannot do (who can do most) he doth desire, and especially endeavour to bring to pass. Among whom I perceive thee (most unhappy and unfortunate Mistress) to be one, who by too much wealth, ease and idle pleasure hast entered into these new and unbeseeming cares."

Whom, after I had a good while heard, I answered thus again : "Hold thy peace, thou old and foolish dotard, and prate not thus against my God. Thou speakest voluntarily against him, thyself being no less impotent for these effects, than justly cast of all men, blaspheming him now, whom in time of thy younger years thou diddest religiously adore. If other Ladies, more noble, wiser and more famous than myself, have heretofore thus entitled him, and cease not yet to call him by the name of a mighty God, how can I then alone give him any new or devised name ? To be plain with thee, I am become his Subject, but from whence the occasion of this allegiance doth spring, I neither know nor can tell thee. And what can I do more ? My feminine forces, conjoined oftentimes with his celestial power, are overcome, and constrained to retire back again. Wherefore there resteth no more for the end of my new and mortal pains but my near death, or else the enjoying of my wished love, which woes I pray thee to mitigate (if thou art so wise as I esteem thee) by thy sage counsel and speedy help, which will perhaps lessen them at the least, or else by thy bitter reprehensions surcease to exasperate and make them greater, blaming that in me which my soul (not able to do otherwise) with all the power and force it hath is wholly disposed to follow." She departed therefore out of my Chamber somewhat offended (as she had indeed good cause) at this my peremptory answer, not giving me one word again, but murmuring (I know not what) with herself, leaving me all alone.

Now was my loving Nurse I say gone, without speaking any more to me, whose counsels though un-*In this place* advisedly rejected of me, yet I, remaining *one may* all alone, pondered all her words in my care-*see how* ful breast. And (although my understanding *contrary* *sensuality* was obscured with misty clouds of senseless *is to reason* love), I found in them nevertheless a sweet and relished taste, which making my heart, touched as it were with repentance, with a wavering and un-constant mind I did consider better of that which (even now I told her) I had resolved to follow. Where-fore beginning now to think and to persuade myself to let this doubtful and dangerous matter pass away, I thought it good to call her back again for my needful comfort : but this good motion was quickly *Venus doth* countermanded by a new and sudden acci-*appear* dent. Because lying all alone in my secret *unto her* Chamber, a most fair Lady (not knowing from whence she came) appeared before mine eyes, glittering with such shining light, that compassed her round about, that my dazzled eyes might scarce behold her, who standing thus before me, without either moving or speaking, as much as by the golden light I might illuminate and sharpen my eyes, so far forth did I cast their beams, until at last her beautiful form, and formal feature of her body, was fully arrived to my perfect knowledge. Whom when I did *A fine de-* clearly see to be all naked, saving only a *scription* thin veil of fine purple silk, which (although *of a fair* *woman* it covered some part of her snow-white body) did nevertheless abridge my sight in looking at her no more than if I had beheld some goodly figure or Image enclosed in crystal or clear glass. Her majestic head, the hair whereof did so much exceed gold in brightness as the golden colour of ours passeth the yellowest and softest in fairness, was crowned with a fine Garland of green Myrtles, under the shadow of which, I saw two eyes of incomparable beauty, and passing lovely to behold, did cast forth a marvellous and splendant brightness, and all the rest of her fair face was in like proportion adorned with such divine beauty that her like on earth might not (I think) be found. She spake not a word, glorying perhaps in herself, to see me gaze on her so much, or else to please and delight me, perceiving me so greatly content and desirous to behold her, yet at length, by little and little in the transparent and shining light, more clearly discovering to me the fairest parts of her dainty body, because she knew that with my unable tongue I could not rehearse her exceeding beauties nor (without evident sight of them) imagine any such to live amongst mortal men. Which admirable beauties, when she perceived, that I had severally and earnestly marked, and to marvel no less at the rare perfection of them, as to wonder at her coming thither, with a pleasant and mild countenance, and with an angelical voice, she began to speak thus unto me:

"Young Lady, and of all others most noble, what dost thou intend to do, disturbed by the new counsels *Venus her* of thy old Nurse? Knowest thou not, that *speech to* these are more intricate and harder to *Fiammetta* follow than love itself, from which so fondly thou desirest to flee? Dost thou not conceive what great and intolerable sorrow they keep in store for thee, most foolish woman, once and even now ours, and by the babble of the old woman dost now fear to be ours again, like her who is yet ignorant of the quantity of our great delights, and quality of our sweet joys? Unadvised as thou art, uphold and maintain him by our speeches, whom the heavens and earth can scarce contain with his might. What dost thou know how much our winged Son without resistance doth reign, and command, as much as Phœbus, rising with his golden beams out of the rich Ganges, and plunging in the Hesperian waves with his wearied Chariot, to give some rest to his fainting steeds, and to ease his own labours, seeth in a clear day? And how he dilateth his signory over all that which is shut up between cold Arture and the burning Pole, who is not only a God in heaven amongst other Gods, but is so much more mighty than all the rest that there is not anyone there who hath not been sometimes wounded with his inevit-

The great force of Love able weapons. With golden and coloured feathers, flying swiftly throughout his kingdoms, in a moment of time he doth visit them all, and governing his strong bow upon his stretched string, cunningly directeth his arrows, wrought by us and tempered in our holy waters : and when he findeth out someone more worthy and fit for his service than another, he shoots them speedily wheresoever it pleaseth him. He doth stir up and augment in young men cruel and fiery flames, and in tired and old men doth renew their spent and wasted heat, inflaming the chaste breasts of virgins with an unknown and hidden fire, and kindling lively and lovely coals, as well in wives as in widows. He commanded, when he list, the Gods (scorched with his firebrands) to leave the Heavens above, and with counterfeit shapes, and false habits, to sojourn on the earth. Was not Phœbus, who conquered swelling Python, and first tuned the melodious Citterns of Parnassus, many times his vassal, some-times for foolish Daphne, sometimes for Climene, and sometimes for Leucothoe, and for many more ? Yes, truly. And at the last, hiding his great light under the shape of a poor enamoured Shepherd,

C

kept Admetus his flocks. Jupiter himself, who doth
govern the heavens, and controlleth all the Gods, by
his compulsion took upon him forms far unbeseeming his omnipotent deity. Sometimes, spreading his
wings under the shape of a lily white bird, sounded

*All these
fables are
touched of
Ovid in his
transforma-
tions*

forth more sweet and pitiful notes than the
dying Swans of Meander. And sometimes,
transformed into a young and goodly
white Bullock, with rude horns on his
mighty Godhead, bellowed out, amidst the
meadows, fields and plains, his amorous plaints,
and deigned not to stoop and prostrate his back to
the knees and feet of a silly maid, and so with his
enjoyed and sweet prey, with cloven hoofs, instead
of cutting oars, his broad and strong breast parting
the waves, and making way through the deepest and
raging billows, he passed his brothers' kingdoms,
who for Semele in his own form, and who for the
love of Calysto, turned himself into the likeness of
Diana. And to tell of that which in times past he did,
metamorphasised into a shower of gold, for the love
of fair Danaë, and transformed into other shapes
for many more, it would be too long. And the fierce
God of War, whose angry and stern countenance,
and whose boisterly behaviour, doth make the very
Giants afraid, hath tempered his terrible and mortal
effects under his power, and was content to become
a Lover. And Jupiter, his blacksmith, who never
stirreth from his fiery forge, continually beating and

framing thunderbolts, hath been also kindled with his fire, and smitten with his golden bolts, which are more mighty and wound more deep than his, though made of hard iron and sturdy steel. And myself likewise (although I am his mother) could not defend myself from his might, whose streams of mourning tears poured forth for sweet Adonis his untimely and cruel death can sufficiently testify. But wherefore do we trouble ourselves with recital of so many examples? There is no deity in Heaven which hath escaped him, but only Diana. And she, delighting herself in woods and hunting, hath fled (nay as some think) rather hid herself from him. But if perhaps (as incredulous) thou dost not allow of this true and tried examples of the Gods, whose mansion places are in the heavens above, and art desirous to know who hath in earth beneath felt the like, so many there are, that I scarcely know where to begin, promising and giving thee to understand, that they were no base, poor or simple men, but the stoutest and most valiant wights that ever lived. And first of all let us behold the most strong and invincible son of Alcmena, who laying aside his dizzy arrows, and casting of his huge and rough Lion's skin, delighted very often to pass his loving times away in framing and fitting Emeralds for his martial fingers, and afterwards to prescribe Laws for his rugged and bushy locks, and by one and one to set them in effeminate and fine order.

" And that mighty hand, with the which he had but erst carried his strong and knotty club, killed great Antheus and beat down and drawn from Pluto his Palace gate the hellish triple-headed Dog, did now draw forth small threads, which he span on Iole her distaff. And those shoulders, on which high heaven was imposed (Atlas changing shoulders with him), were first tenderly pressed, and beclipped of Iole : and afterwards (to please her the more) covered with embroidered garments of fine purple and gold. What amorous Paris did for his sake, what fair Helen, what Clytemnestra, and what Egistus did, all the world doth know too well. And therefore as (as needless also) I omit to speak of Achilles, of Scylla, Ariadne, Leander, Dido, and many more.

" Believe me (Lady) this is a holy fire, and of great force. Now hast thou (therefore) heard how mighty *Love doth work his force even in brute beasts* Gods in heavens, and no mean men in earth have been under the sweet yoke of my princely Son. But what wilt thou say of his force extended in irrational and brute beasts, as well in the air, as in the earth. For him the mournful Turtle Dove doth follow her mate : and our pretty Pigeons, with a marvellous kind of affection, do kiss and bill their loving ones also. And there is not any beast living in the wide earth that can, or doth, at any time escape his gins. The fearful Harts in the Wood, waxing fierce and cruel amongst themselves when he doth wound them with his darts, fighting and braying after their desired and loving Hinds, show bloody signs of this burning heat. The enraged and wild Boars foaming at the mouth with hot and fiery froth, provoked by the instinct and laws of natural love, prepare and whet their tearing tusks, to fight. And the hot Lions of Libia, smitten with love, make all the woody hills and hollow valleys to resound with their roaring outcries. But leaving the woods and champaigns, I say, moreover, that the Gods of the Seas and running Rivers, even in their coldest waters, feel the burning and unquenchable heat of my Son. Nor do I think that it is unknown to thee, what approved testimony Neptunus, Glaucus, Alfeus, and others have given thereof, who were not able to extinguish, no, not so much as to mitigate, these flames with their cold and frozen floods : which although it hath been of everyone long since known in earth, and in the deepest waters, yet penetrating further into the bowels of the earth, it doth violently make open way to the dreadful King of the dark Stygian Lakes. Heaven and earth, therefore, the Sea and Hell have assayed the virtue and force of his arrows. And because thou mayest in few words comprehend everything concerning his mighty strength, I say that all things are subject to nature's lore, and no power is free from it, and that this itself also is under his laws. For if he doth once command, old hatreds and grudges are forgotten, and new angers and ancient rancours give place to his forcible fires.

" And last of all, his power stretcheth forth so far, that it doth make mothers-in-law become gracious and grateful to their stepchildren, which is no little wonder. What dost thou therefore seek ? What dost thou doubt of ? What dost thou foolishly fly ? If so many divine Gods, so many and so mighty men, and so many fierce and cruel beasts have been conquered of him, wilt thou then think it a shame to be overcome ? Alas, thou knowest not what thou hast to do ? But it may be, in submitting thyself to him thou dost expect some bitter reprehension, and dost (perhaps) fear some shame to ensue thereof, which can by no means fall unto thee, since a thousand more excellent women than thyself, having committed ten thousand greater faults than this, shall sufficiently excuse thee, and, as great presidents of this thy reasonable lapse (if so it be) exempt thee from reproach : who, as thou art not so mighty as they, hast not erred so much as they have done. But if those motives do not alter thy mind, and yet perhaps will obstinately still resist, think that thou canst not join with Jupiter in virtue, with Juno in riches, with Apollo in wisdom, and with me in beauty. And if all we have been overcome, dost thou only think to triumph in thy sole conquest ? Thou art deceived, if thou art of this opinion, and shalt suffer a base foil in thine own proud conceit. Let that suffice thee which heretofore hath been enough, and too much, for heaven and earth, and make not thyself so timorous in saying, 'I have a husband, and holy laws and promised faith forbiddeth me these things,' because they are but vain conceits and frivolous objections against his virtue. For like a strong and mighty Prince he doth plant his eternal laws, when, not caring for other of meaner substance, he doth account them but base and servile rules. Pasiphæ likewise had a husband, and Phedra, and I myself, when I loved. Nay, husbands themselves for the most part love other women, when they have wives of their own, as Jason for example, Hercules and wise Ulysses. No injury therefore is offered unto them, if that they are counterchecked with those laws which they themselves use towards other. No prerogative is granted more to them than to women. Wherefore abandon these foolish and unconstant thoughts, and love securely as thou hast begun. Behold if thou wilt not submit thyself to mighty love, of necessity thou must fly away, and whither wilt thou take thy flight but that he will pursue, and overtake thee ? His power is alike in every place, and wheresoever thou goest, and how goest, thou art still in his kingdoms, in the which none can hide themselves no longer than it pleaseth him to suffer them. Let this suffice thee (young Lady) that thou art not molested with such abominable and wicked lust as Mirra, Semiramis, Biblis, Canace and Cleopatra

39

were. My Son shall work in thee no strange and
new things. He doth rule by laws as well as other
Gods, in following which, thou must persuade thyself that thou art not the first, and shalt not be
the last. And if peradventure thou dost believe
that thou dost at this present love alone, thy belief
is but vain, and false. For to let the other world
pass in silence, which is full of them, let us only look
into thy noble City, in the which thou hast many
brave and infinite companions. And note this withal,
that what hath been, and is, done of so many wise
and judicious persons, may not justly be thought
vain and accounted frivolous. Follow us therefore,
and with thankful words and grateful deeds requite
our deity for thy peerless beauty, and intermit not to
remember her, who hath out of the number of simple
and ignorant souls chosen and took thee, to make
thee know and participate the pleasure of our gifts."

Alas, good Ladies, what should or could I answer,
to such persuasive or forcible reasons alleged by so
mighty a Goddess, but only this: "Dispose with me
as it pleaseth thee best." I say therefore, that now
she held her peace, when I having gathered all her
words into the depth of my capacity, and felt them
full of infinite excuses, and knowing her also better
now (than at the first), resolved with myself to embrace and follow her sweet and pleasing counsels.
Wherefore rising quickly out of my bed, and with
an humble mind casting my knees on the ground,

being full of fear, I began softly to say thus unto her:
"O eternal and singular beauty, O heavenly deity,
The force of love is felt most sens- ibly and stronger in them that look to expel it
O only Lady and mistress of my resolute mind, whose force the more it is resisted, the more it is felt, pardon my simple and foolish encounter, which I have made against the piercing weapons of thy unknown and puissant Son: and work with me at thy own pleasure. And stooping to thy will, guerdon my faith as thou hast promised at fit time and convenient place, because that others praising thy effects in me, and wishing themselves the like, the number of thy subjects may without end increase."

I had scarcely spoken these words, when, moving from the place where she stood, she came to me, and with a fervent kind of affection and merry countenance embracing me, she first kissed my forehead, and afterwards, as false Ascanius breathing secret and burning fire into Dido her mouth so she, respiring the like into mine, made my first desires more hot, and my passions more fervent, as after to the ruin of my tormented heart I felt them. And opening a little her purple veil, she showed me between her delicate paps, the lively image of my beloved gentleman, enfolded in a fine garment, whose sweet face seemed to be full of many cares, not much unlike to mine, and said thus: "Behold, young Lady, thy loving and loyal gentleman. And we have not given thee Lista, Gera nor Birria for thy lover, nor one

41

like to any of these. But being most worthy for many brave parts, and a beautiful personage to be beloved of any Goddess, doth love thee (as we have ordained) more than himself, and will continue the same for ever. Wherefore driving all foolish fear away, addict thyself joyfully again to his pure and deserved love. Thy meritorious prayers have with pity penetrated into our ears, and therefore assure thyself that thou shalt without fail according to thy will and works reap no small benefit of them." And thus without speaking any more she vanished suddenly out of my sight.

Alas, poor wretch that I am, could I otherwise think, trying the sequels of her sugared suggestions, and of my ensuing miseries, but that this counterfeit Goddess was rather cruel Ctesiphone than gentle Venus that thus appeared unto me, who laying aside for a while her ugly and hideous hair, no otherwise than Juno the shining glory of her deity, and taking upon her a divine form, as she did an old and crooked shape, represented her before my eyes, as she came to Semele, giving me, as she did also her, sweet counsel mixed with revenge and poison of my final overthrow and helpless fall : receiving which into my miserable breast, was the greatest occasion, and only cause, O godly faith, reverend shame, and most holy chastity, to drive and banish you from the same, from that then chaste (I ween) but now unworthy and spotted breast of mine. But pardon, sweet virtues, pardon me, if due penance of a sinner, and sustained punishment of this guile, may impetrate any remission or favour at all. But now after the Goddess was gone from my sight I remained as one resolute to follow her pleasures. And although this furious passion which I passed troubled my wits, and dulled all my senses, one only spark of all that good, and wisdom, which was lost and gone, kindled (I know not for what desert of mine) a prudent counsel, and knowledge of this true rule in my smothered and consumed heart, which was, that *To disclosed* love once discovered doth never or very *love a happy* seldom come to a happy and good end. *end is sel-* *dom or never* And therefore amongst other profound *granted* thoughts (although it was hard for me to do) I intended not to prefer will before reason, in bringing such desires to their wished end. And though I was truly by divers intermediate chances greatly constrained, yet so much favour was granted me, that without overcharging the mark, and stoutly enduring the grief, I passed it well away. And yet in truth the forces which I yet have are of sufficient power to uphold and conserve such counsel. Because (although I write most true things) I have in such order set them down, that except he, who doth know them as well as I, being the occasion of them all, no other, were he of never so sharp a wit and ready conceit, could understand and know that it was I. And even him I pray (if this little book

43

chance ever to come to his hands) that, for that
love which sometimes he bare me, he would conceal
that, which in manifesting it, would not turn to his
honour or profit. And if he have taken that love
from me without any demerit of my own part, that
at the least he would not dispossess me of that
honour which (admit that unjustly I have it) he
cannot (though he would) render unto me again.
Adhering therefore to this determination, and brid-
ling my eager desires, and too to forward in their
own discovery, with a strained and unpatient rein
of sufferance, I endeavoured with all diligence (and
at my fittest opportunity) by alluring means, and did
practise fine and subtle demonstrances to kindle the
young gentleman with those coals, with the which
myself was inflamed, and to warn him to be as wary
and cunning in his proper affairs, as I was wise and
circumspect in my actions.

In bringing which to speedy effect, dangerous delays were not deferred, and thought not my travail
The condi- in the same, either too long or too great,
tion of the because if the true testimony of the
heart is
oftentimes qualities of the heart is comprised in those
compre- which are not different in passions, I quickly
hended in
those which perceived, that wished effects did follow
are alike my desires : whereupon I saw him not only
full of amorous heat, but very wise also and expert
in pursuing his amorous enterprises, which things did
yield me no small joy and great contentation. With

as earnest care therefore and due consideration,
tendering my unsuspected honour as also to satisfy
his deep desires, when time and place did grant him
fit opportunity, he did seriously solicit me, and (as
I believe) not without great pain (trying the utmost
of his skill) to gain the familiarity of everyone that
was nearest allied, and did daily converse with me,
but especially, and last of all, to insinuate into the
acquaintance of my husband and firmly to purchase
his friendship. The which he did not only obtain,
but did with such show of great goodwill and favour
enjoy it, that there was nothing that might content
or please either of them, if mutually and lovingly the
same was not made known to each other. I believe
(fair Ladies) that without writing it, you may easily
know, or at least may imagine, how greatly this
pleased me. For what woman is there so foolish,
who would not especially conceive as much?

This singular and wished privilege I enjoyed by
this happy familiarity, that publicly, and in all
companies, I might talk with him, and he
Not with words only, but with actions and gestures, love may be manifested discourse with me again. Who, thinking
it now high time to proceed to matters of
greater effects, sometimes with some other
(perceiving that I might both hear and
understand him) discoursed of such things,
by the which I knew (most willing to learn the
principles of this new law), not by his talk only,
which he had with others, that he could cunningly

45

and subtlely declare his affection, and finely have
an answer thereof again, but with divers motions
also of his hands, and gestures in his countenance,
and body, he could passing well perform the same.
And thus with pretty lessons pleasing my willing
mind so much, I learned also to be so diligent and
wary a scholar, that I would not tell him anything,
or he to me again, but by these unsuspected means,
whereby equally and justly we conceived our hidden
conceits. Nor being yet content with these honest
helps, by figurative speeches and invented names
he taught me how to speak in open company, to
make me thereby more assured of his fervent love,
calling me by the name of Fiammetta, and himself
Panphilus. Alas, how many times in the presence
of myself, and of my dearest friends, being prettily
heated with feasting, and love's cates, did he devise
(feigning Fiammetta and Panphilus to be Grecians)
how I with him, and he with me, were first combined
in loving bonds. And afterwards what accidents did
ensue of this Grecian love, colouring his forged novel
with fit and feigned names. It made me truly
many times to laugh, not so much at the gravity
and counterfeit modesty in his discourse, as at the
simplicity and good meaning of those who gave ear
and belief to his tale.

And yet I was sometimes afraid lest that both
his disordinate heats might have unadvisedly
(perhaps) transported his tongue thither whither it

would afterwards have repented that it had runned.
But as he was a more prudent and perfect scholar
than I took him to be, so did he craftily take heed of
speaking of false Latin. O gentle and pitiful Ladies,
what doth not love teach his subjects : and whom
doth not he enable to learn his wise discourses,
and acquaint him with brave and commendable
fashions ?

Myself being but a young and simple woman in
such pastimes, and scarce able, amongst other
Love a gentlewomen my companions, in plain
cunning and common things to untie my unperfect
matter tongue, by giving a willing and an affec-
tioned ear to his speeches, did reap thereby so
much fruit that in a short time, in feigning and
talking, I thought I did excel every famous Poet.
For there were few or none of his presupposed positions but with a fictitious and painted tale I would
have effectually argued, and fitly answered to the
same (a very hard thing in my opinion for a young
gentlewoman to learn so soon, and more difficult to
tell, or put into practice). But all these shifts would
seem but shadows, and of no consequence, if I did
write and set down (if present matter should require),
with subtle flights I did experiment the faith of one
of my most familiar and trusty women, to whom we
both purposed to commit the secrecy of our hidden
love (not as yet by speeches manifested to anyone),
considering with myself, that enclosed in my burning

47

breast it could not be kept there long without
great trouble and grief, and perhaps without some
violent and sudden issue, unless there were some
means and remedies applied to the contrary. It
would be besides this a tedious labour to recount
what counsel, and how many devices were excogi-
tated between her and me (perhaps in vain and
foolish matters) and never put in use, no not so much
as imagined of any before. All which, although I
have seen them put in trial, to my great prejudice
and hindrance, I am not sorry, nevertheless, that
I have known them.

If I do not err (Gentlewomen) in my opinion, the
great firmness of our young years was very strange
With what to behold, if that with a due and perfect
difficulty consideration it is well weighed how hard
lovers are a thing it is for the enamoured minds of
contained
in the bonds two young and raw lovers to continue
of reason any long time united together, but that
on the one or other side, spurred on with superfluous and overruling desires, they should alter and
wander out of reason's course. But the bonds of our
loves were so fast knit, and of such rare tenour, that
the gravest, wisest and strongest personages in like
passages should have got them high and worthy
praises. But now my stained pen, with an unbridled
and wanton desire, doth prepare itself to write of
those final terms of love, beyond the which none
can pass further with deed or desire whatsoever.

But before I come to this point, as humbly as I may, I implore (gentle Ladies) your pity, and therewithal that amorous force, which, possessing your tender breasts, doth also draw your burning desires to such an end. And pray you moreover, if my speeches seem offensive unto you (I speak not of the deed, because I know that if you have not as yet attained to such felicity, you have in your minds a thousand times wished to have felt the same), that then most prompt you would arise in my excuse and defence. And though seemly and honest shamefastness too late (alas) entered into my wilful mind, pardon me, most earnestly entreating thee to give place a little while, too timorous young Gentlewomen, because secure and free from thy restraint and menaces, they may read that of me which, in their fervent loves (I know) and hot desires, they also wish might handsomely befall unto them. With hungry hope (therefore) and full of fearful cares, our longing desires, yet lingering delays drew one each day after another, which both of us with painful thoughts did hourly endure, albeit that one did manifest the same in daily meeting, and secret talk together, and the other did show herself in granting of it very coy, and in show repugnant (though against her will) as you yourselves in seeking that (which perhaps most of all doth please your wanton appetites) do know well enough that

The slack dealing in conducting amorous desires to their end is very bitter

D   49 enamoured young gentlewomen are wont to do. He therefore, giving but little credit to my words in these denials, attending fit time and place, more audacious than advised in that which he did, and more fortunate than wise, obtained that of me which I as well as he (though with a feigned face, and a little rigorous resisting to the contrary) did most greedily desire. But if I should for all this affirm, that this was the occasion that made me love him more, I must confess that every time that the remembrance thereof touched my guilty mind it brought with it an incomparable grief. Wherefore let the Gods above (the secret teachers of our hearts) be witnesses with me herein, that this inevitable accident was then, and yet is, the least cause of that great love which I bear him. Albeit not denying, but that this was then, and evermore since, a most sweet, wished, and welcomed delight unto me.

And what simple and slender-witted woman is she who would not wish that thing which she dearly loved to be rather near unto her than far off from her, and by how much she loved and desired it, by so much more to feel the same nearest of all unto her. I say therefore, that after such a quickly passed chance, not fallen in the compass of my belly before, though not seldom times tossed in my thoughts, with exceeding joy and favourable fortune, not once, but many times by means of our proper wits, and new inventions, we recreated ourselves with this manner of dainty disport, although the pleasures of the same is now (alas) lighter than the winds flown from me, unhappy woman. But yet while these pleasant times passed on, as love itself can make true report, and give sole testimony thereof, sometimes his unlawful coming unto me was not without great fear, when by some secret means or other, and at unseasonable times he would be with me : yet how dear was my Chamber unto him, and with what joy, and how willingly did it evermore receive him, whom I did also know to use more reverence in the same than in any holy Temple. Alas, how many pleasant kisses, what infinite number of loving embracements, and how many sweet nights more gracious and dear to us than the lightsome and clearest days, did we pass together without sleep in pleasant devices and dainty discourses. How many other *Maidenly* delights, most dear to every Lover, have *shamefast-* *ness a most* we felt in that blessed Chamber in that *hard bridle* *to wanton* merry prime of our happy days. O most *and forward* holy shamefastness (a pinching and hard *minds* bridle to wanton and youthful minds), wherefore once again at my request dost thou not depart ? Why dost thou withhold my pen ready to unfold our past joys and pleasures ? Alas, in thinking perhaps to gratify me, thou dost grieve me, and to help me, thou dost hinder me. To those women therefore to whom nature hath granted so large and

51

ample a privilege, that by those things which are
spoken they may comprehend and imagine the rest
which are concealed to others, not so wise as these,
let them be manifest and laid open. Nor let not
any call me fool, as ignorant of so much, in knowing
well enough, that it should have been more honestly
for me to have concealed, than to manifest that
which is already written. But who can countermand Love, when, with working all his might and
force, he doth oppose himself? At this point
many times I let my pen fall out of my hands, and
as often again (molested by him) I took it up, and
put it to his former task.

And finally like a subject and bond woman I
must needs serve him, whom (when I was free in the
beginning) I knew not how to resist. He
Delights showed me that hidden delights and privy
which are
hidden are pleasures were as much worth again as
as much
worth as hoarded Jewels and secret treasures. But
buried wherefore do I feed and please my humour
treasure
about these words? I say, that then I
thanked infinite times the holy Goddess, the
promiser, and performer, of these sweet joys. Oh,
how many times crowned with her green leaves
did I visit her sacred Temples, offering up sweet
incense to her divine Altars, and how often did I
condemn the old Nurse, and her simple counsel: and
did besides this (rejoicing and glorying in myself
above all other enamoured young Gentlewomen

and Ladies, that I knew and kept company with)
scorn and laugh at their ridiculous and appassionated loves, blaming that in my speeches which was
dearest to my soul, saying many times to myself:
" There is no woman beloved so as I am, nor any
Lady, be she never so noble and fair, that doth love
so brave, so wise, and so worthy a young Gentleman
as I do, nor that doth with so great delight and
pleasure reap such amorous fruit in a paradise of
all joy, nor in so great abundance, as I most happily
and hourly do taste."

And to be short, in respect of this, I esteemed the
whole world as a trifle of no account, and thought
that I reached the highest heavens with my thrice
happy head, and wanting (as I thought) nothing else
to attain to the highest top of felicity, and to the
full accomplishment of all my pleasures and sweet
contents, but only to have had the occasion of all
my blissful joy and blessed fortune manifested, and
made openly known to the world, thinking with myself, that that which delighted me so much should
(as myself) have pleased everyone alike. But thou,
O bashfulness, on the one side, and thou, fear,
on the other, you have (I say) withheld me, the
one threatening me eternal infamy, and the other,
the loss of that, of which indeed envious fortune
did afterwards miserably despoil me.

Thus therefore I passed this golden and gladsome
time many days and months (as it pleased Love)

without emulating any loving Lady or enamoured Gentlewoman, loving most happily, and living most joyfully in a world of sweet content, and swimming with full sails in Seas of heavenly felicities, and of all manner of delights, not entertaining so much as a thought of discontent and sorrow, and never imagining that these pleasures, which then my merry heart was so amply and thoroughly possessed of, should be the root and plant (in time to come) of my miserable woes, and woeful miseries, which at this present, without any hope or remedy at all to my hapless pain and endless grief, too well I know, and most sensibly feel.

THE
SECOND BOOK OF BOCCACE
HIS FIAMMETTA

WHILST that, O dearest Ladies, I spent my merry days in so pleasant and jocund a life, as is above written, never thinking of future chances, cruel fortune did secretly prepare her malicious poison for me, and with continual courage (myself not suspecting anything) did at an inch pursue my joyful life. And thinking that (in maikng me become a vassal to love, and in my chiefest time of joy and liberty), she was not well appaid, but perceiving how this my sweet servitude did yield me great delight, she endeavoured with a more stinging nettle to torment and prick my poor and silly soul. And her appointed time being now come, she tempered (as after you shall perceive) her bitter galls and wormwood for my unwilling and feeble stomach: which (maugre my teeth) compelling me to drink, turned my present mirth into sudden sadness, and my wonted laughter into woeful lamentations: which things not only enduring, but yet thinking it my duty in writing them, to show them to some others, I took such compassion of myself, that taking almost all my force from me, and bringing infinite tears to mine eyes, it did hardly permit me anything effectually to execute my purpose herein : which, albeit I may very ill do, yet will I forcibly go about to perform the same.

After that he and I (the weather falling out very cold and rainy) were in my Chamber together, reposing and solacing ourselves upon a sumptuous and sweet bed, and Lady Citherea wearied, nay almost overcome, the dark and silent night with her long tariance favourably granted to our pleasant and desired sports fit opportunity of time and place. And a great light hanging in the midst of the Chamber glutted his eyes and mine (viewing each other's beauty) with exceeding joy : of which, while I recreated my mind in gazing and discoursing of his, mine eyes did drink a superfluous kind of sweetness, which making their lights inebriated (as it were) with the same, with deceitful sleep (I know not how) a little while oppressed, and my words (interrupted also in the midst) remained locked up close in their lids.

Which pleasant and sweet slumber, passing so mildly away from me, as it came, my ears by chance heard certain doleful mutterings and sorrowful bewailings uttered forth by my best beloved. Wherefore suddenly troubled in mind, and my thoughts, at war within themselves for his welfare, made me almost interrupt him with these words : "Sweet heart, what dost thou ail ? " But countermanded by new counsel I kept them in, and with a sharp eye

and subtle ears, secretly beholding him turned now
on the other side of the bed, I listened a good while
to his sorrowful and silent words, but mine ears did
not apprehend any of them, albeit I might perceive
him molested with great store of lamentable sobs
and sighs, that he cast forth, and by seeing also his
breast bedewed all with tears.

What words (alas) can sufficiently express with
how many cares my poor soul all this while (being
ignorant of the cause) was afflicted ? A thousand
thoughts in one moment did violently run up and
down in my doubtful mind, meeting all at the last,
and concluding in one thing, which was, that he,
loving some other Woman, remained with me here,
and in this sort against his will.

My words were very often at the brink of my
mouth, to examine the cause of his grief, but doubting lest he lamenting in this sort, and being suddenly
espied and interrupted of me, he might not be
greatly abashed thereat, they retired back, and went
down again : and oftentimes likewise I turned away
mine eyes from beholding him, because lest the
hot tears distilling from them, and falling upon
him, might have given him occasion and matter to
know that I perceived his woeful plight. Oh, how
many impatient means did I imagine to practise,
because that he (awaking me) might conjecture that
I had neither heard his sighs, nor seen his tears :
and yet agreed to none at all.

But overcome at the last with eager desire to know the occasion of his complaint, because he should turn him towards me, as those who, in their deepest sleep, terrified by dreaming of some great fall, wild beast, or of some ghastly thing, give a sudden start, and in most fearful wise rouse up themselves, affrighted out of their sleep and wits at once, even so with a sudden and timorous voice I shrieked, and lifting up myself, I violently cast one of my arms over his shoulders. And truly my deceit deceived me not, because (closely wiping away his tears) with infinite (though counterfeit) joy he quickly turned towards me again, and with a pitiful voice said:

" My fairest and sweetest soul, of what wert thou afraid ? " Whom without delay I answered thus: " My Love, I thought I had lost thee." My words (alas) I know not by what spirit uttered forth, were most true presagers and foretellers of my future loss, as now too true I find it.

But he replied: " O dearest dear, not hateful death, nor any adverse chance of unstable Fortune whatsoever, can work such operations in my firm breast, that thou (my only joy) shalt leese me for ever." And incontinently a great and profound sigh followed these pitiful words, the cause of which not so soon demanded of me (who was also most desirous to know the offspring of his first lamentations) but suddenly two streams of tears from both his eyes (as from two fountains) began to gush out amain, and in great abundance to drench his sorrowful breast, not yet thoroughly dried up by his former weeping. And holding me, poor soul (plunged in a gulf of griefs, and overcome with floods of brinish tears), a long time in a doleful and doubtful suspense, before (even so did the violence of his sobs and sighs stop the passage of his words) he could answer anything to my demands again.

But after that he felt the tempest of his outrageous passion somewhat calmed, with a sorrowful voice, yet still interrupted with many heavy sighs, he said thus again: "O dearest Lady and sole Mistress of my afflicted heart, and only beloved of me above all other women in the world, as these extraordinary effects are true records of the same: if my plaints deserve any credit at all, thou mayst then believe, that my eyes not without a grievous occasion shed erst such plenty of bitter tears, whensoever that is objected to my memory, which (remaining now with thee in great joy) doth cruelly torment my heart to think of, that is when I remember with myself that thou mayest not (alas, fain would I that thou couldest) make two Panphilowes of me, because remaining here, and being also there, whither urgent and necessary affairs do perforce compel me (most unwillingly) to retire, I might at one time fulfil the laws of love, and my pitiful, natural and dutiful devoyre: O my aged and loving father. Being therefore not able to suffer any more, my pensive heart, with remembrance of it, is continually with great affliction galled more and more, as one whom, pity drawing on the one side, is taken out of thy arms, and on the other side with great force of love is still retained in them."

These words pierced my miserable heart with such extreme bitterness as I never felt before. And although my dusked wits did not well *All these reasons are* understand them, notwithstanding (as much *condemned* as my ears and senses attentive to their *of lovers which per-* harms did receive and conceive of them) *turb their* by so much more, the very same, converted *joys* into tears, issued out of my eyes, leaving behind them their cruel and malicious effects in my heart. This was therefore (good Ladies) the first hour in the which I felt such grudging griefs envious of my pleasures : this was the hour which made me pour forth innumerable tears, the like never spent of me before, whose course and main streams not any of his comforts and consolatory words could stop and stanch one whit. But after I had a long time together remained in woeful wailings, enfolding him lovingly between my arms, I prayed him (as much as I could) to tell me more clearly what pity, and what due piety that was, that did draw him out of my arms, and threaten me his absence; whereupon, not ceasing to lament, he said thus unto me :

" Inevitable death, the final end of all things, of many other sons hath left me sole to survive with my

60

aged and reverend father, who burdened with many
years, and living without the sweet company of his
deceased wife, and loving brothers, who might in
his old years carefully comfort him, and remaining
now without any hope of any more issue, being determined not to marry, doth recall me home to see
him, as the chiefest part of his consolation, whom he
hath not seen these many years past. For shifting of
which journey (because I would not, sweet Fiammetta,
leave thee) there are not a few months past, when
first by divers means I began to frame some just
and reasonable excuse. But he in fine, not accepting
of any, did not cease to conjure me, by the essence
which I had by him, and by my impotent childhood
tenderly brought up, and nurtured in his lap, by that
love, which continually he had borne me, and by the
duty and that love, which I should bear him again,
and by that requisite obedience which every child
should bear unto his father, and by all other things
that he thought most effectual and persuasive, did
like a familiar friend (whose part is rather to command) pray me, that, to commiserate his aged and
declining years, and to tender his welfare, I would
with speed return to visit him. And besides this,
with solemn oaths, and serious observations, he
caused all his friends, and agents in these parts, and
with most earnest entreaties provoked them incessantly, to prick me on in this behalf, saying, that if
he did not see me shortly with him, his miserable

soul would utterly forsake his old and comfortless body. But (alas) how strong and forcible are the laws *The laws of nature are most strong* of nature! I could not presently assent, nor yet can scarce resolve with myself, that, by reason of the great love I bear thee, these piteous exorations should take place in me. Whereupon having with thy good leave determined to go see him, and for his great comfort to remain some short space of time with him, and not knowing also, how I could live without thee, all these (I say), occurring and accumulated in my sorrowful memory, do make me every hour (sweet Lady) most justly and sorrowfully complain." And thus he held his peace.

If there was ever any of you (fair Ladies) that in her most fervent and jealous love had ever had so hard and bitter a Pill as this, even she I think doth know with what incomparable grief my mind (nourished long since with food of his love, and set on fire with unspeakable flames of my own) was then afflicted: but others, free from such amorous passions, could not conceive, because as allegations of extravagant examples, so all my speeches besides would not be *The force of an amorous passion* sufficient to induce them to believe the same. In brief therefore I say, that hearing these words, my soul did seek to leap out of my body, and it had (I think) flown away, if between his arms whom most of all I loved, it had not been straitly embraced, and forcibly retained.

62

But all the parts of my body remaining nevertheless full of shaking fear, and my heart puffed with swelling grief, and weltering in the passions of these agonies, they bereaved me a pretty while of my speech. But afterwards, by quantity of time made more pliable to sustain these never-felt sorrows and unwonted pains, a certain feeble and fearful force was restored to my daunted spirits. And my eyes, whose conduits, stopped by the violence of this unexpected accident, did now burst out into great plenty of tears, and the strings of my tongue, contracted together with sharp sorrow, were now dissolved to utter and breathe out the confused anguish and conceived sorrows in my mind. Wherefore turning me to the Guardian and Lord of my life, embracing him, I said thus :

" O final hope, and sovereign comfort of my afflicted soul : let these my pitiful words take place with force in thy fleeting mind, divert thee from thy new purpose, because if thou dost so dearly love me as thou showest, thy life and mine, before their natural and prefixed period cometh, may not jointly be deprived of this joyful and sweet light. Haled on by dutiful pity, and drawn back again by zealous love, thou puttest all thy future fortunes in doubtful hazard. But certes, if all thy words are true with which thou hast not once but many times heretofore affirmed that thou didst love me, no other pity therefore than this should be more mighty, and of greater force to resist, nor (while I live) to withdraw thee to any other place. And hearken why. It is not unknown to thee, if thou followest that course which thou seemest to do, in what a doubtful and miserable estate thou leavest my poor life, which heretofore hath hardly passed one day not without great sorrow when I could not see thee. Then mayest thou by this be more ascertained, that when thou dost omit to visit me so long together, all my joys will utterly forsake me, and this (alas) would be too much. But who doth not doubt that all kinds of woes, sorrow and anxieties will assail me, and succeed in their place, which (without any resistance that I can possibly make) will perhaps dissolve my vital powers into nothing. Thou shouldest have already known how weak and impotent young women are to reback such cruel and adverse occurrences, and what feeble force they have, with a strong and resolute mind to endure them. If peradventure thou wilt object and say, that in the first beginning of my loves, I have both wisely and stoutly suffered greater adversities than these, I will truly agree with thee herein, but the occasions of them and of these are divers. My hope placed in my own valour made that seem light unto me which, now being put in another his will, will be too heavy for me to support. Who did ever deny me, when burning desire had beyond all measure kindled my breast, and surcharged it with furious passions,

64

that being enamoured of thee, as thou wert also of
me, I might not enjoy thee ? Truly nobody. Which
comfort (when thou art so far sequestered from me)
will not so easily fall to my lot. Besides this, I enjoyed no more then, but the sight of thy sweet face
and goodly personage, and knew thee no more but by
the outward figure, lineaments and proportion of thy
body, although in my heart I made great account
and prize of thee, but now have by good proof perceived, and felt indeed, that as thou art now to be
esteemed a great deal dearer of me than the reach
of my imagination could then extend unto, even so
art thou become mine own with that assured sureness, and those indissoluble bonds, with which true
lovers may possibly be held and united to those
It is a   that love them again. And who doth not
greater grief doubt, moreover, that it is a greater grief
to leave a to lose that, which one hath to hold, than
certainty
for an un- that, which he hopeth to have, although
certainty his hope therein be not afterwards frustrate. Wherefore considering this matter well, I
plainly see my death will soon approach. Shall
therefore the love of thy old father be preferred
before that great affection which thou oughtest
to have of me, and be the ominous occasion of my
untimely death ?

" And if thou dost so, thou art certes no lover, but
an open enemy. Ah, wilt thou make more account
of those few years reserved for the miseries of thy

old father, than of these many, which by great
reason and likelihood I have (living joyfully with
thee) to spend. Alas, what indiscreet folly were this !
Dost thou believe that anyone conjoined to thee in
parentage, nearest in blood, or most firm in mutual
friendship, doth love thee so much as I do ? If this
be thy belief (believe me, Panphilus) it is erroneous.
For truly none can love thee better, and hold thee
He that doth (sweet Panphilus) dearer than I do. If
love most
deserveth therefore I love thee more than others, I de-
most pity serve then to be requited with greater love
and pity than others. Prefer me therefore worthily
before the rest, and being pitiful towards me, forget
all other pity, that might offend and prejudicate this,
and let thy old father, as he hath lived a long time
without thee, enjoy (a God's name) his wonted rest
without thy company. And let him from henceforth (if so he please) live amongst the rest of his
other friends and allies : and if not, let him die. If
it be true (as I have heard) he hath a good while
since escaped the deadly stroke of death, and hath
lived longer here than was convenient for his necessary health, and if he live in pain and with much
trouble (as commonly old men do) thou shalt in thy
absence show thyself more pitiful towards him, to
let him die, than with thy presence to prolong his
troubled and tired life. But thou oughtest rather
to succour me, poor soul, whose life hath not been,
a good while since, but by thy sweet company pre-

served, nor cannot tell how, without the same, to enjoy this mundane light, and who, being yet in the prime of my tender age, doth hope to live and lead with thee many joyful months and years together. If thy journey were to such purpose, and could *Medea her* work such supernatural effects in thy old *medica-* father his body as the charms of Medea and *ments re-* *stored to old* her medicinal spells did upon old Æson, *Æson his* then would I say, that by just piety thou *youth again* wert instiged, and would highly commend this requisite pity, and although it would seem repugnant to my will, yet would I wish and allow of this devotion in thee, and exhort thee to the performance of it.

" But such a miracle, passing the laws and bounds of nature, can never come to pass, according to thy natural reason, as thou knowest well enough. Behold then if perhaps thou showest thyself more cruel and rigorous to me (than I believe or imagine thou wilt) or dost so little care for me, whom on thy own mere choice, and not by compulsion, thou hast loved, and yet dost, that above my love, thou wilt for all this advance the lost and helpless charity of the old man, take some pity at the least of thy own estate, and caring little for him, and bemoaning me less, rue thy own condition, whom (if first thy countenance and afterwards thy words have not deceived me) I have seen to be more dead than alive, as even now thou wert (without perceiving me, that did mark thee) by some uncouth accident, is a most extreme and sorrowful passion, and deprived once *By long* of my sight, and debarred of my company, *grief and* dost thou believe to live so long time, as *sorrow men die* this pitiless pity doth require. Alas, for the love thou bearest to the Gods, look better to thyself, and see what likelihood of death (if by long and lingering grief men die, as I see it daily by others) this journey (ah, this inopinate and unlucky journey) will yield thee : which, how hard moreover and unpleasant it is to thee, thy sorrowful sobs and tears, and the unwonted mourning of thy heart, which panting and beating up and down in thy breast I feel, do plainly show. And if not apparent death (which is most like), a worser and more cruel condition of life than any death (be assured) will accompany thee. Alas that my enamoured heart, urged with great pity that it hath of my own distress, and constrained by that tender compassion which I feel for thee, must now play the humble suppliant, to pray and entreat thee, and to advise thee also, that thou wouldest not be so fond (what kind of pity soever moving thee thereunto) as with evident and imminent danger to hazard thy safe person.

" Why, think that those who do not love themselves possess nothing in the wide world. Thy father, of whom (forsooth) thou art so pitiful, did not give thee to the world because thou shouldest be thy own

minister and occasion of taking thyself away out of
it again. And who doth not believe but that if our
Who loseth estate were as manifest, or could be law-
not himself fully told unto him, that he (being wise
possesseth
nothing in and of mature judgment and experience)
this world would rather say : 'Stay there still.' And
if discretion and reason would not, pity at the least
would induce him to it, and this (I am assured)
thou knowest well enough. It is therefore great
reason, that what judgment in his own tried cause
he hath given, he should (and is most likely) that he
would in our cause (if he knew it) give also the very
same. Wherefore omit this troublesome journey,
unprofitable to thee, unpleasant to me, and prejudicial to us both. As these (my dearest Lord) are
reasons forcible enough (if followed) to keep thee
from going hence, so are there many more not a
little effectual (if put in practice) to dehort thee
from going hence, as first for example, considering
the place whither thou goest. For put case thou
dost bend thy journey thither where thou wert born,
thy native soil and natural country, and a place
beloved more of thee than any other (as I have
heard thee say), in certain things annoyous, and for
certain causes hated of thee. Because thy City (as
thou thyself hast told) is full of haughty and boast-
ing words, but more replenished with pusillanimous
and unperformed deeds. And that they are not only
slaves to a thousand confused laws but to as many

different opinions as there are men. All which (as well foreigners as Citizens), naturally contentious and full of garboyles, do daily rage in civil broils, and intestine wars. And as it is full of proud, covetous and malicious people, so is it not unfurnished of innumerable and intricate cares, the least of which is (I know) most contrary to the good disposition of thy quiet mind.

"But this noble City which thou dost intend to forsake (I am sure) thou art not ignorant, *Naples* with what joyful peace it doth continually flourish, how famous it is for plenty of all commodities, how opulent, shining in glory and magnificence, and how heroically administered, *It is sometimes lawful to praise oneself* under the sole regiment of a mighty and invincible king. All which things, I know (if ever thy appetite I have known) are most pleasant to thy dainty taste. And besides all these rehearsed pleasures, here am I (here am I, Panphilus), whom thou shalt neither find there nor mayst live with in any other place. Leave off therefore thy sorrowful determination, and, changing thy unadvised counsel into better consideration, have regard (I pray thee, by tarrying here still) to the comfort and weal of both our lives."

My words increased his tears in great abundance, of the which, with intermingled and sweet kisses, I drunk up some. But after many a heavy sigh, that he fetched, he answered me thus again:

AMOROUS FIAMMETTA

"O chiefest and singular felicity of my soul, I (doubtless) know thy words to be most true, as by every manifest danger included in them, thou hast plainly set down before my eyes.

"But because (since present and urgent necessity doth require, which I would it did not) I may briefly answer thee, I tell thee, that to pay and acquit with a short grief, a long and great debt, I think (my Fiammetta) thou wilt easily grant that I may and must justly do. Thou must therefore think, and rest assured, that (although I am sufficiently by the pity of my sick and aged Father duly obliged) yet am I no less (nay rather more straitly) bound by the same, which I ought to have of us both, which, if it were lawful to discover, it would of itself seem excusable enough, presupposing that what thou hast said should be judged of my Father, or of any other else for him, I would then leave and let my old Father die, without seeing him at all. But since it behoveth that this pity must be covert and kept close, and accomplished, also, without manifesting the cause of it, I see not how, without great infamy and reprehension, I might anyway desist to perform the same.

"To avoid which due slander in not discharge of my duty, frowning Fortune shall but three or four months at the most interrupt and suspend our wonted delights, which no sooner expired, but without all fail thou shalt see me joyfully return to thee

again, and make both our hearts as glad at our
merry meeting, as they are now dolefully daunted
with their sorrowful parting. And if the place to
which I go is so unpleasant as thou makest it (and
as it is indeed compared with this, thy sweet self
being here) then this must greatly content thee,
thinking, that if there were no other occasion,
that should provoke me to depart from thence, the
qualities of the place, most contrary to the disposition of my mind, would be forcible motives to make
me return and come hither again. Grant me therefore (sweet Mistress) this favour, that I may go
thither, and as thou hast been heretofore most careful of my estate and honour, so now likewise tender
the same, and arm thy mind with patience in this
cross of frightful Fortune, because knowing this
accident to be most grievous unto thee, I may
hereafter make myself more assured, that in any
chance of Fortune whatsoever, my honour is as dear
to thee as myself."

He had now said, and held his peace when I began thus to rejoin as followeth : "Now do I clearly
see that which framed in thy inflexible mind thou
dost bear inexorable. And I scarcely think that in
Things that the same thou dost admit any thought at
are wont all of those great and infinite cares with
to hurt a
lover's mind which thou leavest my distressed soul so
heavily burdened, dividing thyself from me, which
not one day, night nor hour can possibly live here

72

without a thousand fears. And I shall remain in continual doubt of thy life, which (I pray the Gods) may be prolonged above my days, to thine own will and desire. Alas, what need I with superfluous *Dangers* speech prolong the time in discoursing and *that hang* reciting of them by one and one, thyself *daily over* *mortal men* knowing well enough, that the Sea hath not so many sands, nor heaven so many stars, as there be doubtful and dangerous perils that are immin- ent, and commonly incident, to mortal men? All the which (if thou goest from hence) as doubtless they will not a little fear me, so will they greatly offend and hurt thee. Woe is me for my sorrowful life, I am ashamed to tell thee that, which now cometh to my mind: but because by the which I have heard it seemeth a thing possible and likely, constrained therefore I will tell it thee. Now if in thy country, in the which (as the common fame is, and as myself particularly have heard) there is an infinite number of fair and dainty Ladies, who spending their young years in cunning love, and solemn sports and feasts (the first a passion especi- ally incident to them, and the second a common thing used there), with wanton and alluring means are most expert to entice and procure love again, thy wandering eye should espy some one of these, which might perhaps please thy absent heart, and so for her love shouldest neglect and forget mine, ah, what a miserable life should I then lead!

Wherefore if thou dost bear me such fervent affection (as thou sayest and seemest to do) imagine how thou wouldest take it, if for exchange of another (which thing shall never come to pass) I should deny thee (Panphilus) my love : but before my true heart should harbour one treacherous thought thereof, these hands of mine should rent it from my breast, and be the executioners of my just death.

" But let us leave these imaginations, and that which we desire may never happen let us not with ominous augury divinate, and tempt the Gods in vain. But if thy mind be resolutely bent to depart, and forasmuch as there is nothing that can please me which may anyways displease and discontent thee, I must of necessity dispose myself to be agreeable to thy will herein. Notwithstanding, with earnest prayers I request thee, that it would please thee in one thing to follow my mind, in delaying (I mean) yet a little longer (if possibly it may be) thy sudden and sorrowful journey, during which time, imagining in the meantime thy departure, and with continual thinking thereof, presupposing thy absence, I may, with less grief of mind, learn and frame myself to live without thee : which is no strange thing for me to request, nor hard for thee to grant, since that the weather, which for this time of the year is most unreasonable, doth greatly incline to the help and favour of this my desire, and is most contrary to the drift of thy determination.

"Why, dost not thou see how the skies, full of dark and black clouds, with tempests, storms and *Virgil imi-* floods of pouring rain, and Hills of thick *tated in the* snows choking up the ways, with raging and *4th Book of* boisterous winds, and horrible thunders, *Æneas* do daily threaten the earth and earthly creatures with manifest dangers.

"And (as thou canst not otherwise know) how every little River and Brook is now by these continual showers of rain swelled into dangerous and mighty floods. What senseless man then is he (pardon me, good Panphilus) who (having so small regard of his life) would in this blustering, stormy and ill weather take any voyage or journey in hand? Do therefore my pleasure in this reasonable advice, which if thou wilt not do, then tender thy own safety, and do the duty which thou owest to thy own self herein. Let these lowering and doubtful times pass on, and stay for calmer wind and weather to travel at thine ease, and with less danger. And myself in the meanwhile (accustomed by little and little, and inured to pensive and sorrowful thoughts) will with more patience attend thy joyful return."

To these words he deferred not his answer but said: "The tormenting pains, and variety of painful cares, in the which (O dearest Mistress), against my will, content and pleasure, I leave thee, and those which unfeignedly I carry with me in mine own breast, let the comfortable hope of my speedy

75

return assuage and mitigate. Nor is it (pardon me, sweet Lady) a point of wisdom to busy thy thoughts about that (death, I mean) which may as well prevent me here, as surprise in another place, when my destinies must needs yield to their time, and to her stroke. Nor to conjecture and prognosticate of those accidents possible perhaps to annoy me as more likely to be prosperous unto me. Where and whensoever the wrath of the Gods or their favour doth light upon one, even there and then, without vain resistance, must he be content to suffer good or ill. Refer therefore all these things to their disposition, with never thinking or once looking after them, who knowing our necessities can provide better for us than we ourselves : desiring thee tò apply thy mind rather, and employ thy whole cogitations, in humble supplications and requests to them (the gracious Gods, I mean), that they may have a prosperous and happy event. But that I ever become Lover to any woman than to thee (Fiammetta), to whose loyal and everlasting service I religiously dedicate my heart and with oath bind myself, Great Jove himself (yea, though I would myself) with all his might can never bring to pass, for with so strong and sure a chain, Love hath linked my heart to thine, sweet affection hath made my soul subject to the signory, and deep desire hath bound me for ever to thy dispositions. And assure thyself of this besides. That the earth

76

shall first bring forth glittering Stars, and the
heaven (ploughed with Oxen) shall bring forth ripe
corn, before Panphilus shall or will in anything trans-
gress the laws of thy peerless love, or entertain any
other woman into the closet of his constant heart.
The delay of my departure into my Country, which
thou dost request of me, if I knew it could any
ways avail thee, or be profitable unto me, I would
more willingly perform than thou dost require. But
since the daily deferring of it is an hourly augmenta-
tion of our sorrows, and in departing now, I should
return again before the time of my long tariance
here should be (according perhaps to thy mind)
fully finished, I think it therefore a great deal better
to hasten my journey. Which space of time thou
dost also crave to learn (as thou sayest) supposed
sorrows, wherein thou dost simply deceive thyself,
considering that in this meantime thou shouldest
have (myself not being here) that selfsame grief so
forcible and extreme, which at my departure indeed,
and in my unfeigned absence thou wouldest conceive. And as for the foulness of the weather, I will
use (as other times I have been accustomed to do)
a good and wholesome remedy, which I would (the
Gods granted) that I had now occasion to practise
returning from thence again, as in departing from
hence I know to work well enough. And therefore
with a cheerful and strong mind (my loving Fiammetta) dispose thyself to this, which (when thou

77

must do) thou mayest better pass away in doing it on a sudden, than with successive fear and lingering sorrow expect every hour when to begin it."

My tears (at the end of his persuasion somewhat relented) attending some other answer, and hear-*The manner* ing this sorrowful discourse, did redouble *of those that* their falling drops. Wherefore laying my *love* heavy head upon his breast I stayed a good while without speaking any more unto him, and revolving many things in my mind, I could not assent to his consolatory persuasions nor dissent from his alleged assertions. For (alas) who would have answered otherwise to his words but thus: "Do that which pleaseth thee best, and come quickly again." Truly I believe none. But not without great grief and effusion of many tears, after a long while I gave him that answer, telling him, moreover, that undoubtedly it should be a great wonder to find me alive at his return. After I had spoken these words, one comforting up the other, we wiped and dried up each other's tears, and for that night did defer them till some other time.

And he (keeping his old custom) came to see me many times, which were but a few days (alas) before his departure, much changed in habit, and more (as it seemed) altered in mind, from that, since first he saw me. But that woeful night (ah, that black and thrice cruel night) being come, which was the beginning of all my annoys, and the last conclusion of all my joys, with divers and sundry discourses, but not without great anguish of mind, grievous wailings, and Seas of tears, and of sorrowful sobs and *The* sighs on both sides, we passed soon away. *description* Which (although for that time of the year *of the day* was very long) yet to me it seemed the shortest night in all my lifetime. And now the open day (the menacing enemy, and divider of Lovers) began to overcome the light of the stars, the sign of which (coming on very fast after it) appeared to my eyes, embracing him most straitly I said thus:

" O the sweetest Lord of my life, what cruel one is he, that doth take thee from me? What angry God is that, which with so great force doth wreak his ire on me, that while I live it may be said Panphilus is not there where his Fiammetta is? Woe is me therefore, poor soul, that knowest not whither thou goest now, that live desolate, and destitute of thy company. When will that happy time come when once again I shall between my stretched arms enfold this lovely and sweet body? Alas, I fear me never. And as I know not, so am I not able to express that, which my miserable heart divining, went up and down, saying and lamenting in this sorrowful sort." But oftentimes, recomforted of him again, I kissed him infinite times. And after many loving embracements, both of us very loath to rise, yet at the last, the encroaching light of the new day

79

compelling us, unwillingly we did forsake the receptacle and secret testimony of our delights. And he preparing now to give me his last kisses, and farewells, with plenteous tears I first began to utter these words : " Behold, my only love, thou goest, and in short time dost promise thy return. Wherefore assure me thy faith hereof (if so it please thee), so that expecting the same (not accounting for all that thy bare words as vain) I may have of thy future firmness some lively hope and pledged comfort."

Then he intermingling his tears with mine, and hanging about my neck, wearied I think with heavy grief of mind, with a feeble voice said thus again :, " By illuminate Apollo (sweet Lady), I swear unto thee, who with most swift pace coming into our hemisphere (contrary to our desires) doth minister a sorrowful occasion of our sudden departure, and whose golden beams I do attend for my gladsome guides : and by that indissoluble love, which I . bear thee, and by that due and forced piety which doth divide me from thee, that four months shall not fully pass but (if the Gods be gracious to me herein) thou shalt see me here returned to thee again." And then, taking my right hand in his, he turned himself to that side where he saw the Images of our Gods hanging and said : " O most holy Gods, coequal and just governors of Heaven and earth, be present witnesses of this my faithful promise, and of my inviolable given faith.

And be thou also present (O mighty Love) the secret knower of all these things.

"And thou most stately Chamber, more pleasant to me than the heavens and divine habitacles to the Gods, as thou hast been a secret witness of our desires, so likewise keep these words enclosed in thy Walls, in the least of which if (by my own fault) I do fail, let the just indignation of the angry Gods be such towards me, as Ceres her ire was (in times past) towards Erisichthone, as Diana's scorn was wreaked upon gazing Acteon, or such as jealous Juno's envy appeared towards simple believing Semele."

And when he had so said, with a zealous affection and earnest desire he embraced me, and with a feeble and interrupted voice he gave me his last *A dio.*

After he had thus taken his leave, overcome, poor wretch, with extreme anguish of mind, and woeful wailings, I could scarce answer him anything again, but yet at the last by plain and main force, I did fetch these trembling words out of my sad and heavy mind : "Thy assured faith solemnly promised to me, and sincerely given by thy right hand to mine, let Jupiter confirm in heaven with the effect, as Isis did the prayers of Teleteuse, and make it so perfect and entire in earth, as I do effectually desire, and as thou dost with sacred oath require." And accompanying him to my Palace Gate, and opening my lips to bid him farewell, suddenly my words

were taken from my tongue, and the light of heaven
from mine eyes. And like a ruddy vermilion Rose

The effect cut down with scythe in open fields, feel-
of an en- ing the parching and contracting heat of
amoured
woman the Sunbeams, doth fall down amongst
the green leaves, and losing by little and little
his former colour, doth die: so half alive and
dead I fell between my Maiden's arms, and not a
little while after, by her diligent care and help,
who was most faithful unto me, with cold liquors
(recalled back again to this sorrowful world) I did
begin to feel the recovery of my former strength and
forces. And hoping that he was yet at the gate,
like a fierce Bull, having received a mortal wound,
furiously rouseth himself, running and leaping here
and there, so I amazed and lifting up my dimmed
eyes, which had scarcely yet received their perfect
sight, ran eagerly upon my Maid with open arms
to embrace her, thinking to have clasped my Panphilus between them, and with a faint and hoarse
voice, broken as it were in a thousand pieces with
incessant weeping and wailing, I said: "O my soul,
farewell." The maid held her peace seeing my error.
But afterwards having the full feeling of my senses,
and perceiving indeed that I was deceived, I hardly
kept myself from falling the second time into the
like trance. It was now clear day in every place,
when seeing myself in my chamber without my
Panphilus, and looking round about me, and being

ignorant (almost) and astonied for a great while
how this might come to pass, I asked my waiting-
maid what was become of him, and the poor soul
with lamenting answered: "It is a good while since,
Madame, that he bringing you hither in his arms,

The the bright day stealing on, hath by force
curiosity (and not without infinite tears) separated
of lovers and taken him from you." To whom I
said again: "And is therefore gone?" "Alas, good
Madame, yea," said she. And yet consequently I
asked her again: "With what kind of countenance
did he depart?" "With the most sober, saddest
and most sorrowful look" (said she) "and like one
who had the picture of grief, care and anguish lively
depainted in his demiss visage." Afterwards I
followed and asked her what kind of gesture he did
use, and what words he did speak, when he went
away. And she answered: "You being, good Lady,
half dead between my arms, and your soul wandering (I know not where), he got you quickly and
softly into his arms, as soon as he saw you in so
strange a plight, and searching up and down with
his hand in every place, if your fainting soul was
yet contained in your appalled body, and finding
your heart panting, and beating strongly against your
tender sides, bewailing and complaining, a thousand
times and more, with the secret virtue (I think) of
his last kisses he called you back again. But when
he saw you still immovable, and as cold yet as the

83

marble stone, he brought you hither, and doubting of some worse mishap, weeping oftentimes, he kissed your pale visage, saying: 'O ye high Gods, if there be any harm committed and caused by my departure, let your just doom light upon me and not upon the faultless Lady: reduce her vagrant soul into her proper place again, so that of this last joy that doth remain (that is to see me at my last departure, and to give her last ambrosial kisses, with her angelical voice once again saying farewell), we may receive a little comfort.' But after that he perceived no feeling in you, as one devoid of counsel in this cause, and ignorant what to do, laying you softly on the bed, and like the surging waves of the Sea (tossed up and down with stormy winds) wallow and rush violently sometimes forward, and immediately with as much force totter back again, even so he suddenly, flinging from you to the chamber door, espied through the windows the threatening lightsome air (enemy to his abode) with hasty speed to come on. And coming running from thence to you suddenly again, and still calling and crying on you, rejoining as many sweet kisses, as raining bitter tears upon your fair and fainting face. But when he had done so many times together, and seeing that his stay with you could be no longer, embracing you, he said: 'O sweetest Lady and only hope of my heavy heart, whom now (of force departing from thee) I leave in doubtful state of life, the pitiful Gods restore to thee again thy lost comfort, and preserve thee so long in life, that we may see ourselves once again joyful and merry together, as now (deprived of all consolation) this bitter departing doth divide us asunder.' And all the while he spake these words, he did so extremely lament, that the vehement sobs and sighs, that seemed to cleave the heavens, and his loud plaints, did oftentimes strike a great fear into me, lest that they had been not heard of those only in our house, but of our next neighbours also.

" And not permitted now to tarry any longer, by reason of the clear brightness of the day that more and more came creeping on, with greater abundance *An ominous* of tears than before, he said: 'Ah, my *and ill* sweet heart, farewell.' And drawn away *presage* as it were by force, hitting his foot a great blow against the threshold of the door, he went out of our house.

" From whence being gone (S.T.) he said, looking back, meaning that he could scarce go forwards, and still looking back at every step, thinking that when you came to yourself again, I should call him back again to you." She now held her peace.

And I (good Ladies) as you may imagine, sorrowing and lamenting for the departure of my dear lover, remained the most comfortless and distressed woman, bewailing with continual tears his sudden and unfortunate absence.

THE
THIRD BOOK OF BOCCACE
HIS FIAMMETTA

S you have heard (gentle Ladies) before, even in such sort (my Panphilus being gone) did I remain, and with many tears not a few days after I woefully bewailed his sorrowful departure. And there was not anything else in my mouth (although I spake it softly to myself) than : "O my Panphilus, how may it be that thou hast forsaken me ?" This name truly, when I remembered the sweet accents of it, amongst my many bitter tears, did yield me no small *Fond* comfort. There was no part of my chamber *thoughts of* which I did not with a most desirous eye *lovers* behold, saying to myself : "Here did my Panphilus sit, here did he lie, here did I kiss him." And in brief, every place in the same, by representing such sweet objects to my memory, was most dear unto me. Sometimes I feigned with myself, thinking, that (returned back again) he came to see me, and, as if he had been indeed, I looked towards the chamber door, and perceiving myself deluded with my vain fancy, I was angry with myself, knowing that I was deceived indeed. And because I would drive away vain cogitations, I remembered that

87

oftentimes I began to busy myself about many things, but overcome of new imaginations, and leaving the same undone, my miserable heart with an unaccustomed beating did begin to molest me. I called to my mind many things which I would at his departure have said unto him, and repeating also many times with myself those words which we had to each other spoken. And in this manner, not setting my mind firmly on anything, I lived many days together a most sorrowful and pensive life. But after that this great grief (conceived by his departure) by length of time was somewhat alleviated, more forcible and violent thoughts began to enter into my mind, and, being lodged there, did with probable and apparent reasons keep and defend themselves there. And not many days after, remaining all alone in my chamber, it came to pass that I began to say to myself:

"Behold my lover is gone, and is going on his weary way, and thou, poor soul, couldest not at his departure once say farewell, nor pray the Gods to be his guides, nor kiss his troubled countenance, no, not so much as see him: which things if he keep *Lovers* in mind, and if any infortunious accident *oftentimes* (which the Gods forbid) happen unto him, *blame and excuse them-* conjecturing some ominous sign by thy *selves again* silence, may greatly (perchance) blame thee for it." This thought troubled my mind very much at the first, but a new counsel and conceit of other

· 88

matters removed it again from me, because among my sundry thoughts, I said with myself: "I ought not to incur any blame herein, because he, being endued with great wisdom, will sooner expound my sudden ecstasy for a lucky presage, saying: 'She said not farewell, which is commonly wont to be said to them who mean to absent themselves for a great while, when they depart, or else utterly to take their leave,' but holding my peace, he will rather think with himself that it was a sign whereby to note that short time assigned for his stay there."

And recomforting myself again with this flattering imagination, I let it pass, and entered into other new and divers thoughts. And being thus beset with sorrow on every side, I remained all alone, my heart being wholly pensive for him, walking sometimes up and down in my solitary chamber, sitting down now in this place, and now standing in a muse in that, and other sometimes leaning my heavy head upon my hand against my bedside, I said to myself: "O that my Panphilus were come hither now again!" And then from these fancies I passed into other new conceits. As sometimes (for example) with great grief I called to mind how with smiting his foot against the threshold of the door he went out of my chamber, as my trusty waiting-woman had told me. And remembering also that Laodameia did gather no greater token of Protesilaus his long absence, and unperformed return, by no other sign

than by this, it made me many times fall into great
and ruthful considerations thereof, fearing lest the
selfsame thing (which the Gods grant not) might
as unfortunately befall to me. But not conceiving
yet, in the depth of my mind, what should happen
unto me indeed, I let these, as vain and frivolous
imaginations, pass away, which did never the sooner
at my will and pleasure depart, but when others
coming afresh in their places, then did these forsake
my melancholy mind.

And recounting those now in my mind, that were
come, which were so many and so great, that to
Troubles think of their number only (if of nothing
and cares else) it was no small pain to my poor heart,
are wont to for I did not once remember (amongst my
extinguish
love in other thoughts) that I had read in Ovid
young men his verses that troubles, cares and painful
affairs did drive love out of young and tender minds,
but rather, so often, when I remembered that he
was on his way. And thinking, that these were
no small annoyances unto everyone, and especially
to him, whom I knew had been ever accustomed to
rest, and acquainted with ease, and now most of all,
when he was constrained to them against his will.

Wherefore I did first greatly doubt with myself
lest the smallest of these griefs might not have
been means forcible enough to have taken him from
me, and feared again, lest his unwonted travails,
and the hurtful and unseasonable weather, might

90

have been an occasion of sickness, or of some worse mischance, that might have hindered his designs, and so hurt my desires. And in this doleful imagination (I remember) my mind was no longer busied than in any other, although that I did oftentimes argue, by the induction of his unfeigned tears, which I did see trickle down his cheeks, and of my painful troubles, which never changed my firmness, that it could not be a true conclusion, that for so little grief, so great love should be extinct, hoping also, that his young age (mastered with singular discretion and wisdom) would defend and keep him from any other hurtful accident.

Thus therefore, in opposing, answering and dissolving my own objections, I spent so many days, that I did not only think that he was now arrived in his country, but I was also certified thereof by his letters, which for many causes were most welcome and acceptable unto me : in the which he certified me, that with greater flames of affection he burned more in my love than ever he did, and with stronger promises did revive my hope of his return. Wherefore my first thoughts being gone, from this hour forward, new fancies did quickly arise in their places.

For sometimes I said: "Now my Panphilus, the only beloved son of his old father, who many years before had not seen him, received of him with great joy, feasted of all his kinsfolks, and dearly entertained of all his friends, doth not only forget me, but doth (I think) accurse the months, days and hours in the which, with divers occasions hereto-*They that love are always in suspicion* fore, my love hath stayed him here. And honourably welcomed of all his compeers, and with joyful congratulation of all Ladies and Gentlewomen, doth blame me (perhaps) who knew not how to feed his dainty fancies in anything else than in simple unfolding my secret love, and the strange effects of my new affections unto him, when he was here. And minds full of mirth and jollity are apt to be drawn from one place, and to be bound to another, according to the mutability of their pleased and displeased fancies. But (alas) may it now be, that I should lose him in this sort.

"Truly I cannot hardly think it. The Gods forbid that this should come to pass : and grant that as amongst my parents, and kinsfolks, and in my own and native City, they have made and kept me only his, so amongst his kindred, and in his natural country, let them vouchsafe to preserve him only mine."

Alas, with how many salt tears were these words mingled, and with how many more should they have been, if I had believed that that which they themselves did truly prognosticate should afterwards have proved true : albeit that those, which then came not forth, I have afterwards in treble-fold spent all in vain. Besides such speeches, my mind (divining oftentimes of her woes to come) surprised (I know not with what fear), did greatly tremble and quake, which fear was most commonly resolved into these stinging thoughts, and words :

"Panphilus, abiding now joyfully in his City, full of most famous and excellent temples, and by reason of most solemn and high feasts, with exceeding pomp and glory celebrated there, doth with great pleasure visit them : where he cannot choose but find many fair and noble women, which, as in surpassing beauty, gallant behaviour and good graces they excel all others, so most of them being skilful practitioners in their enticing art, with subtle snares and amorous allectives are passing cunning to entrap young and gentle minds, thereby to draw them to their liking, and so to lure them to their love. Alas, who can then be so strong a guardian of himself, where so many motives do concur, but must (maugre his beard) at some time or other by plain force be overtaken : as I myself, not many months sithence, by like powers also assailed, may be an approved and hapless president of such strange and strong virtues, which in my simple breast prevailed. And besides this, new things are wont to delight more than old. It is therefore but an easy matter, that he (being newly arrived, and a stranger) may please them, and they him again."

Alas, how grievous was this imagination to me, the which that it should not come to pass, I could scarce drive out of my mind, saying thus : "How may Panphilus, who loveth thee more than himself, receive into that heart, enclosed in thine, any other new love ? Why, dost not thou know, that there is here perhaps some brave Lady well worthy of his love, who with greater force than with that of her eyes hath oft assayed and endeavoured to enter into his heart, but could not find any way whereby, he being yet scarce thine, as now he is, so many more Goddesses also of beauty passing up and down in this City, and yet not any one of them able to move his mind ? How canst thou then think that he may be so soon enamoured as thou sayst ? And besides this, dost thou believe, that he would violate that troth, which so religiously he avowed unto thee, for any other faith ? It may never be, and therefore thou must trust to his fidelity, and rely upon his good discretion. With great reason thou oughtest to think that he is not so meanly wise, but that he knoweth, well enough, that it is but mere folly to leave that, which already he hath, to get that, which he hath not, yea, if that which he would forsake were but a small thing, and of great deal less account, in respect of that which he seeketh to attain, being of greater estimation and value. And of this also thou must have an infallible hope, that this cannot so easily come to pass : because if the great fame and general report of thy beauty be true, which thyself hast often heard, thou mayest (placed amongst the number of the bravest Ladies in his Country, and to the fairest

of them all paragoned) be prized above the best,
which hath not in it any one richer, braver or more
nobly born than thyself. And besides this, whom
can he find amongst all the Gentlewomen in his
City, that would, nay that could, love him so dearly
as thou dost.

"Again, he is not ignorant (as one expert in amorous
affairs) how hard a labour, and intricate a matter it
is, so to dispose and work with any woman, to make
her like at the first, or at the first assaults to make
her yield to love. And although he did not love
thee at all, yet being troubled about many affairs of
his Father, and occupied with his proper business, he
could not now be at vacant leisure to acquaint himself with other new women. Wherefore let not this
only fall into thy thought, but hold it for an infallible
Maxim, that as much as thou lovest, so much thou art
beloved again." Alas, how falsely and sophistically
were these arguments coined against the truth. But
with all my disputing, I could never refel and put
out of my mind the obscure and miserable jealousy
entered into it for advantage, and accomplishment
of my other griefs. But yet somewhat lightened
(as if I had argued truly), and eased a little thereby,
I did to my feeble power remove such injurious
thoughts from my mind. O dearest Ladies, because
I will not spend the time in recounting every one
of my uncouth thoughts, what were my most careful deeds you shall now hear. At the strangeness

of which marvel not, since I must needs follow, not
those which I would, but such as it pleased Love to
give me, ah, those was I constrained to perform.
Very few mornings escaped me when, risen out of
my weary bed, I went not up to the highest turrets
of my Palace, and from thence no otherwise than
the Mariners, climbing up to the top (of their main
Mast, do pry on every side, to see if they can espy
any dangerous Rocks, or ken any land that is near,
which may hinder their continued course), I first
looked about me on every side. And afterwards,
fastening mine eyes steadfastly towards the East, I
did mark how much the Sun, elevated above the
Horizon, had spent of the new day, and the more
I saw it higher, the more I said (to myself) that
the term of Panphilus his return drew on, and many
times I did with great delight, as it were, see it
rise and come forth, and discerning sometimes my
own shadow, by the ascended quantity of it in the
Merediall line, made less and less, and sometimes
looking to the space of his body, made bigger by the
earth in his setting, I said with myself, that he went
more slowly than ever he did before, and did lengthen
the days more in Capricorn than he was wont to do
in Cancer, and so likewise, mounted up to the middle
circle, I said that there he stayed too long to delight
himself in overlooking the wide earth. And although
he glided down swiftly towards the west, yet methought he was too long in his course again, whose

light after that our Hemisphere had lost, and that
the twinkling stars had full scope to show forth
theirs, thus partly contented, I went numbering
Lovers and calling to mind many times with myself
mark their the days that were past, and with little
days with
stones stones did mark those with other days
also that were to come, no otherwise than in times
past (dividing their merry and happy days from their
sorrowful and dismal times with little black and white
stones) were wont to do. Oh, how many times do I
now remember, that before their due time I did put a
stone there, thinking that so much of the prescribed
term should be diminished how much the sooner I
adjoined it to that which was already past, sometimes counting the little stones assigned for the
days past, and sometimes telling those which stood
for those days which were yet to come, although I
kept the number of every one of them very well in
my mind (thinking every time to have found some of
them increased, and that the other should have been
diminished). So did my eager hot desire transport
me to the wished end of the prefixed term. Using
therefore these vain cares, I returned many times
to my desolate chamber, more desirous to be there
all alone, than willingly in any company. And when
I was alone, to drive away sorrowful cogitations, I
opened a certain casket of mine, out of the which
I took many things (sometimes his favours bestowed
on me) by one and one, and the delight and great

G

desire which once I had in beholding him I did now take in gazing upon them, which when I had seen, scarce able to contain my swelling tears, yet fetching great sighs, I kissed them, and as if they had been rational creatures, and things of understanding, I did ask them saying, " When will your M. be here ? " and laying them up again, I drew forth many of his letters which he had foretimes sent me, and reading almost every one of them over, and imagining that I did talk with him, I felt no little comfort. I called oftentimes my faithful and secret maid unto me, with whom I had much and divers communication touching him, sometimes asking her what her hope was of his return, and sometimes what she thought of him, or if at any time she had heard anything of him.

To all which demands, either to please me, or else according to her opinion, answering the truth, it was a great comfort to my desolate mind. And thus many times I passed away the greater part of the day with less grief and sadness. I took no less *Variety of* pleasure and content (than in the foresaid *talk doth* things) to visit the holy Temples, and to *diminish* *sorrow and* sit at my Palace Gate with other Gentle- *sadness* women of my acquaintance, where oftentimes with sundry discourses my infinite cares were somewhat removed from me. To which places sometimes resorting, it fell out often, that I saw divers of those young Gentlemen whom I did know to keep Panphilus company : and whensoever I espied them, I did never forget to look amongst them, if happily I might see Panphilus with them, as sometimes I did. Oh, how oftentimes was I vainly deluded with this foolish imagination. And although I was thus deceived, yet it did me much good to see them, whom (as by their pitiful countenances they bewrayed as much) I saw full of like compassion, that I had in seeing themselves alone (as it were) and deprived of their sweet companion, and who (methought) seemed not half so merry as they were wont to be.

Ah, what a great desire had I many times to ask them what was become of their gentle friend and associate, if reason and modesty had not counter-checked my eager will herein. But Fortune truly was sometimes favourable to me herein, because in talking of him in suchlike places, and thinking that I did not hear and understand them, they said that his return was almost at hand : and how sweet these words were to mine ears it were a bootless labour to express. In this sort therefore, and with such sundry thoughts and superstitious deeds, and with many other like these, I did study to pass the tedious days away, which were so irksome to me in their length, desiring therefore still for night, not because of both I thought of it more profitable or comfortable for me, but because when it was come there was the more time spent, and the less to pass away. After that the cumbersome day therefore (whose long hours being finished) gave place to silent night, fresh fancies and new cares came also in company with the same. And I, who from my cradle being *Love doth* naturally given to be afraid in the solitary *assure* *lovers in* darkness of night, accompanied now with *darkness* mighty love, was free from all manners of fear. And perceiving everyone in my house to take their quiet rest, sometimes I went up alone to that place where I had not long since seen the Sun rising in the morning, and as Arontes did speculate the celestial bodies, and their orbicular motions, between the white Marbles in the hills of Lucca, so did I (the night creeping on with overlong minutes, and feeling the great cares and careful thoughts to be enemies unto my wished sleep) behold the Heavens from that place, and the swift revolutions of them, imagining with myself that they were wonderful slow in their course : and sometimes turning mine eyes steadfastly towards the horned Moon (having recourse to her wane, and to her roundness), I perceived, by the increase and decrease of it, some nights to be longer and shorter than other. And so much the more my desire was made more fervent, by how much sooner I wished, that the four months by her sweet course had been brought to an end. Oh, how many times (although it lent a dimmed and obscure light) did I behold it a great while together with great delight, imagining that my Panphilus his eyes were then fixed on it as well as mine. Whom for all

100

that I do not now doubt that (I being now quite out of his memory) he did not once care to look on the Moon, but not having so much as a thought thereof, he did rather at that time of the night take his rest in his bed.

And I remember, that aggrieved at the slowness of her course, with divers sounds (following the old *Lovers who* and ancient errors of those many years ago) *expect the* I helped her forwards in her slow course, *return of* *their be-* to grow to her full roundness, to the which *loved think* after that it was come, contented with *every hour* *to be longer* her perfect and full light, she cared not *than other* (as it seemed) to diminish the same again, and to return to her new horns, but to remain still in her round form, albeit with myself I held her excused for the same, esteeming her abode more favourable and gracious with her joyful Mother than desirous to return to the dark kingdoms of her infernal Husband. But I remember well, that the devout petitions and earnest prayers, which many times I offered up unto her, to accelerate her easy and slow pace, I turned now into threatening speeches, saying:

"O Phœbe, an evil rewarder of the devout service done unto thee, with pitiful prayers I labour to lessen thy travel and weary journey, but thou, not esteeming them, with long and slow tariance (injurious to thyself and to me) dost not care to increase mine. And therefore if, to the necessity of

my help, thou dost not return more bicorned, thou
shalt then perceive me as slow in thy honours and
sacrifices, which I mean to offer up unto thee, as
now I find thee careless and slack in thy duty to
the world. Why, dost not thou know, that the
sooner thou shalt four times horned, and as many
times round, have showed thy lights to mortal
creatures, by so much the sooner my Panphilus
shall return to me again : who being once come
back, then as slow or as swift as thou wilt thou
mayest run out thy compass and circles."

Truly that selfsame madness which did induce
me to make such prayers, that very same did so
bereave me of myself that it made me sometimes
think that she (afraid of my threatenings) made
greater haste in her course only for my pleasure :
and other times, seeming not to care for me, to be
more slow than she was before. This often beholding on her, made me so skilful in her nature and
course that, when she was in her wane, or in any
part of heaven, or conjoined with any star, I might
have fully judged and known how much of the night
had passed away, and how much was to come.

Both the Bears likewise (if she had not appeared)
did by long experience make me very skilful and
certain thereof. Alas, who would have believed that
love could have taught me such Astrology, a science
more fit for finest wits, and profound judgments, and
not for a troubled mind occupied with his fury.

AMOROUS FIAMMETTA

When the heavens, full of darkest clouds and overrun with boisterous and tempestuous winds, and choked with misty fogs, did from this place take my sight away, sometimes (if I had no other matters to busy myself withal) calling my waiting-maids and Gentlewomen together in my Chamber, I did myself tell and (to please my strange humour) willed them also to recount divers tales, the which the more they were elonged from the truth (as for the most part such kind of people are wont to tell) so much the more (methought) they had greater force to drive away sighs, and to make me merry, who gave diligent care unto them, so that sometimes, notwithstanding my melancholy fits, I laughed apace at them. And if perhaps such feigned jests and invented tales could not (as true matters) be *To have* justly set down in divers fabulous Books, *company* yet in searching out of other's mysteries *in misery* by them, and applying these with mine, *doth make* and perceiving myself to have company *the grief* *the lighter* in my sorrows, I passed the time away with less grief. Neither do I know which of these was most gracious unto me, to see the nights passed away and spent, or else (my mind busied about other things) to see the days run on and spent.

But after that the foresaid operations, and many other devices, had occupied my senses for a good while, I went, enforcing myself (as it were) to sleep, although I knew it was but in vain, and therefore

went rather to lie down to sleep. And being all
alone in my bed, and troubled with no rumours
and noise, all those thoughts almost, which in the
daytime had sursaulted me, came now afresh to my
mind, and in despite of myself made me, with many
more arguments pro and con, to repeat them against
myself.

And I would many times have entered into others,
which thing (alas) was not so easily granted unto
me, but yet sometimes by very force leaving them,
and lying on that side where sometimes my Panphilus was wont to lie, which place reserving yet
(as it were) a sweet savour and scent of his body,
methought my drowsy senses therewith revived,
and, my mind greatly contented, I did call him
softly with myself, and (as though he had heard
me indeed) I did sweetly pray him that he would
Divers return quickly again. I did after imagine
thoughts of that he was come again, and feigning many
lovers frivolous things with myself, by one and
one methought I did tell them unto him, and he
demanding many of me again, I did answer again in
his place : and sometimes it happened that carried
away with such foolish thoughts I fell at last asleep,
which was sometimes more pleasant and more
welcome to me than any watching and waking, because when I was awake I did falsely suppose these
imaginations with myself.

But this, if it had endured but any small time,
104

did make them appear no otherwise to my fancies than if they had been true indeed. Sometimes *Dreams* methought he was returned, and that in *represent* most fair Gardens (free from all suspicion *many times* and fear) decked with green leaves, sweet *those things* and fear) decked with green leaves, sweet *which are* flowers, and divers kinds of pleasant *beloved* fruits, I sported and played with him as other times we did accustom to do. And there, I holding him by the hand, and he me, unfolding his fortunes good and bad, and telling all his accidents unto me, methought that many times before he had perfectly told out his tale, with often kissing I did interrupt him in his delightful discourses. And as if the same had been true indeed (which but with feigned eyes I did contemplate) I said : "And is it true (sweet Panphilus) that thou art returned again ? Certes it is. For here I have thee." And then I kissed him again. Methought that other times with great solace I was walking with him up and down the sea banks. And sometimes my imagination was so strong herein that I did affirm it with myself, saying : "Well now I do not dream that I have him between my arms." Oh, how it grieved me when it came to pass that my pleasant dreams and sweet sleep were both ended, which (going away) did continually carry that away with them which, without any trouble or grief to him, I must needs confess did oppress me. And although that I remained in great melancholy by remembering of them, living nevertheless all the next day in good hope, I was somewhat content and eased, desiring still that night would quickly draw on, because I might in my sleep enjoy that, which waking I could not attain to. And although my sleep did sometimes yield me such needy favours, notwithstanding it did not permit me to receive such dreams of pleasure mingled without much bitter and poisoned gall of sorrow, because many times (methought) I saw him apparelled with ragged and forlorn garments, besmeared all over (I know not) with what foul and black spots, and very pale and fearful, as though he had been pursued of some cruel enemy, with shrieks and outcries calling to me: "Help me, O my Fiammetta, help me!" Other times (methought) I heard divers talk and mutter of his death.

And sometimes these fantasies of horror pierced so far into my mind that (methought) I saw him lie dead before me: and in many other uncouth and pitiful forms, so that it never came to pass *Things seen* that my sleep was of more force or greater *in dreams* than my grief. Wherefore suddenly awaked, *are some-* *times true* and knowing the vanity of my dream, as *or else* one contented yet but to have dreamed *figures* *of true* these terrors and terrible dangers, I *things* thanked the Gods, remaining yet somewhat troubled in mind, and fearing that the things which I had seen, if not in all, in part at least they had been true, or else figures of true things to come. Neither I was content at any time or persuaded by the contrariety of these (although I said with myself, and heard of others, that dreams were but vain) until I did hear some news of him, of the which I began now carefully and warily to inquire after. And in such sort (as you have heard, fair Ladies) I passed away the tedious days and irksome nights, attending one still after other in their long course. But the truth is that, the time of his promised return approaching, I deemed it the best and safest counsel to live merely in the meantime: by which means my beauty (a little altered and decayed by reason of this long unacquainted grief) might return again into her proper place, because at his arrival I might not seem ill favoured and not gracious in his sight, and so might not (perhaps) please his dainty and curious eyes.

Which was not hard for me to do, because being, since his departure, accustomed and well acquainted with sorrows, it made me endure and pass them away with very little trouble or no pain at all. And besides this, the near hope of his promised return made me every day feel a little more joy, and content of mind. Wherefore I began to frequent the feasts again, not a little while before intermitted of me, ascribing the occasion thereof to my obscured and cloudy days, perceiving now the clear and new times to be at hand.

Nor no sooner did my mind (contracted erst with
most bitter and pinching griefs) begin to dilate
and enlarge itself in such a pleasant and joyful life,
but I became fairer than ever I was before. And
I trimmed up my gorgeous and rich vestures, and
made my precious ornaments fairer, no otherwise
than a valiant Knight at arms doth clear and make
bright his Complete Harness, challenged to some
worthy and famous combat, because I might seem
more stately and bravely attired with them at his
return, the which (as after it fell out) in vain I
did attend. As then therefore these actions were
changed into another tenour, so did my thoughts
also change their copy.

It came never now into my mind that I could
not see him when he departed, nor the remembrance
Vain of the sorrowful sign of his smitten foot
thoughts against the door, nor any thought of sting-
of lovers ing and envious jealousy, nor his sustained
troubles, nor my suffered toils, nor his dangers, nor
my dolours did now molest my peace, but rather days
next before the end of his promised return I said
to myself: "Now it doth grieve my Panphilus to be
long from me, and perceiving his time near, according to his promise, doth make short preparation
and haste for his speedy return. And now perhaps,
having left his old father, he is on his way."

Oh, how pleasant were these words unto me, and
how often did I most sweetly descant upon this note,

thinking many times with myself, with what kind
of most loving entertainment, gracious gesture,
and sweet and friendly shows, I might at the first
represent myself unto his person, and welcome him.
Alas how many times said I to myself:

" At his return he shall be more than a thousand
times embraced of me, and my zealous kisses shall
be multiplied in such store that they shall not suffer
one right and perfect word to come out of his mouth,
and I will make restitution of them a hundred times
redoubled, which at his departure (without receiving
on his part any again) he gave to my pale and half-
dead visage." And in these kind of thoughts I
doubted many times with myself that I could not
bridle that burning and fervent desire that I should
then have, at the first sight of him, to embrace
him, if I did (perhaps) see him in open and public
company.

But the ungentle Gods (as you shall hereafter
perceive) found out a sorrowful means, which persuaded no fear, doubt or mistrust of the due performance of any such circumstances, and ceremonies,
denying me the chiefest thing indeed. Remaining
therefore continually in my chamber, and as often
as anybody came into the same, so often did I believe
that they were come to bring me tidings that he was
coming, or else to tell me that he was already arrived,
I never heard any talk in any public and private
place, but with open and attentive ears I noted it

well, thinking that either they did, or else should, speak of his return.

And sitting in my chamber I rose (I think) a thousand times out of my place to run to the window, as though I had been busied about something else, and looking from thence afar off, and beneath also at the door (driven on by the suggestion of a foolish conceit, and fond belief of his being near), I said : " Is it possible, Fiammetta, that Panphilus being now returned doth come to see thee ? " And afterwards, finding my mind illuded, confounded with myself, I went to my place again. And saying, that at his return he should bring certain things to my husband, I did oftentimes ask, and caused many to inquire, if he was arrived, or when his friends in these parts did look for him. But receiving no joyful answer of my diligent and careful inquiries, but only such an one as of him that should never come any more (as afterwards indeed he did not), caused me to live in a most sorrowful and solitary plight. Wherefore wrapped (most pitiful Ladies) in these cares, as you have heard, I came not only to the greatly desired and (with infinite pain) expected term, but I passed it, also many days after, in great and grievous woes. And uncertain with myself whether I should blame him or not, my hope began by little and little to relent.

Wherefore I partly left off my former and pleasant imaginations, into the which (giving perhaps my

mind too great a scope) I had entered too far.
And new thoughts now (the old being gone) began
to toss and turmoil my soul afresh, and holding my
mind (in divers doubts and perplexities) to know
what was the occasion of his tariance longer than
he promised, I began to excogitate many things care-
They feel fully with myself. And before many other
incredible doubts that were objected to my mind, I
passions
who, after found many things so ready in his excuse,
the end of and many more than he himself (if he had
their pro-
mised time, been here) could have perhaps alleged.
see not the Sometimes I said : " O Fiammetta, what
return of
their beloved reason doth make thee think that thy
Panphilus doth stay without returning to thee but
because he cannot : divers sudden changes and unexpected affairs do many times hinder forward men
in their determinations, and do quite dissolve their de-
signments. Nor is it possible to prescribe so precise
a time to future things as many unwisely believe.
And who doth doubt also that present, near, ancient
and dutiful piety doth not bind more than that
which is absent, strange, new and but mere voluntary? I know it very certain, that he loveth me
most of all, and doth now think of my sorrowful
life, and hath no small compassion of my pains.
And pricked on by force of love is many times
in hand and most willing to set forwards, and to
come unto me. But the old dotard (his injurious
father) with his tears (perhaps) and prayers, hath

111

somewhat more prolonged his appointed time, and, opposing his commandments to his forward will, hath retained him still there. Wherefore as soon as fit opportunity is answerable to his desirous mind, he will come to me again."

But after these speeches and friendly excuses, my thronging thoughts did drive me on farther to imagine more strange, unlucky and more grievous occurrences. Sometimes I said:

"Who can tell, if he, more wilful (than his due love required) to see me again, and too precise to come just at the end of his appointed month, laying aside the great pity of his aged father, and neglecting all other business, hath embarked himself in some slender vessel, not attending the calms of the tempestuous waves (and crediting too much deceitful and lying Mariners, who for their gains are too adventurous and desperate of their own lives, and too prodigal of those of their passengers, and having committed himself to the rage of the merciless winds, and surging waves of the dangerous Seas) is perhaps drowned and perished in them. Unfortunate Leander by no other occasion and lamentable means than these was taken from his hapless Hero. Again who knoweth if, constrained by his froward fates, and fortune, he is thrown upon some unhabitable and desert rock, and, escaping danger and death by water, in exchange of that hath gotten a worse by famine or ravening fowls, or else left upon any rock by forgetfulness (as Achimenedes was) doth in vain attend that some should come, or by chance touch by, to fetch him from thence. For who is ignorant how full of deceits the lawless seas are ?

"For it may be also that he is taken by enemies, or with gins by wicked Pirates bound fast and kept in prison. All which perils, as they are common, so do we daily see them come to pass." But on the other side afterwards it came to my mind that his journey was more safe by land, yet I did imagine likewise of a thousand sinistrous chances that might hinder and stay him as well that way. Wherefore judging that he might (when such inopinate and unlucky hazards of fortune came suddenly and soonest objected to my mind) find the more just and better excuse (as he did allege the greater and worser dangers) sometimes I said :

"Behold the Sun, hotter than it was wont to be, doth dissolve the huge hills of Snow congealed in *The effect of* the middle region of the Air, whereupon *the Sun in the Spring-* with furious and flowing stream they came *time* pouring down into the plains, of the which he hath not a few to pass over. Wherefore if now, with more audacious rashness than advised reason, he hath adventured to pass over them, and with his horse is fallen into any of them, and stifled there amongst them hath miserably lost his life, why, how can he then come ? Floods have not learned of late, neither is it a strange thing to them, with these injuries to molest travellers, and cruelly to swallow up unawares those that pass over them. But if he hath happily escaped these unhappy dangers, he may be perchance fallen into the hands of some pitiless thieves, and (despoiled of all that he hath) is perforce kept, and without hope of redemption stayed of them.

" Or else peradventure may be overtaken by some malady in the way, where now he abideth for the recovery of his health, and after he is well again will without fail come joyfully to us." While these careful imaginations occupied thus my perplexed mind, a little cold sweat did overrun all my body, and I was so greatly afraid of the event of these uncertain dangers, and so strongly persuaded of their truth, that I turned my break-brain thoughts into pitiful prayers to the divine powers, that they would take the same from me, apprehending them so forcibly in my mind, and no more nor less, than if before mine eyes, I had seen his imminent danger, and instant death. And sometimes I remember that with firm belief I bewailed his woeful end, as if I had seen any of these intellectual adversities indeed.

But afterwards I said to myself: " Alas, what strange causes are these which my miserable thoughts cast before my eyes. The Gods forbid that any such may befall. Let him stay still, and as long as pleaseth him, and let him rather (than to content me, or to offer himself to any dangerous

114

jeopardy, which may chance indeed, though now they
do but delude my troubled wits) not return, nor see
me at all.

" All which perils (though they are indeed possible)
yet are they impossible to be kept close, being most
like that the untimely and violent death of so noble
and famous a young Gentleman as he is cannot
long be hidden, and concealed, especially from me,
of whose estate and welfare I do carefully cause, and
with secret and subtle investigations do continually
procure, diligent inquiry to be made.

" And who doth doubt moreover if that any of
these supposed perils were true, but that flying
Fame a Fame, the swift reporter of ill news, would
swift re- have long since brought the manner of his
porter of all
ill things death hither ? By means of which fortune
(but my least friend in this) would have given me an
open way to have made me the most sad and most
sorrowful woman that might me.

" Wherefore I rather believe, that he remaineth
in as great grief as I am in, if that his most willing
return is forbidden only by the heavy commandments of his father, and therefore he will come
quickly or else, excusing his staying so long, will for
my great comfort write to me the occasion thereof."

Truly (the foresaid thoughts) although they did
fiercely assault me, yet were they easily enough
overcome, and the hope, which by the term determined was enforced to fly from me, with all my

115

power I did retain, laying down before it the long and fervent love which he bare unto me, and I to him, his pawned faith, the adjured and sacred Gods, and his infinite tears, in which things I did affirm and think it impossible that any deceit or guile might be hidden. But yet I could not so rule my sorrowful mind, but that this hope, thus forcibly kept, must needs give place to many vagrant and vain thoughts, that were yet left behind, which, driving hereby little and little out of my woeful breast, did work amain to return to their former places, reducing eftsoons to my mind divers prodigious signs and tokens, and many other unfortunate accidents. And I did scarcely perceive, the peaceable hope being almost quite expelled out of my heart, but I did immediately feel their mighty and new forces planted in her place. But amongst all other murdering thoughts that did most of all massacre my grievous soul (hearing nothing at all in process of many days of my Panphilus his return) was sharp and stinging jealousy. Ah, this spitefully galled and wounded my breast more than I was able to endure. This did disannul all excuses (which I had made for him), as knowing and consenting to the occasion of his absent deeds. This did oftentimes induce me to those speeches condemned of me before, saying:

" Alas, how art thou so foolish to believe that either the love of his father, urgent affairs or delightful pleasures may now keep Panphilus from coming hither, if he did love thee so as once he said he did? Dost not thou know that Love doth overcome all

Love doth overcome all things things, for he hath (fervently (perhaps) enamoured of some other Gentlewoman) quite forgotten thee, whose pleasures, being as forcible as new, do hide and hold him there, as sometimes thine did keep him here.

" Those foresaid Ladies, passing gracious in everything they do, and (as thou saidst) in every point most apt to love, and with brave allurements endeavouring to be beloved again (he himself being likewise, by the delicate pureness of his clear complexion, naturally inclined to feel such passions, and for many rare and commendable qualities in him most worthy to be beloved), applying their whole studies to his service, their pains to his pleasures, and he his desires to their devotions, have made him become a new Innamorato. Art thou so assotted with the fame and glory of thine own beauty that thou dost not believe that other Women have shining eyes in their heads, fairness in their faces, and that they are not as full of courtly behaviour and good graces, and all things else, that may command young men's minds, as well as thou art? And dost thou think that they are not so skilful (who are (alas) a great deal more than ever thou wert) in these amorous attempts as thou art? Why, thou art deceived. And if this be thy belief it is false. And dost not likewise believe that he on the other side

117

can please more than one Woman ? But yet I think
that if he could but see thee, it would be a hard
thing for him to love any other. But since he cannot
see thee, nor hath not seen thee these many months,
how canst thou deem otherwise than so ? Thou
must needs know that no worldly accident is per-
manent and eternal, for as he was enamoured of
thee, and as thou didst please him, so is it possible
that another may like him, and he (abandoning thy
New things love) may affectionate some other. For
always new things are ever wont to please a great
please deal more than those which are daily seen.
And everyone doth with greater affection desire that
which he hath not than that which he hath already
in his own possession.

" Again, there is nothing, be it never so delightful, which by long time enjoying and using the same
doth not wear irksome at last, and of less (if of none)
account at all. Who will not moreover sooner and
more willingly love a fair and new Lady at his own
house, than one whom he hath long since served in
a foreign Country and unknown place. He did not
also love thee (perhaps) with so fervent and zealous
affection as he made thee believe. And neither
his tears nor any of his passions were to be held so
dear, and so sure a pledge of such great love, as he
did still affirm, and as thou didst think that he did
bear thee. Many men also, departing from their
beloved, are tormented with anguish, and grief of

mind, with bitter wailings, taking their woeful *congies*, swearing deeply, and promising many things profoundly, which with a good and firm intent (perhaps) they mean to perform, but some sudden and new chance controlling the same, is an occasion to make them forget all their former oaths and protestations.

"The tears, oaths and promises of young Men are not now, and of late, become arres and pledges of ensuing deceits for simple and credulous Women. They are generally more skilful and more apt to know all these things, than in knowing how to love, such is their vagabond wills, leading them to these inconveniences. And there is not any of them who would not sooner change ten Women every month than to adhere and keep himself ten months only to one. These continually believe to find out some new customs, forms and devices, and do greatly glory to have had the love (ah, the spoil) of many Women. What dost thou therefore hope for? Wherefore dost thou suffer thyself to be abused with vain and false belief? And yet (Fiammetta), though thou knowest not the means, and art not able to withdraw him from this, yet continue thou still in loving him: and show, that with that art, that he hath betrayed thee, thou hast not deceived him."

And many other words followed these, which did kindle me with fierce and burning anger, and which did with a most timorous heat so inflame my mind,

that it brought me almost to unbeseeming, furious
and frantic actions. Nor the confected rage did first
pass away, before the infinite tears (bursting it
asunder) did most abundantly issue out of my watery
eyes, which were accompanied also (the same nevertheless remaining sometimes with me a good while)
with great and grievous sighs, that came smoking
out of my smothered heart (which to comfort and
cheer up myself again), condemning that which my
presaging mind did foretell me of, by main force
as it were, the well-nigh lost and fugitive hope,
with most vain reasons, did return again. And in
this sort recovering almost again all the joy that
whilome had left me, I lived many days between
hope and despair, being always careful and beyond
all measure desirous to know exactly what was
become of him that came not.

THE
FOURTH BOOK OF BOCCACE
HIS FIAMMETTA

MY tears (pitiful Ladies) have been but light hitherto, and my sighs pleasant, in respect of those which my sorrowful tongue (not so pressed to write them, as my heart so prone to feel them) doth now prepare to set down before you. And truly, if the pains which I have passed hitherto are well considered, they may be rather termed dalliances of a young and wanton gentlewoman than woes of a tormented Lover. Arm your minds therefore with firmness and patience, and let not my promises so make you afraid, that (the things which are past, seeming grievous unto you) you would not be desirous to hear the sequels, which are full of more sorrow, and greater grief. And I care not (gentle Ladies) to comfort you any whit in these sad reports, because you might take the more pity of me, and the more, by how much knowing his malice the greater, by whose impiety all these sorrows did fall upon me, you might be more wary, and less wilful in committing your fond dispositions to young Men's fleeting discretions, and in putting your trusty hope into their trothless hands. And so in talking with you, I

shall (perhaps) oblige myself unto you, and in counselling you make myself unbound, or else, admonishing you by these perplexed accidents (allotted and
befallen to me) I shall help, if not heal, your amorous
maladies. I say therefore (good Ladies) that with
such divers imaginations (which you have a little
before comprised by my discourse) I was continually
molested, when, after more than a month past of
his promised return, I heard certain news on a day
of my beloved young Gentleman. And thus it was.
That going with a devout mind on a day to visit the
sacred and religious places, and to offer up to the
Gods some orisons for the release of my hard mishaps, that, restoring Panphilus to me again, or else
driving him utterly out of my mind, I might recover my banished comfort, it came to pass, that
being in company with many wise and discreet Ladies
(some nearly allied to me by blood and affinity, and
others conjoined to me by ancient familiarity) set
upon pleasant discourses, and in merry veins, there
arrived by chance a Merchant, who, no otherwise
than Ulysses and Diomedes did to Deidameia,
began to show forth his gems and precious Jewels,
and such especially as he thought most fine, and
fitting best the dainty minds of such young and
curious Gentlewomen.

Who also (as I gathered by his speech, and he
being also demanded of one of the company) saith
that he was an inhabiter of that City where my

Panphilus was born, and dwelled. But after having shown many of his knacks, and some of them bought of the Gentlewomen, others priced and given him again, they entered into pleasant and merry talk amongst themselves, and whilst he did look for his money, one of them, who was of a young and flourishing age, of a most beautiful countenance, and of noble blood, commended of many for her rare qualities, and of most for her courtly and nice behaviour, and the very selfsame Gentlewoman who had asked him before what he was, and from whence he came, demanded of him again, if he had ever known one Signor Panphilo his countryman. Oh, how much with these and many other demands did she please my humours, and fulfil my like desires. I was in sooth greatly glad that they fell into such talk, and did most willingly lift up my ears to hear the arguing of them both, but especially to know the effect of his answers, who without delay said :

"And who is he that doth know him better than I do ? " To whom she said again, striving (as it were) and importunately forcing herself to know what was become of him : "And where is he now ? " "Oh" (said the Merchant), "it is a while since his Father (having no more Children but him) called him home unto him " : whom the young Gentlewoman yet asking again : "How long is it since thou knewest any certain news of him ? " "Truly " (said he), "never since

123

I came from thence, which is not yet (I think) full fifteen days." She continued still inquiring and said: "And how doth he now?" "Very well," said he, "(it seems) for the very same day that I came from thence, I saw a most fair young Gentlewoman, with great solemnity, feast and joy, enter into his house, which (as I partly understood) was newly married unto him."

Whilst the Merchant was speaking these nipping words, although I gave a doleful ear unto them, yet I stared the inquisitive young Gentlewoman steadfastly in the face, marvelling with myself, and imagining greatly in my mind, what the occasion might be, that should move her to examine such strait particulars and interrogatories of his estate whom I would before this time have believed that no other woman but myself had scarce known. For I perceived, as soon as the sorrowful words (that Panphilus was married) came to her ears, that casting her eyes down, there appeared in her cheeks a red and hot colour, and that her prompt and ready words died presently in her mouth, and by as much as I could perceive, with the greatest pain in the world she stayed her tears (ascended already up into her eyes) from trickling down her cheeks. But I (especially desiring the same), oppressed with sursaults of unspeakable grief, and suddenly after assailed with another as forcible and as great (jealousy, I mean), I scarcely stayed myself with most vile

and scolding terms, from reprehending her altered
countenance, and disturbed senses, as one grieved
at the very heart, that she should show towards
Panphilus such manifest tokens of Love, greatly
fearing thereby that she had (perhaps) (as well as
I) some just occasion to be discontented with the
report of these bitter news. But yet I moderated
myself, and with great pain and fretting anguish
of mind (the like I think was never heard of),
I bridled and kept still my troubled and ireful
heart, under a modest and unchanged countenance,
though more desirous to complain and bewail than to
hearken any further after such heavy news, or to see
such apparent and wounding signs of corrivality.

But the young Gentlewoman, perhaps with that
same forced courage and strength, forcibly retaining her grief within her like myself, and passed it
away, as though it had not been she who was before
so much troubled in mind and in face, and showing
a semblance that she believed his words, the more
she asked, the more she found his answers contrary
to her desires, and alas most repugnant to mine.
Whereupon, leaving the Merchant, of whom so
instantly she had demanded news, and disguising
her sadness with a visard of feigned mirth, we stayed
longer together (than I would), talking diversely of
this and that. But after our talk began to grow
to an end, everyone went away, and I myself, with
a soul fraught full of anger and anguish, fretting

within myself, no otherwise than the enraged Lion
of Libia after he hath discovered the Hunter and
his toils, my face burning sometimes by the way
as red as fire, and sometimes waxing suddenly pale
again, sometimes with a slow pace, and sometimes
again with a hasty gait, and broad steps, more than
womanly modesty did require, sorrowfully returned
to my sorrowful lodging. Where, after that it was
Passions of lawful for me being all alone, to do what I
jealousy would, and entered now into my Chamber,
I began most bitterly to lament. And when a good
while together my infinite tears had washed away
a good part of my grief, my speech being come to
me more frankly than before, with a faint and feeble
voice I began to lament, saying :

" Now dost thou know the occasion, so greatly
desired of thee, of his unjust stay ? Now dost thou
know (miserable Fiammetta) why thy Panphilus
doth not return to thee again ? Now hast thou
found out that, which so seriously thou didst search
out ? What dost thou then desire to seek more,
miserable wretch as thou art ? What dost thou
demand more ? Let this suffice thee. Panphilus is
no more thine. Cast away now thy flattering hope
for ever seeing him again, and thy desires to have
him ever any more. Abandon thy bootless tears,
lay down thy fervent love, and leave off all foolish
and vain thoughts. Believe from henceforth divine
presages, and credit hereafter thine own divining

mind. And now begin to know (though too late) the perjuries and deceits of young men.

"Thou art come just to that miserable point whereto other silly women (trusting too much like thyself) have already arrived." And with these words I rekindled my incensed rage, and reinforced my grievous lamentations. And afterwards with most fierce words I began to speak thus:

"O ye Gods, where are you now? Where do your just eyes now behold? Where is now your *Blasphem-* due anger? Wherefore doth it not fall upon *ies of those that be* the contemner and scorner of your might? *jealous* O mighty Jupiter, whose divine Godhead can brook no wicked perjuries, and yet is by an execrable imp forsworn, what do thy thunderbolts, and where dost thou now bestow them? Who hath most justly now deserved them? Wherefore are they not cast upon that most irreligious and perfidious man, to terrify others, by his perpetual fall, not to forswear thy holy name? O illuminate Phœbus, where are now thy Darts, with mortal steels, of which fierce Python (in respect of him who so falsely called thee to witness of his detested treachery and deep deceits) did so ill deserve to be pricked? Deprive him of the comfortable light of thy shining beams, and become his pursuing enemy, no otherwise than thou showedst thyself to miserable Œdipus. O ye other Gods and Goddesses whatsoever: and thou mighty Love, whose celestial

127

power this false lover hath mocked, why do you not show your force, and pour thy condign wrath upon his guilty head ? Why do ye not turn heaven and earth, and all the cruel fates and the infernal sisters, against this new bridegroom, that in the world for a notable example of a detestable deceiver, and for a wicked violater of your righteous laws, a despiser of your might, he may not survive any longer to laugh and flout you to scorn ?

"Many less faults than this have procured your heavy indignation not to so just a revenge as this. Wherefore then do you delay it ? You are not scarce able to be so cruel towards him that he might for his heinous offence be duly punished. Alas, poor wretch, wherefore is it not possible, that yourselves, injured also, should not feel the effects of his fraudulent dealings as well as I, so that the ireful heat of his deserved punition should be as well kindled in your revenging breasts as in my injured heart. O Gods, throw all those dangers down, or else turn some of those least plagues upon his hateful head, of the which I did of late doubt. Kill him with any cruel kind of death that pleaseth you best, because I might in one hour feel my total and final grief, that I should ever after have sustained for him, and so revenge yourselves and me at once.

"Do not partially consent, that I alone should bewail the grief of his vile offences, and that he, having mocked both you and me, should merely rejoice and disport himself with his new spouse."

But incensed afterwards with less anger, and yet provoked with more fierce and sharp complaints, coming to Panphilus, I remember that I began thus to say :

" O Panphilus, now I know the cause of thy staying there. Now are thy deceits most manifest unto me. Now do I see what kind of love doth hold thee back, and what pity doth keep thee there. Thou dost now celebrate the unhallowed Hymens and espousal rites (nay, wrongs), and I (poor soul, enchanted with the pitiful charms of thy fair tongue, and with thy Crocodile tears deceived) do now consume and waste myself away with mourning and lamenting, making with my floods of tears an open way to my speedy death, which with ignominious titles of thy cruelty and homicide shall quickly ensue.

" And these pleasant years, which I desired so much to prolong, shall be now cut off by thy unjust occasion. O wicked man, and worker of my woes, tell me now with what heart thou hast entertained thy new spouse, with intent to beguile her, as thou hast done to me ? With what eyes diddest thou behold her ? With those eyes that thou diddest entrap me (most miserable and credulous woman) ? What faith diddest thou promise her : that which thou diddest so solemnly swear to me to keep uncorrupted ?

Why, how couldest thou do it? Dost thou not remember that the thing which is once bound cannot
be bound any more than once? What Gods diddest
thou adjure? Ah, what perjured Gods? Alas,
The thing miserable woman, I know not what Siren
that is once flights and Circean pleasures have so be-
bound for- witched thee that (in knowing thyself to
ever can be be mine) thou shouldest transform thyself
bound no into so wicked a mind, and sink into the
more
deceitful gulf of thy pleasing fantasies. For what
fault (alas) did I deserve to be so smally regarded
of thee? Whither is the great love between us so
suddenly flown away?

" Alas, what wicked fortune doth so miserably
corrote and oppress doleful creatures? Thou hast
now committed thy promised fidelity to the winds,
and thy faith also of thy right hand given me to the
same, the perjured Gods, by whose sacred Godheads,
with great desire or show thereof, thou diddest
swear to return, and thy flattering words, wherewith
thou wert very well stored, and thy feigned and forced
tears, with which thou didst not only bathe thy
cheeks, but also mine, all these (I say) lightly and
rudely heaped onc upon another, thou hast rashly
committed to the careless winds. And now, scornfully deriding me, thou livest merrily with thy new
mistress.

" Alas, who would have ever believed that such
vile and bitter gall had been hidden in thy honeyed

and flattering speeches, and such accursed disloyalty in thy unsuspected dealings ?—or would have ever

How needful it is to be merry trusting lovers words

imagined that thy tears had been with such deceitful art sent forth ? Certes, not I. But rather as thou diddest seem faithfully to speak them, and no less sincerely to lament, so I did with assured integrity give credit to thy words and tears.

" And if peradventure thou wilt affirm the contrary, and say that thy tears were true, thy oaths simply protested, and thy faith given with a pure and upright heart, let it be granted : but what seemly excuse wilt thou allege for not performing them so entirely as thou didst promise ? Wilt thou say that the enticing beauty of thy new Lady is the occasion thereof ? Why, this will be but a weak reason, and a manifest note of thy inconstant mind. And shall this be besides a sufficient satisfaction of my loss ? Alas, no. The sin is not pardoned unless the thing which is taken away be restored again. O most wicked man, was not the fervent love which I bear thee sufficiently known unto thee, and yet (woe is me therefore) do still bear thee against my will ? Alas, yes. Thou didst not therefore need so great skill and such subtle wit to deceive me.

" But, because thou wouldest show thyself cunning in the highest degree, thou diddest therefore use all possible art, and malice in thy filed speeches. But boast not (Panphilus) of thy brave victory and

131

goodly conquest that thou hast got, in deceiving a simple and young woman, and her especially who did put so great trust in thee. My simplicity did merit greater sincereness than thine was. But what ? I believed the reverend Gods no less invoked by thee than thy own self.

" The which with bended knees, and bowed heart, I pray that they would make this thy greatest part of thy eternal fame, to have deceived a young Gentlewoman, who loved thee more than herself.

" Ah, Panphilus, tell me now, did I ever work anything against thy mind, or was I at any time so *It is a great* oppugnant to the feeding of thy humours, *shame to* whereby I deserved so slyly to be affronted *deceive a* and so injuriously betrayed ? I never com-*young wo-* mitted in sooth any other fault against *man that* *loveth truly* thee (if this be a fault) but when I did so foolishly enamour myself of thee, and did bear thee (more than was due) so great faith and extreme love. But this offence did not deserve such accursed penance in thy cruel conceit. In one thing only (I know) I have too much failed, for doing of which I have justly deserved the anger of the Gods : and this was, to receive thee (wicked man and vile monster) into my chaste and then undefiled bed, and in suffering thy naked side to lie so near to mine. Admit that I was not (as they themselves did well perceive and say) but thou especially wert culpable of this crime, who with thy bold subtlety and cunning practices,

132

surprising me alone, and fast asleep in the dark and silent night (as one, who at other times was accustomed to deceive me) first taking me softly in thy arms, my dear honour and unstained honesty being almost violated, before I was thoroughly awaked, what could I do then (alas) when I perceived this ?

" Should I have cried out, and with my bootless clamours have blotted my undoubted virtue with perpetual infamy, and for thee, Panphilus, whom I ever loved more than myself, procured a certain and sudden death ?

" I strived apace (the Gods know) and with my feminine forces (as much as I could) resisted thy eager will, which (not able to control) being overcome, and myself wearied, thou didst enjoy thy greedy prey.

" Oh, that that black day, which did in course bring on this damned and wicked night, had been my last, to have ended in the same my virtuous and unspotted life, with an honest and patient death !
How dearly Oh, how many bitter griefs and what grip-
honesty ing corsives will assail me from henceforth :
ought to be
esteemed and thou, with thy Wedded wife, wilt (for thy own pastime and to delight her) by one and one unrip thy old loves, and make me (miserable woman) culpable in many matters, abasing my beauties to commend and flatter hers, and discommending my qualities, to set hers forth the more. Both which, and all things else in me, were with

133

high praise wont to be extolled of thee above all other women's in the world.

"And all those unspeakable favours (which compelled by mere pity and extreme love I did so gently bestow on thee) thou wilt, perhaps, injuriously affirm, that they sprong of hot and burning lust. But amongst many other things, which thou wilt untruly declare, remember (disloyal Panphilus) to speak of thy own deceits, by means of which thou mayest truly swear and say that thou hast left me in a lamentable and miserable estate. And with these forget not also to tell of thy received honours, and infinite courtesies done thee, because thou *Ingratitude* mayest make thy ingratitude sufficiently known to thy hearer. Nor let it pass thy mind, nor escape thy mouth, to reckon up how many worthy, valiant and noble young Gentlemen have attempted many times to get my love, and the divers means which continually they practised for the least hope of it, as their glorious and daily musterings before my windows in goodly troops, in the daytime, their jealous contentions by night, and their divine prowess showed in feats of arms, and yet could never unwind me from the labyrinth of thy enchanted love.

"And forget not to tell that (notwithstanding all this), for a woman scarcely known, thou hast of me made a sudden and dishonourable exchange. Who (if she be not perhaps so simple as myself) will with great suspect receive thy dissembling kisses, and will warily defend herself from thy deceitful dealings, from which alas I had never the power to keep myself, and whom I wish may by such an one to thee as Atreus his Philomena was to him, or as the daughters of Danaus to their new husbands, or as Clytemnestra to Agamemnon, or (at the least) as myself (thy iniquity being the occasion thereof) have lived with my dear husband, most unworthy of all these injuries.

"And that she may bring thee to such extreme misery (which now for very pity of myself I do woefully bewail) that it may force me against my will to pour out abundant tears for thee. All which things I pray the Gods (if that with any pity they behold miserable creatures) may quickly fall and light upon thee."

Although that I was greatly troubled with this intolerable grief, and not that day only, but many more after, notwithstanding the alteration that I perceived in the foresaid Gentlewoman did sting me cruelly on the other side, the which drew on my mind sometimes to so ruthful and jealous thoughts as I was not other times accustomed to imagine. And therefore said with myself: "Alas, wherefore do I sorrow (Panphilus) for thy long absence, and that thou art combined to a new wife, knowing that if thou wert here present, thou shouldest be mine never the more, but another's. O most wicked man, into how many parts was thy love dissected, and

how fit doth the etymology of thy name and calling
agree with thy nature and condition, since being
(Panphilus) thou art a friend to all. To her with
whom thou livest there, to this, who lives without
thee here, to me, who lives and dies for thee, so that
to her, to this, to me, and yet perhaps to none at
all. And so, false wretch, by these means thou wert
in league with many, when I thought that thou
diddest defy all women besides me. And so it came
to pass, that thinking to use my own goods, I was
too bold in usurping that which belonged to others.
And who can tell (this being now known) if any of
these (more worthy of favour at the Gods' hands
than myself), objecting them for the injury received
by me, and craving revenge for the harms that I
have done them, have impetrated so much grace,
to make me feel these unacquainted woes and
undeserved griefs of mind. But whosoever she be
(if any there be) let her forgive me, because I have
ignorantly offended.

"And my simple ignorance doth deserve some
favourable pardon. But with what fine art didst
None can thou feign these things, with what a vile
love at one conscience didst thou practise them, by
and selfsame what kind of love, or of what tenderness
time more
than one of mind wert thou drawn to this? I have
at once heard it more than once said, that none
can love no more but one, at one and selfsame
time. But this rule took exception in thee.

136

" For thou diddest love many or else diddest carry a show thereof too much by one. Ah, careless wretch, diddest thou give to all, or to this one (which could not so well nor so craftily conceal that which thou diddest so maliciously hide from me), that faith, those tears, those sighs, and promises, which thou diddest so prodigally bestow on me. If thou diddest this thou mayest then securely live, and at thy liberty love all, and yet not bound to any woman. Because that which is distinctly given to many cannot be properly said given to one.

" Alas, how may it then otherwise be but that he who robbeth so many simple women of their yield-*Why Nar-* ing hearts must needs be despoiled of his *cissus was* by some woman again. Narcissus beloved *enamoured of himself* of many, and being most rigorous to all, was at the last overtaken with the shadow of his own beauty. Atalanta, most swift and pitiless in her race, left her miserable lovers behind, combatting between love, life and death, until Hippomenes with a brave and mastered deceit overran and overcame her, she consenting also willingly to the same.

" But why do I allege old examples ? Myself, who could never be taken of anyone, was at last (ah me, therefore) unfortunately surprised by thee. Hast not thou therefore amongst so many of thy spoil found out some brave one who hath entangled thee ? I do not think, but do assuredly believe,

137

that thou wert once subdued by him, who may tame thee, and subject to her, who had but little cause to be proud of her captive.

"But if thou wert (whatsoever she was, that with so great force did conquer thy subtle heart) why dost thou not apply thy love only to her likings? But if neither to her nor to me thou hast desire to return, at least come back again to this, who could not cover thy secret and false love, nor conceal her own fond passions. And if thou wilt needs have my fates and fortune so contrary to me (which perhaps according to thy erroneous opinion I have deserved), let not my offences prejudicate the right of other women. Return again to them at the least, and keep thy faith first perhaps promised to them, and then to me, and to hurt me only, offend not so many, as I believe thou hast left here, and elsewhere, in vain and fond hope. And let not one prevail more there, than many here.

"She is already thine, nor cannot (although she would) but be still thine. Leaving her therefore in safety, and with infallible assurance of thy love, come, because those which are not able to be made thine, but with thy presence, thou mayest with the same keep them also thine."

After many of these vain speeches, because they did neither smite into the ears of the Gods, nor sound in those of that obdurate and ungrateful young man, it came to pass, sometimes, that suddenly I changed

my counsels into these speeches, saying: "O miserable young woman, wherefore dost thou desire
that Panphilus should come hither again? Dost
thou think with greater patience to suffer that consuming corsive near thee, which being so far off
is most grievous to thy thoughts? Thou desirest,
fond woman, thy own harm. And if now thou
remainest in (peradventure) that he loveth thee.
So if he did return thou mayest be assured that
he were come not for thy sake, but for the love of
some other woman. Let him therefore remain
still there, and from henceforth being far from thee,
let him rather hold thy love in doubtful suspense,
than living here, by contrary examples, and by too
apparent demonstrations, show that he doth not
love thee at all. And content thyself at the least,
that thou dost not remain alone in these consuming
pains, and forsake not that comfort that miserable
and distressed women, when they have companions
in their miseries, are wont to take."

It were too hard a task for me (good Ladies) to
show with what incensed ire, with what quantity
of tears, with what burning sighs, and choking
sobs, with what gripping griefs of my poor heart,
Every hard and with what vehement and doleful
thing
waxeth soft passions, I was almost every day wont to
in time meditate on these thoughts, and to think
of these matters. But because every hard thing
in time is mollified and changed, it happened that

139

having many days together led this kind of life, and not able to sink any further into the Gulf of grief than I was already fallen, by little and little it began somewhat to relent. And the more it departed from my affected soul, the more was my fervent love and lukewarm hope kindled there again, both which remaining in the place of my surceasing sorrows, made me change my present will, and alter my first desires of having my Panphilus again, and to descant somewhat of his return to me again. And as even now the despair of never enjoying him again was most contrary to me in this, so much the more did my repugnant desire of the contrary increase. And as kindled flames tossed abroad, and blown about with boisterous winds, do grow into greater flakes, so Love, by contrary thoughts in me, was not only nourished, but made of greater force. Wherefore I was moved with repentance of these foresaid frantic passions, and superfluous speeches. And now considering well of that in my mind which unbridled anger had provoked me to say, I was as much ashamed as if they themselves had heard me. And therefore I gently blamed that senseless rage, which in the first assaults of it, with so great force and fury doth take hold of our blind minds that it doth not permit any truth (be it never so much apparent) to be manifest unto them. But notwithstanding, the more it is kindled, the more in space of time it

weareth cold again, and doth make that afterwards
clearly known which rashly before it condemned
in words and deeds. Wherefore having recovered my
right mind again, and after my senses were better
settled, I began thus to say: "O most foolish
young Woman, wherefore dost thou thus molest
thyself? Wherefore without any certain
occasion or knowledge dost thou consume
thyself in the heat and rage of thine own
anger? Say that this is true that the
Merchant told (which perhaps is not), and
admit that he hath married a wife, is this
so great a matter? An inopinate thing indeed
(I must confess), which thou didst not think would
so soon fall out. And yet it is most requisite that
young men in these causes must please and obey
their Fathers' wills. For if his Father would have it
so, with what face or colour could he deny it? And
thou must also believe, that most of them that take
wives, may love them as well, and yet esteem of
others more. And, that the copious plenty which
busybodied wives yield to their quiet Husbands is
an occasion of sudden cloying, although they never
did so much please and delight them in the beginning. And what dost thou know, how much, or
whether, she doth content him or not? Perhaps
Panphilus took her by mere compulsion, and loving
thee more than ever he did her, it is (perhaps) no
small grief unto him, and doth think the time too

Lovers sometimes blame and sometimes excuse their beloved again

141

long and tedious in being with her. And if she please him, thou mayest yet hope, that she will quickly seem unpleasant, and irksome unto him.

"And of his promised faith and religious oaths thou canst not truly, with any reason, accuse him, because, coming to thee again, he shall in thy Chamber fulfil the one and the other, and what else he hath avowed to our mutual and great joy. Have therefore recourse to the Gods with prayers, that Love, which is able to do more than pledged oaths, or pawned faith, may move and make him return to thee again. And besides this, why shouldest thou have any suspicion of his disloyalty, persuaded thereunto by the troubled mind, only, and altered countenance of the young Gentlewoman? Dost thou not know how many young Gentlemen love thee in vain, who if they knew thee to be Panphilus his Mistress could not choose but be greatly aggrieved? So must thou think it possible, and no strange thing, if he is beloved again of many women, who would be as sorrowful and as heavy to hear that of him which grieved thee so much, although for divers occasions everyone might be especially discontent."

And in this manner, forging sundry fancies with myself, I came (as it were) again to my first hope. And whereas I had before thundered forth many blasphemous curses against his dealings, now with humble and mild petitions I entreated him, and persuaded myself to the contrary. Thus hope re-

142

covered once again, my tormented heart had not, for all that, any force to be merry, but there appeared rather in my countenance signs of sorrow, and I felt in my mind a continual molestation, so that I knew not what to do, or how to think of these *The con-* perplexities. My first cares were fled away, *ditions* and in the first fury of my sudden anger *of angry* *lovers, and* I had in rage cast away all the stones *of those that* which were memorial testimonies of the *are overcome* *with their* overpassed days, and had burned all the *passions* Letters I received from him, broken all his favours, and rent in pieces all his other trash.

I took no pleasure now to gaze upon the heaven, as she, who was uncertain and doubtful of his return, being thoroughly persuaded of it before. The desire that once I had to hear amorous histories and tales, and to pass the night away in such exercises, was quite dead, and the present time, which had abbreviated now the Summer nights, did not grant these things, of which oftentimes either all or some great part I passed away without sleep, continually spending them in pitiful plaints, and in sad cogitations. And if I enjoyed sometimes the benefit of sweet sleep, my fancies were nevertheless troubled and tossed about sundry dreams, some of them seeming very joyful unto me, and some full of sorrow and care. The resorting to public places, temples and feasts was irksome now unto me, and I did never (or else very seldom,

143

when I could do no other) visit or desire to go to them. My face being on the sudden become lean and pale caused so many marvels, doubts and sadness in my house that everyone talked diversely of the same.

And looking and living in this pitiful case, and making semblance that I knew of nothing, I remained the most pensive and the most sorrowful woman that might be. My doubtful thoughts did draw on and waste most part of the day, uncertain whether I might resolve myself to mirth or moan. But seeing the nights fitting best my unpleasant humours, and finding myself alone in my Chamber, after having first lamented my woes, and talked many things with myself, stirred up and inspired as it were with better counsel, I turned my devout prayers to Venus, saying :

" O singular beauty of the Heavens, O most pitiful Goddess, and most holy Venus, who in like- *Fiammetta's* ness of thyself, in the beginning of my *prayer to* anxieties, didst appear unto me in this *Venus* Chamber, afford me now some comfort for my great griefs, and by that reverend and internal love that thou didst bear fair Adonis mitigate my extreme pains. Behold what tribulations I suffer for thee. Behold how many times the terrible Image of death hath been presented before mine eyes. Behold if my pure faith hath deserved so much pain as I wrongfully sustain. Being but young, and not knowing thy darts, I suffered myself at thy first pleasures and without denial to become *The Image of death terrible* thy subject. Thou knowest how much good thou didst promise me : and I cannot truly deny, but that I have enjoyed some part thereof, but if thou wilt comprehend these sorrows, which thou diddest give me, as part also of that good, then let Heaven and earth perish in one hour, and let all laws like unto these be annihilated, and made new again with the world. But if they seem unequal in thy sight (as I hope they do) then let (O gracious Goddess) thy promise be fulfilled, because thy holy mouth may not be thought or said to have learned to dissemble (as mortal men's do). Send forth thy Son with his golden arrows, and with thy firebrands, to my Panphilus, where he doth now remain so far distant from me, and inflame his heart in such sort (if peradventure, for not seeing me so long time, it is waxen too cold in my love, or too hot with the present beauty of another) that, burning as I do, none occasion whatsoever may withhold him from coming back again. Because taking again some comfort and ease under the heavy burden of these calamities, I may not so quickly die.

"O most fair Goddess, let my words sound into thy ears, and if thou wilt not set him on fire, pull out of my poor heart thy wounding Darts, because I may (as well as he) spend my days without such great grief." With this form of prayers (although I saw their effects but vain, yet thinking that they were heard) I did with small hope somewhat lighten my torments, and beginning new thoughts I said :

"O Panphilus, where art thou now ? Alas, what doest thou ? Hath now the silent night surprised *Jealous* thee without sleep and with so many tears *thoughts* as it hath taken hold of me ? Or doth thy young spouse perhaps (not heard of me at all) hold thee in her arms, or yet, without any remembrance of me, dost thou sweetly sleep ? Alas, how may it be that Love can govern two Lovers with so unequal Laws, both loving so firmly, as I am too assured that I do, and as perhaps thou dost, I know not ? But if it be so, that these thoughts do occupy thy mind, as they do overcome mine, what wicked prisons or merciless chains do hold thee, that in breaking of them dost thou not return to me ? I know not (certes) what might stay me from going to thee, unless my beauty (which would without all doubt be an occasion of my utter shame, and a great impediment to me in all places) did not only keep me back. What business soever, and what other occasions of stay thou diddest find, should be by this ended, and now thy Father should have glutted himself with thy daily company, who is I know (and for whose death, the Gods know, I do continually pray) the only occasion of thy stay there. And if not of this, at the least of robbing thee from me, he was undoubtedly the only cause and means. But I fear me, poor soul, that going about to pray for his death thou dost prolong his life, so contrary are the Gods to thy requests, and so incroyable in everything I crave of them. Ah, let thy love (if it be such as it was once wont to be) conquer their opposite force, and come again. Dost not thou think that I lie sadly all alone a great part of the tedious nights in the which thou diddest once bear me faithful company, though accompanied (I must needs confess) with millions of martyring thoughts. Alas, how many long Winter nights lying acold without thee, in a great and solitary bed, have I passed heavily away. Ah, call to thy forgetful mind the sundry kinds of these pleasures, which in many things we were wont to take together, remembering which, I am then certain, that there is no other Woman able to divide thee from me. And this belief doth make me (as it were) more surer than any other thing that the news of the new spouse are but false, which if they were true, yet she cannot (I think) take thee from me, but for a time. Return therefore, and if sweet delights have no force to draw thee back again, let the desire which thou hast to deliver her (whom above all other Women thou lovest, from sudden and shameful death) persuade thee to be reclaimed. Alas, if thou wert now returned, I hardly believe that thou couldest know me again, for so hath exceeding sorrow and anguish of mind extenuated, and altered my former and fair countenance. But that which infinite tears hath taken from me a short gladness (in seeing thy sweet face) shall quickly restore to me again, and I shall be once again that Fiammetta which I was before. Ah, come, Panphilus, come, because my heart doth still call upon thee, suffer not the flower of my young days to perish in dole, altogether prest for thy delights, and vowed to thy pleasures. I know not, alas, with what modesty I could bridle my sudden and exceeding joy if thou wert here again, but that unmoderately it should be manifest to every public person. Because I doubt (and justly) that our love, with great wisdom and patience a long time concealed, might not be perhaps discovered to everyone. But yet wert thou come to see, and to try, whether ingenious lies could as well take place in prosperous events, as in adverse and crooked accidents. Alas, I would thou wert for all this come, and if it could not be better, then let everyone that would, know it, because I would think quickly to find out a plaster for every wound."

This being said, I suddenly rose up and ran to the window as if he had understood my words, *The vain belief of Lovers* but I perceived myself (alas) deceived in my foolish imagination, in thinking that I heard that which I did not, and that he knocked at the door, as he was sometimes wont to do. Oh, how many times, if any of my other careful

Lovers had known this, might I have been dis-
honourably dealt withal, if any malicious and crafty
person had feigned himself to be Panphilus in such
a case. But after that I had opened the window,
and looked towards the Gate, mine eyes made me
more assured of this manifest illusion, and so was
my vain joy tossed with a true and sudden turba-
tion of mind, not unlike to the tempestious waves
(after that the strong Mast, broken in pieces by
blasts of mighty winds, with crumpled sails, by
main force of them is thrown into the Sea) without
resistance do cover and hide the endangered ship.
And returning after my old wont to my accustomed
tears, I did miserably begin to lament and bewail.
And forcing myself afterwards to give some rest
to my tormented mind, drawing up the vapours of
sweet sleep into my closed eyes, in this manner
Sleep the with myself I did call upon them again :
rest of all "O quiet sleep, the most pleasant rest of all
things, the
peace of all mortal things, and vain peace of men's
men's minds minds, which dost shun all care like an
enemy, come to me, and with thy operations drive
out of my burning breast these smothered thoughts,
these heavy cares, and these ruthful and restless
fancies. O thou that dost restore wearied bodies,
and hardened in cruel and breathless pains, to ease
again, and dost make them fit and fresh to endure
new labours, why dost thou not come ? Thou givest
repose to others, give also some little rest to me,

whose need is more than any other's else. Forsake
the eyes of merry and pleasant young Gentlewomen,
who holding now their Lovers in their arms, and
passing the time joyfully in the exercise of the
Goddess of Cyprus' games, do utterly refuse and
hate thee. And enter into mine, who lieth here alone,
forsaken, and choked with Seas of sorrowful tears,
and consumed with scalding sighs. O thou the
tamer of fierce and wicked creatures, and the better
part of man his life, let me take some comfort by
thee, and reserve thy absence until that time when
Panphilus with his pleasant discourses shall delight
my weaned ears, which shall be never wearied in
hearing him, and my desirous eyes, with his brave
beauty in looking on him. O feeble brother of dark
death, which dost equally intermeddle false things
with true, enter into my sorrowful eyes. Thou
didst once overspread Argus his hundred eyes, commanded by jealous Juno to watch, and unwilling
The to sleep. Alas, come now into mine, which
property are but two, and which do with great desire
of sleep attend thy grateful entrance. O Haven of
life, rest of light and companion of night, which
doth come [to] all alike, as gracious to high Kings
as to base and poor slaves, enter into my sorrowful
breast, and making a pleasant sojourn there, recreate
a little my daunted spirits. O most sweet sleep,
which dost compel human generation (fearful of
death) with more patience to learn her long and

lingering coming, possess me with the effects of thy
force, and drive from me these infectious hurts, in
the which my unquiet mind troubleth itself without
any profit at all." Morpheus, more pitiful unto
me than any other God to whom I offered up my
prayers (admit that he made delay in granting me
that favour which I besought him by my importunate orisons), after a long space (constrained more by
the force of my pitiful prayers and unpitied disquiet
than of his proper accord) came slowly and silently
stealing into my eyes, and so (myself not perceiving
him at all) crept in by the windows, as yet half open,
Dreams of into my giddy head, which did greatly need
hapless his presence and help : and being most
Lovers willingly entertained there, did wholly turn
himself up and down, possessing every place of it.
But sweet and desired peace, although that sleep
was come, did not yet enter into my unsettled mind,
but in lieu of thoughts and tears, a thousand fearful visions (full of infinite terrors) did make me
greatly afraid, believing, verily, that no hellish fury
remained in Pluto his Cities, but that every one in
most horrible forms and ugly shapes (methought)
did appear many times unto me, threatening me of
divers ensuing stratagems, and oftentimes with their
ghastly looks breaking me out of my momentary
sleep, which afterwards (as though I had not seen
them at all) I was content and glad within myself,
that they were but fantastical and foolish shadows.

And in brief, there were but a few of these nights after the unfortunate tidings of this new bridegroom and his bride, in the which I took any pleasure or ease in my forced sleep, and never representing to my wandering fantasies my Panphilus with such joy as they were wont to do many times before. Which thing did no less beyond all measure grieve me, than the contrary without mean to molest me. Of all these cares at last, of all my streaming tears, ceaseless sobs and sighs, and of all my multiplied griefs, but not of the occasion of them, my dear husband had no small inkling, and knowledge, especially when he perceived that the lively colour of my face was changed into a dead paleness, and that my pleasant and shining eyes (depainted round about with two blue and purple circles) were deeply sunk into my forehead. Seeing which things (I say) caused him many times to marvel, how all these alterations should happen.

But perceiving, at length, that I had lost my appetite to meat, and that my wonted sleep had forsaken me, he sometimes asked me what was the cause thereof. Whom I answered, that the weakness of my stomach was in fault, which had so extenuated and appalled my face with that deformed leanness, myself not knowing no other cause why it was thus gone from me but only that. Alas, how simply did he believe (giving entire faith to my deceitful words) this feigned excuse and false tale,

152

and caused infinite medicines to be made and ministered to me, all which (to content him) I did will-
No help of ingly take, not that I did think to get any
the body can profit or ease at all by them. For what
lighten the
passions of lightening of the body can ease or assuage
the soul the infesting passions of the infected soul ?
None I believe. But my mind being purged of them,
they might (perhaps) alleviate and help my body
much. The medicine available for my malady was
but one, which was very precious, dear, and too far
off, to make me receive my pristiniate health. But
after my deceived husband perceived that all these
drugs did help me but a little, or nothing at all, he
being more tender and careful of me (than I deserved)
by sundry ways and new means endeavoured to
.purge me of this melancholic humour, and to restore
to me my lost and former mirth, but yet he laboured
all in vain.

Sometimes with comfortable words he did assay
to cheer me up, saying : " There are, sweet Lady,
and my dearly beloved wife (as thou knowest well
enough) a little beyond the pleasant hill of Falernus,
Delectable in the midst of old Cuma, delectable Islands
places upon the Sea coasts, the situation of
which is so sweet, pleasant and delightsome that
the like (I think) is not under the cope of wide
heaven. They are environed with most fair hills,
full of all sorts of fruit, and covered all over with
green vines, loaden with goodly bunches of white,

153

red and purple Grapes, in the valleys of which there are no kind of wild beasts that may with pleasure be hunted but are to be found there.

"Nor far distant from thence, there is a great plain full of game, and fit for all manner of flights of preying and sollacing Hawks. There is the Island Pitycusa, and Nisida, abounding in Conies, and the Sepulchre of great Mesenus, leading away to the dark kingdoms of Pluto.

"There are Sybilla of Cuma her Oracles, there is the Lake Avernus, and the great Theatre (a common and ancient place for many brave pastimes and rare spectacles). There are sweet and clear Fish-ponds, the Hill Barbarus, and the vain and prodigal labours of the wicked Emperor Nero.

"All which delights, both old and modern, can-not but greatly recreate men's minds, that never saw them before, who for their pleasure and solace go many times to visit them.

"And besides all this, there are most healthful and wholesome Baths for men and women of all degrees, and most sweet and goodly ones for Ladies of honour and renown. And the air being very temperate and pleasant there, doth continually afford fit times and good occasions and means to visit them. There is no going thither without a merry mind, nor abiding there without great feasts, jollity and pastime, in such brave companies of noble men, Ladies, Gentle-women, and fine and stately dames of this City.

154

AMOROUS FIAMMETTA

" Wherefore I am determined that thyself (not well, as thou sayest, in thy stomach, and troubled worse I fear in mind, and, as far as I can guess, grieved with deep and melancholy passions), for recovery of each sanity again, shall go thither with me : which journey shall not be without great pleasure, assured profit, and speedy help unto thy distempered body and sorrowful mind." But when I heard his words, doubting lest in the very midst of our sports, and abroad there, my dear Panphilus might return, and so I might not (perhaps) see him, inflicted with inward grief, I stayed a good while pausing, before I could answer him again.

But after seeing his resolute pleasure, imagining also that if he came he would seek me out wheresoever I was, I answered him I was ready, at his pleasure, to go whither and when he would. And to be short, not many days after we went thither.

On what contrary medicines did my loving husband excogitate and practise for my helpless griefs. Admit that corporal languors were cured there, yet very seldom or never did any go thither with a whole and sound mind that did return with the same again, whether it was the mere Situation of the place washed with the waves of the Sea (the natural place of Venus' nativity), or the time in which it is more used (in springtide I mean) as more fit for those things that made it. Neither is that (truly) to be marvelled at, which oftentimes

appeared to me there : that the most honest Gentlewomen, and of best account, disposing for awhile
their womanly modesty and shamefastness, did
use in all their merry meetings and sports an
unwonted kind of unbridled liberty and irrequisite
familiarity, and did more lasciviously assemble together in those places (privileged perhaps for such
wanton pastimes) than anywhere else.

And I was not only of this opinion, that with
less stain to their honours, in those places, in that
company, and at those times, they might do it,
but all those almost which were accustomed to
resort to those Islands, then as full of mirth, glee
and feasts as Cypres or Cytherea were, at what time
their Ladies' holidays and divers honours were
celebrated there. The greatest part of the time
there was spent in ease, and passed away some time
more in delightful exercises, and not a few times
in amorous discourses of Gentlewomen amongst
themselves, or else in company of young gentlemen
and Gentlewomen together.

There were no viands but most delicious, and
which were most dainty to be got, and most noble,
Wine precious, old and the purest wines, of
stirreth up force not only to awake drowsy Venus,
to Venery but to raise up to life that vigour which
is already mortified in any man or woman, do follow
there. And how much also the virtue of the baths
doth confer to the same, they do better know who

have sometimes proved them. There the cool Sea banks and most pleasant gardens, and every other place besides, with divers feasts, with new devised sports, with most fine and curious dancings, with all kinds of musical instruments and celestial melody, and with amorous songs and Madrigals, made, played and sung by those lusty youths and sweet Nymphs, did resound forth marvellous and pleasant Echoes. Who is he therefore that can, amongst so many enticing pleasures there, keep himself free from Cupid his darts, who doth without any pain or labour (if I am not deceived) rule there, as in the most principal place of all his kingdoms, and helped by so many friendly allectives doth with great ease, against such willing and capable subjects, use his strength and divine forces.

Into such places (most pitiful Ladies) my husband was wont to carry me to rid me of my amorous burning fever. Into which after that we were arrived, love used no other means towards me than he did towards other, but my soul rather (which could not be wrapped in more strait bonds of love than it was) somewhat (though little enough) cooler, and by the long staying, that Panphilus being from me had made, and by many tears (and sustained griefs) was kindled into so great flames, that I thought I had never felt the like before. And this did not only arise of the foresaid occasions, but remembering with myself that I was oftentimes there in Panphilus his company, both love and grief (seeing myself without him) did not a little increase in my wounded heart. I saw not any Hill, or Valley, that I (accompanied sometimes of many, and of him, sometimes pitching their toils for wild and savage beasts, sometimes leading hounds, and learning water Spaniels, and laying gins to entrap and snare the silly Fowls of the Air, sometimes baiting hooks with Angle cord, to choke the pretty and foolish Fishes in clear rivers and brooks, and sometimes getting some, and other sometimes missing of their purpose) knew not and perceived, that these were evident testimonies of our mutual pastaunce and glee. Moreover, I did not see any rock, shore or Island there but I said:

"Here was I with my Panphilus, this did he speak unto me here, and this did we here." Likewise there *The like Petrarch unfolded most finely in a certain Sonnet* could be nothing else seen there which was not first an especial occasion to me with great efficacy to remember him, and with more fervent desire afterwards to see him either here, or else returned in any other place again. As it pleased therefore my dear husband, so there we began to take our delights: sometimes rising up betimes, and so soon as clear day appeared, and mounted upon our swift coursers, and gentle Palfreys, sometimes with hounds, sometimes with hawks, and with both sometimes, running up and down into the nearest

158

places, and most abundant for vollery and venery, now through the shadowed Woods, and now in the open fields, we went earnestly pursuing our game. And seeing many goodly chases, and brave courses there, rejoicing everyone's heart to see them, did but a little or nothing diminishing my sorrowful thoughts, for when I saw any fair sight, or course, therewithal I presently said :

"Oh, that thou wert here, Panphilus, to see this sport, as sometimes thou wert." But (alas) having now until that point, somewhat sustained, and with less grief endured the beholding, and with some small relaxation of my pains followed these pastimes, by recording them now, and thus in my mind (overcome as it were with secret grief) I left them abruptly off, and let them all do as they listed for me.

Oh, how many times do I remember that in these imaginations my bended bow and arrows did fall out of my hands, in handling of which, in pitching of nets, and letting hounds go, or following them, *Divers pastimes bring to unhappy lovers no pleasure at all* there was not any Nymph that waited on Diana her train, that did (I think) ever excel me. And it fell out very often, that many times in my chiefest sport of hawking like a careless woman, and thinking of other greater matters, I did let those hawks that I carried on my fist (myself flown as it were out of my wits) with sudden flight to soar away, of which pastime being in times past most studious, and as much desirous, and not half so careless to commit such faults, I did not only now take no regard, but found no pleasure in them at all.

But after that every valley, hill and all the wide plains were thoroughly traversed up and down, and our company laden with store of prey, we returned home to our pleasant Pavilions, which oftentimes we found full of glee and mirth, by reason of sundry and divers feasts made in them.

Sometimes afterwards sitting under the hollow dens, and entries of high Rocks, that did with their crooked bodies overhang the Sea, and with fresh air shadowing the Sands, where tables being set and furnished with sundry sorts of meats, in company of many Ladies and brave Gentlewomen we made great cheer together.

From which again we were not so soon risen, but divers sweet instruments sounding melodious music, the young Gentlemen and Gentlewomen in most brave order began to lead divers stately and pleasant dances, in which I must needs (though against my will) make one. But because my melancholy mind was not delighted with them, and that the weakness of my body did also deny the same, I danced but a measure or two, and sat me down again. And withdrawing myself behind all the rest, amongst the cloths of Tapestry and Arras that were spread abroad and hung up, I secretly said to

160

myself, "Where art thou now, my Panphilus?" and so sat me down again amongst other Gentlewomen.

And in these places at the very same time giving a willing ear to the skilful music, and the silver sounds of those instruments, which with passing sweet notes entered deeply into my mind, and, thinking of my Panphilus, I did at one time cover and hide, discord, feasts and grief because, listening to the pleasant noise made, every demi-dead spirit of love did regain their former vigour and force in me again : and the remembrance of those merry times did return again to my mind, in which the heavenly harmony of these instruments, touched with rare skill, was wont in presence of my Panphilus to work divers commendable and sweet effects. But seeing not my Panphilus there, with most sorrowful tears and sighs I would willingly have complained on them, if it had been lawful for me in that place. And besides this the sundry Sonnets sung of many young Gentlewomen there (exceeding the Nightingales in sweet notes) were wont in my joyful times to delight my happy mind, of the which, if there was any (peradventure) that did please my melancholic humours, I gave most attentive ear unto the same, and desiring greatly to have it, because rehearsing and singing it afterwards to myself, I might openly and with less suspect, after a modest kind of sort, learn covertly to mourn, and secretly to sorrow with myself, with those griefs especially that were contained in it.

But after that the reiterated dances and rounds had wearied the young Gentlewomen, every one began to place themselves amongst us, and as it was no rare thing there to see the amorous young Gentlemen thronging about us, did encompass us in the manner of a crown, which thing never happened there, or anywhere else, that I perceived, but it made me call to mind that fatal day, when Panphilus, standing behind a fair knot of young Gentlemen, entrapped me with the virtues of his divine graces. Wherefore I lifted up mine eyes many times in vain, prying and looking between them, being fondly persuaded, by my foolish conceit, that I should in like manner have seen my Panphilus amongst them there.

Wherefore casting mine eyes sometimes amongst them, I marked how some of them with eager looks and pitiful glances did behold the amiable objects of their chiefest desires.

And myself waxed by this time very cunning in those amorous dalliances, with a perplexed eye did view everyone, and note everything they did, and perceived well who loved indeed, and who jested in demonstration, sometimes commending one for the grace that he observed in his discourse, and sometimes another for the pretty invention he used, and for his amorous arguments so well couched

162

together in his loving stints: saying to myself, that
my miserable estate and cursed condition had been
After a much better if I had then played the coun-
known error terfeit, as now they did, reserving thereby
one waxeth
wise at a free soul to myself, as with dallying
length and sporting they did keep to themselves.
Afterwards refelling such an opinion, I said: "Nay,
I am rather content (if in possessing an evil there
is any content at all) to have loved faithfully."

Returning therefore with mine eyes and thoughts
to the wanton behaviour and amorous actions of
these young Lovers, I reaped some small comfort
by their sundry fancies. And when I did perceive
that any of them did love more fervently than the
rest, I did more commend with myself such well-
meaning Lovers. And having thus a long time with
an earnest mind beheld them, I began softly to
say with myself: "O thrice happy and fortunate
are you, who are not deprived of the sight and
sense of your understanding as I am! Alas, how
was I wont heretofore (as you do now) to solace
myself with these indifferent recreations. Long may
you enjoy your felicity, since I alone must remain
an example of scorn, and a pattern of misery to all
the world. If Love at the least (making me discontent with the thing beloved of me) shall be an
occasion to shorten my days, then shall it follow
that with a tragical death (as Eliza did) I will
eternish my lasting fame and memory."

163

THE FOURTH BOOK

And having thus said, I held my peace, and went again to note those countenances, gestures and actions with which these loving Novices,

professed Lovers and retired Soldiers did diversely study to please their dainty Ladies and Gentlewomen. Oh, how many have I eftsoons seen in like places, who (after a great while having looked in every place about for their desired joys, and not seeing nor finding them, deeming and reporting the feast not half so pleasant by reason of their absence, nor so delightsome) with half angry and very sad countenances have gone from thence again. Whereupon some little laughter (although it was but feeble and weak), in the midst of all my melancholy dumps, was permitted to take place, and a little comfort also granted to them, perceiving that I had company in my sorrows, measuring in this sort by mine own miseries other men's mishaps. Then thus disposed (most dear Ladies) as my words do show, the delicate baths, the weary hunting, and the Sea banks had glutted my queasy mind with all kind of pastimes, and cloyed it with superfluities of feasts. Wherefore dismasking my old and former countenance, and discovering the smoke of my choked sighs, and the loss likewise of my appetite to my meat and sleep, to my deceived Husband, and not caring to manifest to the appointed physicians of my health these incurable infirmities, both he and they despairing (as it were) with themselves of my life, we returned again to the City. In the which, the conditions of the time preparing many and divers feasts, it framed also with the divers occasions of my manifold griefs. Wherefore it came many times to pass, that to the solemnizing of new espousals I was especially also invited, as being by parentage near of kin to them, or else, by ancient familiarity, friendship or neighbourhood, acquainted otherwise with them. To the which also my Husband oftentimes constrained me to go, thinking by these means to prevent the ordinary course of my melancholy fits, or else somewhat to ease my mind, so greatly infested by them. Whereupon I was at such times urged to take again my forsaken ornaments, and to put my neglected hair (judged of all men before to shine like gold, but not unlike now to ashes) in the finest order I could,

wherein I was not to learn how to do it. *A passionated young Gentlewomen care not how to adorn themselves* And remembering myself with a more deep consideration whom these fine threads of gold, besides all other beauties, were wont to delight, with a new froward passion I did disturb again my fantastical mind, which made me sometimes so much forget myself that I remember, that (no otherwise than called back again from a deep sleep, or raised out of an ecstasy), taking up again the comb that was fallen out of my hands, I returned to my careless and unwilling office. And taking some assured

165

counsel in my Glass, of the setting forth of those
ornaments, with which I had adorned myself, and
seeing my face to look very pale, and greatly dis-
figured, and deeply therewithal apprehending in my
mind my lost and altered beauty, I was almost in a
doubt whether it was my face or no which I saw in
the Glass, but imagining rather that some infernal
and hideous fury stood by me, turning myself about,
I did verily think and fear that it was behind me.
But yet, after that I was tricked up very brave,
clean contrary to the quality of my mind, I went
with other Gentlewomen to those solemn and
sumptuous feasts, in which reigned nothing but
mirth, joy, and all manner of merry and pleasant
recreations. Merry I term them in respect of others,
because, as He knoweth from whom nothing is hid,
there was never any since the departure of my
Panphilus which was not an occasion to me of most
heavy cheer and matter of continual sorrow. Being
therefore come to the places appointed for the
honours of such marriages, although that in divers
places and at divers times celebrated, yet they
never saw me otherwise disposed than to remain
still at one stay, which was, bearing a counterfeit
countenance of content, and a feigned face (as
well as I could) of merriness, with my inward mind
altogether occupied with subjects of sorrow, deriving
the occasion of this sadness and grief as well from
joyful and pleasant things which I saw as from

sorrowful and unpleasant passions which I felt. But after that amongst other Ladies and Gentlewomen I was with great honour received, my mind not intentive upon new fashions, nor mine eyes desirous to gaze upon brave and rich attire, wherewith all the place did shine, but with a vain imagination deceiving themselves, thinking (perhaps) to have seen Panphilus there (as oftentimes in like places they had done before) they went rolling up and down, and casting their beams in every place round about : and not seeing him, as one now most assured of that of which I was at the first probably persuaded, and like a woman confounded in mine own foolish conceit, I sat me down with the rest of the Ladies, refusing the proffered courtesies, and offered honours, for whose sake (he being now absent) they were wont to be most dear unto me.

And after that the new Bride was come home, and the magnificent pomp used at the Tables was ended, and everyone with his passing dainty cates and heavenly Nectar had cheered up their frolic minds, as divers brave dances, sometimes directed by the tuned voice of some cunning and singular Musician, and other some led and footed by the sound of divers sweet instruments, were begun, every place of the espousal house resounding with a general applause of mirth and joy, myself because I would not be accounted coy and disdainful, but civil rather in such an honourable assembly, and well mannered, having gone sometimes about with them, I began to sit me down incontinently again, entering still into new and fantastical imaginations.

It came then to my mind how solemn and glorious that feast was which, like unto this, was once made in honour of my nuptial joy, in the *Everything refresheth* which being then but a simple soul in *the memory* frantic love matters, and free from melan- *of the Lover of his fore-* choly passions, as abounding in all joy, I *passed and happy life* saw in myself with worthy congratulations of everyone honourably saluted, and nobly entreated. And comparing those times with these, and seeing them beyond all proportion altered, I was with great desire (if opportunity of time and place had granted) provoked to weep. This swift and sudden thought did run also in my mind, when I saw the young Gentlemen and Gentlewomen to rejoice equally together, and to be merry alike, courting and devising one with another, sometimes with many pleasant and sweet discourses, and sometimes with many singular and pretty devices, fit for such purposes, how that once I beheld my Panphilus in like places, and how in his company he and I all alone had passed the time there together, and could not now do the like. And it grieved me no less to see myself deprived of the occasion of making such kind of joy, and enjoying such content, than I was sorrowful for the pleasure which I lost by the not performance of the same. But from thence applying my ears to amorous delights, songs and sundry tunes, and remembering those with myself that were passed, I sighed, and marvellous desirous to see the end of such tedious feasts, being malcontent in the meantime, and sorrowful with myself, I passed them away. Notwithstanding, beholding everything exactly, the companies of young Gentlemen being flocked about the Gentlewomen and Ladies, that now were set down to rest them, and retired into divers places to gaze on them, I did perceive well that many of them, or almost all, did sometimes aim their beams at me, and did talk secretly amongst themselves of divers things touching my beauty, bravery and behaviour, but not so softly but that by manifest hearing of my own part, or by imagination or hearsay of some others, no final part of their speeches came to mine ears.

Some of them said one to another: "Alas, behold that young Gentlewoman, who had not her *Divers op-* paragon for beauty in our City, and see *inions and* now what an one she is become! Dost *speeches of* *men* not thou see how strangely she is altered, and how appalled her once fair face is grown, myself being as ignorant of the cause as amazed to see the effects." And having thus said, looking on me with a most pitiful and mild eye, as they who were greatly condolent of my griefs, going away left me full of compassion, and more piteous towards myself than I was wont to be. Others did inquire of

169

one another, amongst themselves, saying : " Alas, hath this Gentlewoman been sick ? " And afterwards did answer themselves again, saying : " It seemeth so, because she is waxed so lean and pale. Wherefore it is a great pity, especially thinking of her former beauty that is now faded quite away." But there were some of a deeper reach than the rest, whose true surmises grieved me very much, after many guesses and speeches amongst themselves, saying : " The paleness of this young Lady is a manifest token of an enamoured heart. For what kind of infirmity doth bring a Lover to a lower estate of body than the unruly passions of fervent and hot affection ? She is undoubtedly in love. And if it be so, he is too cruel and inhuman that is the cause of such unworthy consequences (grief and cares I mean), that make her look with so pale and thin cheeks."

When I had heard these nipping words, that rubbed up my festered wound, I could not withhold my sighs, perceiving that others were more ready to pity my miseries than he to prevent these mishaps who by greatest reason, and most of all, should have had compassion in his thankless heart. And after I had fetched many deep sighs, with an humble and low voice I earnestly besought the Gods that in lieu of their kindness towards me they might have better success in their Loves. And I remember again, that the value of my honour and honesty was not small amongst some of them, who in talking together did favourably seem to excuse the foresaid true surmises, saying: " The Gods forbid that we should hatch such a thought in our minds, to say, that fond Love should molest this wise and modest young Lady, or that blind affection could trouble her mind at all. For she, as she is endued with as great honesty as any other, so was she (as it ever seemed) never addicted to such vanities as many of her co-equals, and hath not showed at any time so much as a semblance of wanton boldness, but continually arguments of wise and modest behaviour. Nor amongst the divers communications and companies of curious

Love is a passion not supported any long time and inquisite Lovers, there could be never heard any speech of her Love, not once imagined amongst them, which is so furious and forcible a passion that it will not be any long time concealed, but will like restrained flames violently burst out unawares."

" Alas " (said I then to myself) " how far do they roam from the truth, not deeming me to be in love, because (as it is the manner of fools) I make not my love public to the view of everyone, and preach it not openly abroad, to be secretly tossed from mouth to mouth, as others (vainly glorying in theirs) are commonly wont to do." There came also sometimes oppositely before me many young and noble Gentlemen, proper men of personage, of sweet and amiable countenances, in everything gracious, courageous

171

and courteous, and the chiefest flowers of our City, who oftentimes before, by many cunning means and drifts, had to the utmost of their power attempted and laboured to have drawn but the devotions of my eyes to the desires of their hearts. Who, after that a certain while they had seen me, so much deformed and altered from that I was wont to be (not well pleased perhaps that I did not at the first frame my affections to their fancies), disdained now to look at me, and forsook me, saying : " The brave beauty of this Lady is gone and turned to a bleak hue, and the glory of her inflaming desires is now extinct."

Wherefore shall I hide that from you (fair Ladies) which doth not only grieve me to rehearse, but generally all Women to hear ? I say therefore that although it was the greatest grief in the world to think that my Panphilus was not present, for whose sake my then excellent beauty was most dear unto me, yet in such upbraiding sort to hear that I had lost it, it was no less than present death to my soul. And besides all these things, I remember that being sometimes invited to such feasts, I have been drawn perforce into the company of many pleasant Ladies, diversely discoursing amongst themselves of amorous conceits, where with willing ear, harkening what issue infinite Lovers have had in their hot passages, I easily perceived that there was never any of them tormented with so fervent passions as

172

AMOROUS FIAMMETTA

I am: nor their love beset with so many miseries,
nor contrived with such secrecy, as mine was. Although that of more happy and fortunate Lovers,
and of less honourable loves, also the number is
greater.

In this sort therefore, sometimes eyeing, and
sometimes giving ear to that which was done
and spoken in these places, like a pensive and sad
Woman I passed away the weary time. After that
the Ladies and Gentlewomen had rested themselves
a pretty while, it happened that many brave young
Gentlemen rising up, and amongst other Gentlewomen invited me oftentimes to dance, but as
often in vain went from me again. Who remaining
nevertheless in their disports (with minds free from
heavy thoughts and high intentions), some moved
with desire to show perhaps their greatest cunning,
and others pricked on thereunto by spurs of hot
and burning love, but all very curious in the same,
myself sitting by myself alone, with a scornful mind
and coy looks, did mark the new-fashioned tricks,
the gesture and behaviour of many Gentlewomen
there.

And certes I blamed some in my mind, although
I greatly desired (if it might have been) to do as
they did, if my Panphilus had been present there.
Who, as oftentimes as his dear remembrance came
to my doleful mind, so often was it sufficient matter,
and the only occasion of my new melancholy and

173

fresh sorrows : and who doth not (as the Gods know) deserve the great love, which continually I have borne, and yet do still bear him. But after that with no small grief I had a great while beheld these dances, which with the sudden sursaults of other grievous thoughts seeming unpleasant and tedious unto me, urged as it were with some other desires, I rose up most willingly from my place, and to burst asunder my heaped and swelling sorrows (whose

Grief is re- open and sudden discovery I greatly feared) *claimed by* I got myself smoothly away into a solitary *lamentation* and secret place, and there giving full scope and leave to my flowing tears, I acquitted my foolish eyes, for all the vanities that they had seen, with an austere and due guerdon, which were not distrained from them without many bitter words, kindled with burning anger, but knowing also my miserable fortune to be so cruel towards me, I remember that sometimes I began thus to inveigh against her, saying :

"O fearful Fortune, mortal enemy to every happy creature, and only hope of miserable men.

The pro- Thou the sudden changer of kingdoms, *perties of* and of mundane things, dost as a helper *Fortune* with one hand lift up, and as a destroyer with the selfsame throw down again, as thy indiscreet judgment doth direct thy inconstant will, not content to be wholly anyone's, exalting him aloft in one thing, or else in another, casting him utterly down, or, after that thou hast made him happy by any lent felicity, dost heap upon his mind new and uncouth cares, because that worldly men, living in continual want and need, may (according to their vain opinion, and their endless pride) implore thy help, and adore thy deity. Yet art thou still blind and deaf, disdaining to behold the manifest miseries, and refusing to listen to the complaints, of miserable creatures, triumphing only with those whom thou hast unworthily (perhaps) exalted. Who, embracing thy friendly favours, and honouring thee with all their devotions, whilst with a smiling look and flattering promise thou art entertaining them, even on a sudden, with some unexpected accident or other, find themselves utterly thrown down by thee, and then (though too late) do miserably perceive how thou hast changed thy serene smiles into froward frowns.

"Amongst the number of which myself (wretched woman) may be put, who not knowing of my own part any malice wrought against thee, and ignorant of any heinous offence and indignity, whatsoever, perpetrated by me against thee, that might reduce thee to so severe a revenge, am most unworthily and pitifully punished. Alas, whosoever reposeth trust in great and mighty things, and like a puissant Prince ruleth in high and stately palaces, applying always his quiet and credulous mind to joyful and pleasant objects, let him cast his eyes upon me, and behold how, from a high and renowned Lady of felicity, I am now become a most low and wretched handmaid of fortune, and (which is worse than this) how cruelly I am rejected and disdained of the only lord and master of my subjected heart.

" Ah, Fortune, thou didst never give any more effectual example of thy unconstant mutability than myself, if that with a perfect and sound mind my first and latter condition of life be well considered. I was received of thee, fickle Fortune, of thee (false Fortune) was I received into this world, in abundant quantity of goods (if nobility, riches, honours and dignity be any part of them) which were moreover by thy bountiful and large hands (which thou didst never yet withdraw from them) daily and copiously augmented. So that (in sooth) like a mighty Lady I did continually **possess** them, as mutable things use them, and, beyond the common course of women's covetous nature, did liberally impart them to others.

" But being ignorant, Fortune, that thou wert also the same which with unequal passions and careful thoughts didst surcharge the mind, and not knowing that thou hadst also a great portion in Love his Signories, I fell in love as thou wouldest, and with that young Gentleman whom thou only, and none else, didst then present before my wretched eyes, when I thought myself farthest from any such danger. Whom after that with

176

strong and intricate knots thou didst perceive
that he was bound in the Circle of my heart, thou
hast (unstable and changing oftentimes) sought to
work my harm, and wreak thy undeserved injuries
upon me, sometimes disturbing our linked minds
with vain and deceitful imaginations, yea, and
sometimes our eyes with pitiful and public glances,
because our love made manifest might be hurtful
unto us.

"And I am certain that many times thou hast
been (even as thou wouldest thyself) the only cause
that many displeasant and discrepant words of my
beloved young Gentleman have come to my ears,
and hast with mine of like consequences filled his
again, able enough (being credited) to have engendered hatred and discord, and to have hazarded
a sudden mislike, but their issue and thy drifts
were never answerable to thy determinations.
Because, admit thou dost as a Goddess govern all
exterior things as it pleaseth thee, the virtues
of thy mind are never the more subject to thy
might.

"Our wisdom hath continually gone beyond thy
wiliness in this point. But what doth it avail, for
all this, to oppose it against thee, since thou hast
a thousand flights to endomage thy enemies. And
that which thou canst not bring to pass by right,
thou dost contend to work by wrong. Not able
to sow the seeds of malice and envy in our hearts,

M   177 thou hast endeavoured to inculcate into them things of like effect and predicament, and besides this to replete them with the greatest grief and anguish of mind. Thy industries, annihilated heretofore and made frustrate by our provident wisdom, were strengthened again by thy other fraudulent forces and peevish ways, and as a perverse enemy, as well to him as to me, thou hast practised the means with thy ominous accidents, by long distance of place to divide us both asunder.

That which Fortune cannot bring to pass by right, she doth by wrong

"Alas, when would I have thought that in so strange a place, so far distant from this, and divided from me by such great Seas, so many high hills, wide fields, valleys and plains, and by so many great rivers, the only source and cause of all woes should (by thy means) be sprung up, and grow still? Truly never. But yet it is so, and for all that though he be far from me, and I from him, I doubt not but that in despite of thee, Fortune, he loveth me, as I love him, whom above all things else in the world I do most dearly esteem.

"But to what end and effect doth this love serve more than if we were either mere strangers or mortal enemies? Alas nothing at all to no purpose else. Our wits and policy therefore prevailed naught against thy contradictions. Thou hast carried away with him all my delight, all my good, and all my joy: and with these my merry times, feasts

and pastimes, my gorgeous attire, my peerless
beauty and my pleasant life. In lieu whereof thou
hast left me dolours, grief and sorrow. But yet,
thou couldest never make me relinquish his love,
no, nor is thy might so great (as great it is) to
make me by intermediate fits only fancy him.
Alas, if I, being yet but young, had committed
anything against thy Godhead, the simplicity of
my unripened years should have excused my raw
defects. But if thou wouldest nevertheless take
some revenge upon me, wherefore didst thou not
wreak it upon thy own things?

" Thou hast injustly (Fortune) put thy Sickle in
another's Corn. For what hast thou to do or to in-
To put one's termeddle thy laws with love his matters?
Sickle in
another's I have most high and strong towers, most
corn fair and ample fields, many herds of Cattle,
and great store of treasure, which with thine own
hands thou hast bountifully bestowed on me, wherefore with consuming flames, devouring waters,
cruel rapine and sackage, and wherefore with unlucky death didst not thou extend thy wrath upon
them? Thou hast left me those things which may
no more avail for my consolation than Midas his
golden favour, which he received of Bacchus for
his pinching hunger : and hast transported only
him away, whom I accounted dearer than Gold,
than gems, than rich palaces, yea, more than infinite worlds of wealth. Accursed, therefore, be

those amorous arrows, which presumed to be revenged of Phœbus, and which now sustain such base injuries by thee.

" Alas, if these had never pricked thee, as now they pierce me, with better advice (perhaps) and with more mature deliberation thou wouldest molest thy loving associates. But behold thou hast wronged me, and brought me to this extreme point, that of the richest, noblest and highest Lady I am become the most miserable and unfortunate woman in all my country, and this, cruel Fortune, thou seest too well approved in me. Everyone doth rejoice and spend their times in merry feasts and glee, and only I do still lament, and waste my youth in endless moan, which kind of life is not now begun, but hath so long endured, that methinks thy merciless anger should have been ere this time somewhat mitigated.

" But I forgive thee all, if of pity or of courtesy thou wilt let me favourably enjoy the sweet company of my Panphilus again, as thou hast not without great grief divided him from me. And if perhaps thy anger doth yet endure, let it be satiated upon the glory of my goods and possessions. Alas, cruel as thou art, let my unhappy and poor condition of life grieve thee, and move thee to commiseration of my calamities. Thou seest that I am become such an one that, as a fable to the common people, I am carried from mouth to mouth, whereas my several beauties with solemn fame and with sweet praises were wont to be blazoned everywhere. Begin therefore, gentle Fortune, at the last to be pitiful towards me, because I may with grateful and reverend titles (myself enabled justly to praise to thee) incessantly honour thy mighty majesty.

"To whose prayers if thou dost open a gracious ear, and wilt not rigorously deny the easy effects of so reasonable a demand, then for ever do I vow (and herewithal let the immortal Gods bear record) to erect to thee the lively Image of myself, preciously adorned, and gloriously set forth in every place and Temple (dedicated and most dear to thee) in token of thy perpetual honour, and everlasting fame. Which with never-dying memorial of thy miraculous pity, subscribed with these words, 'This is Fiammetta lifted up of Fortune from the deep pit of extreme misery to the highest top of happy joy,' as shall be published to the open sight and view of all the world." Oh, how many other things also did I oftentimes declaim with myself, to recount which would be but a long and tedious labour, but all were briefly ended and resolved into bitter tears, by means of which, sometimes it fell out, that being perceived of other gentlewomen, and with many comfortable words cheered up by them, I was much against my will carried to these festival dances.

THE FOURTH BOOK

But who would think it possible (amorous Ladies)
There is that such anguish and grief should so
nothing that usurp a young Gentlewoman's heart that
maketh a there was nothing, which could not only
miserable not make it merry, but that the same
lover glad was an occasion of greater sorrow, which
but the same cannot but seem incredible to all, though
is an not to me, miserable woman, that hath
occasion of proved it, doth feel it, and doth know it
greater grief to be too true.
again one
way or
another

It came to pass many times that the weather
(according to the season of the year) being very
hot, many other Gentlewomen and myself, because
we might the better pass it away, upon most swift
Boats, winged on every side with flashing Oars,
we ploughed the gentle waves of the calm Sea,
singing sometimes, and with playing sometimes on
divers Instruments, went rowing up and down to
seek out solitary and opacal Rocks, divided from
the main shore, entering sometimes into hollow
caves, at the foots of steep hills, made by nature
itself, under which (being most fresh for wind, and
cool shadows) we did many times sit and pass away
the heat of the day.

These were, alas, especial and chief remedies
offered to me, to refrigerate the corporal heat of
my body only, but they lent me not any new ease
of those never-ceasing sorrows, and no extinguish-
ment at all of those flames which burned my soul

182

inwardly, but did rather bereave me of such needful helps, because the outward heat being now
The fire of past (which to delicate and tender bodies
the mind is doubtless no small annoy) by and by
doth not
receive any a more ample and fit place was made
refreshing for amorous and tedious thoughts, which
or ease by
exterior are not only the preserving matter of
things Venus' flames, but a forcible substance
augmenting the same.

Being therefore come to these places which we had sought out, and shrouding ourselves under them for our refreshing and delight, we went (whither our minds did lead us) up and down, viewing here and there this company and that of young gentlemen and gentlewomen, with goodly troops of which every little Rock, Bank and sandy shore (which were by the shadow of any hill defended from the scorching heat of the Sun beams) not otherwise than a green Meadow with fair and plenteous flowers, were almost all covered. Oh, what intensive pleasure and how great a delight is this to them that have their hearts free from the molesting passions of love. There might be seen in many places fair tables set, and white and fine Diaper cloths spread upon them, and all things so exquisitely done, and with such ornament, magnificence, glory and cost, that the very sight only of them had sufficient force to provoke anyone's mind and appetite, were it never so melancholic, demiss or drowsy, but only mine, which was too much soaked in sorrow. There might in other places (as convenient time did require) divers others have been seen, how merrily they went to their morning repasts, of whom our company (as we did them again) with cheerful countenances and courteous entreaties was invited to their feasts and sports.

But after that we had (as the rest also) with great feasts banqueted ourselves, and after that (the tables being taken away) we had danced certain Neapolitan rounds, and then (after our accustomed manner) had embarked ourselves again, we went by and by rowing up and down in this creek, and that Cliff, where in certain secret and by places of the Seashore, to the gazing eyes of every curious and wanton young Gentleman, were showed delightful and desired sights, which was : many fair and young Gentlewomen stript into their Waistcoats of white Satin without sleeves, and without hose or shoes, swimming, and solacing themselves in the cool water. And gathering Shell-fish amongst these cliffs and hard rocks, in stooping down to take them up, did oftentimes discover the round and snow-white balls of their delicate and fruitful bodies. And in some places again there were others, who with more subtle and with greater industry, with trammels, drags, flewes, and with all manner of nets, and divers others that with angles (to the great delight of the beholders) and with many new devices

184

more, and pretty arts, deceived the silly and simple fish. But what need I trouble myself to declare every particular pastime and pleasure which was practised and taken there ? Let them (though they go not thither at all) imagine the like that have exercised themselves, or have any understanding in such things, how many, and of what force they are to recreate the mind. And if they go thither, then they shall see nothing else but mirth and solace, and all kind of youthful disports.

There the open minds of everyone are free from sorrowful passions, the occasions of the contrary being so many and so great that there is scarce a denial of any demand among them.

In these places I confess (because I would not seem to be devoid of courtesy, and would not be troublesome to the whole company) I took a visard of feigned mirth upon me, though I was still sailing with contrary blasts of tempestuous love and envious Fortune in those Seas of griefs and cares *The grief* in which since my Panphilus his departure *of the mind* I have continually hulled up and down. *is hardly* Which thing how hard it is to perform, *covered with* *a merry* they that have tried it may give sufficient *countenance* testimony thereof. For how could I be merry in mind, calling to mind that I had sometimes seen Panphilus with me, and myself also without him, in like pastimes, whom I did now by distance of many miles know to be denied from me, and

185

besides this without hope to see him any more. If I were not troubled with any other grief than only care and vexation of mind, which continually held me in suspense of many things, was not this sufficient enough to have confounded my soul alone ? And can it otherwise be thought, because forasmuch as the fervent desire that I had to see him had so bereaved me of my true knowledge and understanding, that knowing assuredly that he was not in those places, yet (as though he was there indeed) I did argue in my mind, and, as if this had been true, without any contradiction I proceeded farther to see whether I could espy him out or no. There was not any Boat, Galley, Ship or Bregandine (of all which the Sea coast there was so full, sailing forth, some coming in, some casting and some weighing Anchor, as the azure sky in a clear and frosty night loaden with Golden stars) which I did not first with mine eyes survey, and after by my servants search out and know whither they went, and from whence they came.

I never heard sound of any instrument, although I knew him to be skilful in only one, to the notes and tune of which I did first give an attentive ear, and after ask who he was that played on it, imagining still, that he might possibly be the same, whom I did so carefully seek after. There was not any pleasant Rock, Cool shore or shadowed Cave which I had seen, nor any company left unvisited of me, to see if happily I might have found him.

Certes I confess that sometimes this unfeigned and vain hope did abolish a great part of my sighs, *Fiammetta her sighs turned into tears issued out of her eyes* which sighs (after that it was gone from me) amassed together in the concavity of my brain, whose natural issue was to have been breathed forth, converted now into bitter and brinish tears, were by the conduits of my sorrowful eyes poured forth, and so the counterfeit joys were turned into confected and true anguish of mind.

Our pleasant City, surpassing all other Cities in Italy that are held famous for noble feasts and royal *Naples* shows, doth not only exhilarate her Citizens with generous and solemn Nuptials, refresh them with divers sweet walks, Crystalline Rivers, delightsome sea sands, pleasant shores and green banks, but, copious also in many goodly sports, as sometimes with one public and sumptuous spectacle, and now with another princely and solemn show, doth rejoice her people's hearts, and stir them up to exceeding and general gladness. But amongst all other pastimes in the which it doth appear to the world most famous, in Tilt and tourney (which is almost daily exercised there), and generally in all feats of arms, it is chiefly renowned. This therefore was wont to be an ancient custom amongst us (after that the tempestuous and stormy blasts of shaking

187

THE FOURTH BOOK

Winter are past, and the merry Springtide, with her new flowers and green grass, hath brought again

*A descrip-
tion of
Springtide* to the world her trepassed beauties, the vigour also and courage of young lusty Lords and Gentlemen being by the quality and season of the time rekindled, and their amorous hearts more prompt than before, to discover their fervent desires) that at the greatest and most stately houses of noblemen, the bravest most honourable Ladies, shining in glittering gold, and adorned with their most precious and rare Jewels, did with these frankly assent to meet joyfully together. I do not think that to behold King Priam his Daughters-in-Law, with many other of the Phrygian Ladies, when, attired and beautified in the bravest sort, they presented themselves, and came before their Father-in-Law, and sovereign, to dance, to feast and to make merry, was either a more rich or goodly sight than for to see in many pleasant places of our City the majestical meeting and brave assemblies of celestial demi-goddesses in the same, which, after that in fair troops they came to the public Theatres (every one to the utmost of her power showing herself most brave, and making herself most beautiful) I doubt not but if any Gentleman stranger, but indifferently conceited and judicious, had arrived there (having considered their haughty countenances, their noble behaviour, and viewed their costly apparel and rich ornaments,

188

rather princelike than convenient for many (nay, most) Gentlewomen there) would not have judged them women of this latter age, but would have thought that some of those ancient and magnificent Ladies had been returned again to the world, saying with himself :

" She for her stateliness doth resemble Semiramis." This other (gazing on her sumptuous apparel and Jewels) would rather be deemed Cleopatra. Another (considering her courtly and lovely graces) he would have compared to fair Helen. And another (viewing well her gesture and sweet actions in his mind) he would affirm not to be unlike to Queen Dido. Wherefore proceed I thus in comparison of them all ? Every one by herself would rather seem a divine majesty than any human matter. And how oftentimes have I (miserable Woman), before I had lost my Panphilus, heard many young Gentlemen descant upon myself, contending to whether of these two I might have been best compared : to the Virgin Polixena, or to Venus of Cipres. Some of them saying that it was too much to compare me to a Goddess, and others, alleging the contrary, said that it was too little to resemble me to an earthly and mortal woman. There was not amongst so great and noble company any of them remaining long in their places, nor grave silence was kept there.

But the old and ancient Gentlemen, rising up to behold the lusty young Gentlemen, how lovingly some of them (taking the coy Gentlewomen by their delicate hands to dance) did amorously discourse with them according to the desires of their fancies, and how other some with tuned voice and melodious instrument deciphered the effects of his amorous passions. And in this sort was the hottest part of the day spent in all manner of noble sports and glee that might be devised.

And after that the Sun hath once begun to send forth his beams cooler than before, then do the *A descrip-* honourable Princes of our Ausonian king- *tion of* dom meet together in that habit as their *Autumn.* *Italy* high estate doth require. Who, after that they have beheld the divine graces of every Lady, and fed their greedy eyes with every Gentlewoman's beauty, and marked well their dancing, commending some more, some less, but all generally, going away with almost all the Knights and Gentlewomen (as well married as unmarried men) after a little while, in great and most brave companies, with rich and new-fashioned apparel, and clean contrary to the rest, with Masks, and other goodly shows, they return back again.

What tongue is there, be it never so famous for golden eloquence and choice words, or wit, never so much commended for excellent sentences and exquisite invention, that could perfectly or particularly set down the Noble and gorgeous Habits, and the sundry brave suits of apparel (as pleasant

190

for variety as wonderful for magnificence), which was seen there ?

Not Homer, certes, so worthy amongst the Grecians, nor Virgil, so highly praised of the Latins, which with stately verse did write the infinite adventures and accidents, which both those noble men, and which the Grecians, Trojans and Italians, had of yore in their open wars, private peace and stratagems. I will therefore endeavour to make a brief relation of them to those Women who did openly never see them performed, which description shall not so vainly be inserted in this my pitiful discourse, and not to so small purpose, but that the wiser sort of Women may comprehend my sorrow beyond any woman's past or present, to be without pause or relaxation still continuated : since that with the admirable dignity of so many princely shows and rare sights, it could not by any merry mean (were it never so little time) be broken from that cleaving and cloying grief. I say therefore (to come to the matter) that our noble Princes and valiant Lords were mounted upon Coursers of Naples, and Spanish Gennets, so passing swift in running, that any other beast whatsoever, yea, the very winds themselves (although they made never so much speed), they would in course (invisible almost) leave behind.

Whose youth and lusty years, comely favour, and approved magnanimity and courage, made

them passing gracious, and renowned in every
Gentlewoman's eye and mouth. They came pranc-
ing forward on their barded horses, with caparisons
of purple and crimson Satin, curiously embroidered
with fine threads of shining Gold, and with cloth of
the same artificially woven by Indian hands, with
strange works of divers colours intermingled, filled
and bordered with Gold, pearl and precious stones.
Whose silken, soft and lovely locks, hanging down
upon their stately shoulders, were tied round about
with a fine filament of Gold, beset with Diamonds,
Rubies and Emeralds, and with many other gems,
or else with a little Garland of green Laurel, having
A descrip- on his left hand a light shield, and bearing
tion of Tilt a strong Lance in his right hand, at sound
and Giuoco of Tuscan trumpets making furious and
di canne,
much used courageous encounters either one against
of the
Spaniards, another, or many against many, after the
Italians Morisco guise, but generally in the most
and Moors
brave and admirable sort, before the noble
Ladies and Gentlewomen begin their heroical
sports. Commending him most who with the point
of his Lance carried nearest to the ground, and
closely couched under his shield, without any disordered motion of his body in the saddle, did show
himself in running on his fiery steed.

To such kind of feasts and pleasant shows, as
I was ever wont (poor and miserable Fiammetta), I
was also invited, and certes not without great grief

192

unto me, because beholding these pastimes it came
to my mind that I had whilom seen my Panphilus
sitting amongst our more ancient and reverend old
Gentlemen, to behold suchlike spectacles : whose
sufficiency (according to the admirable gravity of
his youth) deserved so high a place. And sometimes standing (as young Pretextatus amongst the
noble and grave Senators of Rome) with the foresaid robed Knights, to judge of these pastimes,
amongst whom, one for his authority was like unto
Secuola, another for his gravity to either of the
Catos, and some of so pleasant and delectable countenances that they seemed Pompey the Great or
Marcus Marcellus, and others of so stern and martial
looks that they seemed lively to represent the
worthy African Scipio or Quintus Cincinnatus : all
the which, equally and eagerly beholding the running
of every one, and calling to mind their young and
lusty passed years, pricked to the quick with glory
of honour and courage, and muttering and fretting
to themselves, sometimes commended one and sometimes another, Panphilus affirming all their sayings,
and allowing their censures. Of whom sometimes
I heard, how he compared (talking of this and that,
now with one, and now with another) and how he
resembled all those valiant Champions that did
run, to the young and old renowned Heroes of the
other worlds.

Oh, how dear a thing was this to my ears, as well

for him that spake it as for them that attentively
gave ear unto it, and also for my Citizen's sake of
whom it was spoken. So much truly, that the remembrance thereof is yet very grateful unto me.
Of our young Princes, whose heroical countenances
bewrayed their hardy and courageous minds, he
was wont to say that one was like to Arcadius of
Parthenope, of whom it is reported, and firmly believed, that none came better appointed and more
resolute to the destruction of Thebes, at what time
his mother sent him thither, being but a young
youth. The next after he confessed to be like the
sweet Ascanius, of whom Virgil (a singular record
of so brave a youth) wrote so many golden verses.
Comparing the third to Deiphobus, and the fourth
for beauty to Ganymede.

Then coming to those of riper age, that followed
these, he gave them no less perfect and pleasant
semblances. For there might you see one coming
along with a ruddy colour and a red beard, and with
soft, bushy and crisped locks falling down upon
his strong and flightly shoulders, and (no otherwise
than Hercules was wont to have) bound up with a
fine little garland of green leaves, apparelled with
costly garments of silk, occupying no more room
than the just quantity of his body, garnished with
sundry brave works wrought with skilful hand,
with a Mantle upon his right shoulder, fastened together with a button of Gold, and with a fair and

rich shield covering his left side, and carrying in
his right hand a light spear, as was most fit for
that sport, whom he said that he was in gesture,
and countenance, like to great Hector. After whom
another coming along, adorned in like Habits, and
with as stout a countenance as the other, having
cast up the golden fringed border of his Mantle upon
his shoulder, with his left hand cunningly managed
his unruly horse, he judged another Achilles. Another following him, shaking his threatening Lance,
and carrying his target behind his back, having his
soft hair tied together with a fine veil (given him
perhaps of his Lady) he called Protesilaus. After
whom another following with a fine Hat on his head,
of a brown colour in his face, and with a long beard,
and of a fierce countenance, he called Pyrrhus.

And another after him with a more mild look,
and with a sweet and smooth face, and more
gorgeously adorned than the rest, he thought to
resemble Paris of Troy, or King Menelaus.

What need I prolong my narration about this
royal rank any further. In brief, as they passed in
that long and goodly company, he showed who was
like to Agamemnon, who to Ajax, who to Ulysses,
who to Diomedes, or to any other Grecian, Trojan
or Latin worthy of eternal praise and memory.
Neither did he give them these names merely of
his own pleasure, but, conferring and confirming
his arguments with acceptable reasons about the

manner of these paragoned Lords, did show that
they were only and worthily compared unto them.
Wherefore the hearing of these reasons was no
less pleasant than to see the very same persons by
whom and for whom he spake and framed them.

The gallant troop therefore of Horsemen, after
riding three or four times with easy pace up and
down, to show themselves to the lookers-on, cour-
ageously began their fierce courses, and, standing
almost right up in their stirrups, bravely couched
under their Targets, with the points of their Lances
carried so even as they seemed to shave the ground,
The order swifter than the swiftest wind their horses
of those that carried them away. And the air resound-
run a Tilt ing with the shouts of the people that stood
by, and the jangling of the silver and golden bells,
that every horse was almost trapped withal, the
noise also of Trumpets, and of other martial instruments, the flapping and smiting of the caparisons against the horses' sides, and of their bases in
the air, and the flyttering of their Mantles also
against the wind, did prick on their fiery steeds
to a more hot, braver, swifter and more courageous
course.

And thus, everyone with great delight and joy
continually beholding them, and marking the order
of their courses, they made themselves to be worthily
admired, and not unworthily praised in the secret
hearts and open mouths of all the spectators.

196

AMOROUS FIAMMETTA

How many Ladies and Gentlewomen (someone seeing her Husband amongst these here, another her Lover, and some their near Kinsmen) did I see many times clap their hands, and most highly rejoice at the dexterity and courage of their friends ? Not a few truly. And not only these, but strangers also : myself only excepted : who (although I saw my Husband there, and other of my kindred with him) with sorrowful cheer did behold him, not seeing my Panphilus there. And when I remembered how far off he was from me.

Alas, good Ladies, is not this a marvellous thing, that that which I see, should be the material cause and substance of my sorrow ? And that nothing may make me merry. Alas, what soul is there in hell, never so much tormented with endless pain, that seeing these things could not but feel some respective joy ? Why, not one at all (I think). For they, ravished with the sweetness of Orpheus his harp, forgot for a time their cruel pains and torments. But I, set in the midst of a thousand torments, and placed amongst a thousand joys, and continually exercised in many and sundry kinds of sports, cannot (I say) bury my grief in momentary oblivion, nor assuage and lighten it, be it never so little a while. And put case that sometimes at those feasts, and suchlike, I have with an unfeigned and true countenance hid it, and have given respect to my tedious sighs, in the

night afterwards, when I did find myself all alone,
I did prolong, not pardon any part of my tears,
but did pour out rather so many of them as the
day before I had spared and kept in scalding sighs.
And these things inducing me to more pensive
and piercing thoughts, and especially in considering
their vanities, more apt and possible to hurt than
to help, as by proof of them I do manifestly know,
the feast being finished, and myself going from it,
and not without cause complaining and waxing
angry against these vain shadows, and all other
worldly shows, I began thus to say :

"Oh, how happy is that innocent man who
dwelleth in the solitary village, enjoying only the
The praise open air ! Who, employing his sole care
of a solitary and labour to invent subtle gins for simple
life beasts, and to make nets for unwary
birds, with grief of mind can never be wounded.
And if perhaps he suffer any great weariness in his
body, in casting himself down upon the green grass
incontinently he refresheth himself again, changing
his place sometimes in the fresh river banks, and
sometimes under the cool shadow of some great
wood, where the chirping birds, with their pretty
songs, and the soft trembling of the green leaves
(shaken by some pleasant and little wind, as staying themselves to hearken to their silver notes), lull
him sweetly asleep.

"Ah, Fortune, hadst thou granted me such a
198

life (to whom thy desired gifts are but a cloying care, and detriment), it had been better for me. Alas, how my high Palaces, sumptuous beds, treasure and great family, anything profitable, and how little pleasant, unto me, when my mind, surcharged with overmuch anxiety, and wandering in unknown countries after Panphilus, cannot have any small rest, nor when any comfortable respiration may be granted to my wearied and breathless soul. Oh, how delightful and gracious a thing is it to press the green and sweet banks of the swift-running rivers, with a quiet and free mind, and upon the naked turfs to fetch a sound and unbroken sleep, which the gliding river with murmuring bubbles and pleasant noise, without fear doth nourish and maintain. These eases are, without any grudge, granted to the poor inhabitants of the country village freely to enjoy, and are a great deal more to be desired than those toys which with many flattering words I have oftentimes fawned on, and have with such diligent and daily care embraced (as the fine dames of the Cities use commonly to do), and which at last, with the careless coil of the tumultuous family, or negligently, broken. His hunger (if at any time perhaps it prick him) with gathering of Apples in the faithful and secure woods he doth drive away, and many young and tender herbs, which the wide Champaigns or little hills of their own free will bring forth, are also a most savoury and sweet sustenance unto him. Oh, in how many running brooks, Crystalline fountains, and sweet waters, lying down all along, may he quench his thirst, and with the hollow of his hand in clear and streaming rivers ? Ah, wicked and pinching care of worldlings, for whose sustentation nature doth require but little and doth prepare light things. We think with the infinite number and sundry sorts of delicate viands to fill the gourmandize of our bodies, and to please our queasy appetites, not perceiving at all, that in them there lie hidden the very causes, by means of which the ordinate humours and good blood are ever more corrupted than nourished.

" And how many times in cups of gold and silver, richly garnished with gems and precious stones, instead of sweet and delicious wines, do we daily hear that cold and swelling poisons are tasted, and do hourly see that in hot wines and compound drinks, licentious, unbridled and wicked lust is drunk and thrown headlong down. Whereupon, commonly they fall by means of these into a superfluous security : which by wicked words, or damned deeds, doth bring to them a miserable life, *Poetical* or doth pay them home with a most con-*conceits* temptible death, seeing moreover, by daily proof, that these kinds of unkind beverages made the drinkers' bodies in a great deal worser and more miserable case than stark mad. The Satyrs,

200

Fauns, Dryads, Naiads and Nymphs keep him faithful and simple company.

" He doth not know what Venus doth mean, nor cannot skill of her biformed Son. And if he doth perhaps know her, he perceiveth her beauty to be but base, and little amiable. Now (alas) would it had pleased the Gods that I had likewise never known it and that (keeping simple and plain company) I had lived a rustical and rude life to myself all alone.

" Then should these incurable griefs have been far from me which I now sustain, and my soul, *The pomp of the world like to the wind* together with my most holy name, should not have cared nor desired to see these worldly pomps and feasts, like to the flying winds and vanishing smoke in the air, nor (if it had seen them) should have been so full of anguish and sorrow as now it is. The desire of high and princely towers, of rich and sumptuous houses, of great families, and costly trains, of fair and delicate beds, of shining clothes of gold and silver, of pampered, proud and swift horses, and of a thousand other superfluities of nature, doth never disturb his temperate mind, nor clogs his heart, with burdening and burning care to keep them. Not accompanied nor sought after of wicked men, he doth without fear live in quiet and sequestered places, and, without seeking doubtful rest in high and stately lodgings, doth demand only the open air and light for his repose.

" And of the manner of his life the wide firmament is a manifest and continual witness. Oh, how much is this life nowadays unknown, and like an enemy eschewed and condemned of everyone, whereas it should be rather, as the dearest and sweetest content, followed and embraced of all. Truly I suppose that the first age of the world lived in this sort, which piecemeal brought forth Gods and men.

" There is no life (alas) more free, nor more devoid of vice, or better than this : the which our first fathers enjoyed, and with which also he is this day of all others best contented who, abandoning the opulent and vicious Cities, inhabiteth the private and peaceable woods. Oh, what a world had it been if Jupiter had never driven Saturn away, and if the Golden Age had continued still under a chaste law, because we might all live like to our primitive parents of the first world.

"Alas, whosoever he be that doth this day observe the first and ancient riches, even he (I say) is not inflamed with the blind rage of hapless and helpless Venus as I am, nor he, who hath resolved with himself to dwell in Woods, hills, or dales, was ever subject to any careful kingdom, nor to the wavering wind of the unconstant populare, nor to the suffrages, opinions and censures of the trothless common people, nor the infectious plagues and envious pestilences, nor to the frail favour also of

202

blind and inconsiderate Fortune, in all which myself, having put too much trust, love and study, in
the midst of the waters (like Tantalus) do die with
endless thirst. To little things great rest is afforded,
although it be a hard matter without the greater to
be able to sustain the life. But he whose thoughts
are turmoiled about great things, or doth desire to
What they overrule great matters : the same man
are that (I say) doth evermore follow the vain
follow riches honours of fading riches. And high styles
and magnificent titles please for the most part
false and deceitful men. But he is free from fear
and doubt, and cannot discern of the malicious man,
swelling in rancour and cankered envy, nor of the
backbiter by his venomous tongue and viperous
teeth, who dwelleth in the simple and solitary
woods and fields ; and is also ignorant of the sundry
hatreds, and incurable wounds of love, and the
abominable sins of the people committed one against
another in the Cities; and liveth without fear of
breach of laws, and clear of suspicion to be guilty
of riots and mutinies, and beateth not his brains
to forge feigned tales and to use deceitful words,
which are notes to entrap men of pure faith and
plain dealing. But the other, while he is aloft, is
never without fear or peril, suspecting continually
the very same sword that he weareth by his side.
Oh, how good a thing it is to resist naked, and lying
upon the ground securely to take his sustenance.

Never or seldom at all did capital or great sins
enter into little cottages. At the first there was no
care taken for gold, nor the holy stone, nor God
Terminus, was set a bound or Arbiter to divide
fields from fields, and severals from commons.
With tall and stout ships they ploughed the unknown waves of the Sea, but everyone did know
his proper coasts and banks. Nor with strong piles
of timber, with deep ditches, high walls, strong
bulwarks and ramparts did they fortify and compass about the sides of their Cities, nor cruel
weapons and rusty armour were scoured up and
made ready to fight, or borne of warriors in those
days, neither had they any Engines, or devilish
devices, which (with great pity) might ruinate stone
walls, and break Iron gates in pieces.

" And if there was perhaps amongst them any
little war, with naked breast and unarmed arm
they fought it out, in which the broken boughs of
trees and stones served them for their weapons
and pellets. Nor the fine and light spear of horn
was armed with Iron, nor the stabbing dagger,
trenching sword and murdering rapier were girt
to any of their backs or side : nor the bushy crest
and proud plume of coloured waving feathers did
adorn the glittering helmets, and that which in
their happy days was the happiest thing of all,
was, that Cupid was not yet born, whereby the
chaste minds (violated afterwards with his poisoned

204

darts, when he first began to fly with swift wings through the world) might live securely and free from all tormenting thoughts. Ah, I would the Gods had given me to such a world, the people whereof, content with a little, and fearing nothing, followed only their wild and savage appetites.

" And that of so many great goods and felicities that they enjoyed I had not possessed any other than not to be molested with so grievous love, nor to feel so many smothering sighs, as now I am, and do now feel, then should I have lived a more happy life than now I do in this present age, full of so many *Mutations* poisoned pleasures, unprofitable ornaments *of ages* and shadowed pomp. Alas, that the wicked fury of gain and avarice, that headlong and enraged wrath, and that those minds, which of themselves kindled loathsome lust, and violated these first bonds, so holy and easy to be kept (given of Nature herself to her people), and that the thirst after rule (a bloody Sun) came now in place, and that the weaker became a prey to the greater and more mighty ! Sardanapalus came now in, and first of all made Venus (though of Semiramis it was made more dissolute) more dainty and delicate, and then to Bacchus and Ceres prescribed new orders and customs never known of them before.

" Then came in also warlike Mars, who found out new sleights and a thousand mortal ways to death. And then all the world began to be contaminated with black gore, and the Sea to be tainted with red rivers of blood running into it. Then most wicked crimes entered into everyone his house, and in brief there was no great or detestable sin perpetrated without some former and foul example before. Brother killed brother, the father the son, and the son the father. The husband lay slain for the fault, and many times by the proper fact, of his wife. And wicked mothers destroyed daily their own fruit. The infinite cruelty and endless envy of stepdames, which continually, secretly or openly, they bear to their husbands' children, I need not to allege, because their effects are manifestly seen at all times and places.

" Riches therefore brought Pride, Avarice, Lechery, Wrath, Gluttony, Envy and Sloth, and every other *Love the* vice, with them. And with these afore-*worker of* said Fiends the Captain and worker of *all mischief* all mischief, and the only artificer of all sins, entered also (dissolute and unbridled Love I mean), by whose continual sieges, laid to miserable minds, infinite Cities, ruinated and burnt, do yet smoke, and for whom all nations have made mortal uproars, and do yet broil in the lamentable and endless wars.

" And the overwhelmed and drowned kingdoms by his cruel tyranny do yet oppress many people. And concealing all his other execrable effects, let those only which he useth towards me suffice for a manifest example of his merciless mischief and cruelty, which do so sharply environ me on every side that I cannot turn my mind to no other thing, but only to the grievous objects of his immanity."

Discoursing thus with myself, sometimes I thought that that which I did was wicked in the sight of the just Gods, and that my pains were annoyous to me without compare.

But many greater offences committed in times past, and daily practised by others, made me (in respect of them) seem but innocent, and the consideration of those pains which others endured (although I believed that none passed the like grief as I did, seeing myself not to be the first, nor one alone) did so work in my understanding that I became the stronger to suffer my own : the which I pray the Gods determine with hasty death, or else drive them away with Panphilus his speedy return. Thus therefore pitiless Fortune, for this kind of life, or rather for a worse than this, hath left me but small comfort, as you (pitiful Ladies) have heard.

Which consolation understand it not such, that it was able to make me forget my sorrow (as others commonly are wont to do), for this did but only stop my tears (ready to fall out of mine eyes), and did sometimes indeed dissolve my sighs into nothing, without affording me nevertheless any other benefit. Prosecuting therefore the pitiful history of my painful life, I say, that heretofore, with many other young gentlewomen, adorned with singular beauty, I was never wont to omit any great feast in our City, or which was celebrated in our divine temples : the which solemnities, feasts and triumphs without my presence the company did account but little worth, and thought them less beautified. Which times appointed for them my waiting-women, duly knowing to be at hand, were very diligent to solicit and put me in mind of them, and others of my maids also, observing their old order in laying forth, and making ready my noble garments, sometimes said to me : " With what gown may it please you (good Madam) to adorn yourself ? For the solemnity of such a feast is to be celebrated this day in the temple, which doth attend your coming for the only beautifying and accomplishment of it." To whom (alas) I remember that sometimes with an angry *A troubled* voice and austere countenance (turning *mind careth* furiously to them again, no otherwise than *not to go* *brave*   a tusky Bear doth to a company of barking Curs) I answered, saying : " Pack hence, the vilest part of my house, and carry away these ornaments from my sight. A simple and poor garment is most fit to cover this miserable body, nor let not me hear you any more talk of temples, feasts and solemnities, if you esteem of my favour at all. Oh, how many times did I yet perceive well enough that those temples were visited of many noble

208

personages who came thither rather to see me than for any great devotions, and not espying me there, grieved as it were in mind, went from thence again, generally affirming that the feast was dishonoured, and not to be called a feast without my presence there. But although that I refrained thus from them, yet sometimes, entreated and constrained, I must needs, in company of other noble Ladies my acquaintance and companions, go to them : with whom (but simply apparelled in my ordinary holiday attire) unwillingly (the Gods know) I went thither.

And there did not look for any solemn and high place (as I was wont to do), but refusing the honours offered unto me, I humbly betook myself to the lowest places, amongst other gentlewomen of meaner calling and degree. And there harkening to many speeches, sometimes of one and sometimes of another, with secret grief (as well as I could) I passed away the time that I stayed there. How many times (alas) did I hear them that sat nearest unto me talk of me, saying :

" Oh, what a great marvel is it to see this young Gentlewoman (the singular ornament of our City) become now of late of so demiss and abject a mind ! What divine spirit hath inspired her ? Where are her noble robes ? Where are her high and stately countenances ? And whither are her rare and surpassing beauties fled ? " To which words (if lawfully I might) I would have answered : " All these things,

with many other more (dearer to me than these),
Panphilus (ah, my injurious Panphilus) hath carried
away with him." And compassed about there with
many Gentlewomen, and importunately urged with
many questions, with a feigned cheer and countenance of necessity I must satisfy them all. But one
of the Gentlewomen amongst the rest, with these
stinging words began to mock me, saying : " Thou
makest me (Lady Fiammetta), and many other
Gentlewomen more, never cease to marvel at thee,
not knowing what sudden occasion hath moved thee
to forsake thy rich attire, thy Jewels, gems and
ornaments, and many other things, so commendable
and beseeming thy young years, and which (we
know) were once most precious unto thee. Being
yet but in the flourishing prime of thy age, thou
shouldest not put on this grave apparel and these
uncouth Habits.

" Dost thou think, that letting thy youthful time
pass, thou canst call it back again ? Use thy years
Years ought therefore according to their properties and
to be used nature. This homely and honest clothing
according to nature. This homely and honest clothing
their quality which thou hast put on may perhaps hereafter serve thy turn better. And as thou seest here
every one of us (elder and graver than thyself) with
curious and skilful hand adorned, and with honourable and costly garments attired, with such oughtest
thou (Fiammetta) to be set forth and beautified."

To her, and to many other also, expecting what I

would say, with an humble and low voice I made this answer:

"Gentlewoman, and you the rest of my friends, we come to these holy places, either to please the Gods, or else to please men. If to please the Gods, the mind adorned with virtue is sufficient, and it doth not import whether the body be clothed with silk or sackcloth. If to please men, forasmuch as most of them are blinded with false opinions, and by the exterior parts and lineaments of the body conjecture the inward disposition of the mind, I confess that the apparel used sometimes of me, and now of you, is very requisite. But this is now my least care, my chiefest desire consisting rather in a sorrowful repentance of my past vanities, which being most willing to amend in the sight of Gods and men, by this apparel, and in other things else, I make myself (as much as I can) contemptible to the world, and displeasant to your nice eyes."

At which words the tears of inward truth, violently expressed forth, bathed my sorrowful visage, and therefore thus I began to say softly to myself: "O ye pitiful Gods, the searchers of all our hearts, let not these untrue words (uttered by my lying tongue) be imputed to me for a sin, which (not of a malicious will, and flat hypocrisy to deceive them, but of mere necessity to dissemble my grief, and cover the cause of it from them) I was constrained to use as a holy and godly excuse. But let them rather be meritorious unto me, since that in concealing from thy people an evil and scandalous example, in lieu thereof, by these feigned words, I gave them a good president and pattern of better life. It is a great grief (you know) for me to tell a lie, and with what an unpatient and troubled mind I tell this forced and forged tale you know too well, and I can do no more."

Oh, how many times (fair Ladies) for this iniquity have I received pitiful prayers of the Gentlewomen *How hard* sitting about me, saying, that of a most *a thing it* vain woman I was become a most devout *is to judge* *of another's* convertite. Truly I understood, many times, *holiness* that there were some of them of this opinion, that I was so highly in the Gods' favour that there was nothing that I could crave at their hands but I might easily obtain the same of them. And therefore I was many times visited of holy women, for a zealous and devout one also, they being (poor souls) as much deceived in that which with my sorrowful and subtle countenance I did hide my mind, as ignorant how discrepant my fervent desires and my feigned devotions were. O deccitful world, how much can counterfeit looks prevail in thee more than just and well-meaning minds, if that their works be hidden and secret.

Myself a greater sinner than any other, and sorrowful for my dishonest loves, yet couching them under the Veil of honest words, am reputed holy :

but the just Gods know that (if I could without danger of my honour and good name) with true reports I would make satisfaction to everyone whom in fictions, speeches and gesture I have deluded, and would not hide the headspring from whence such streams of tears did flow, nor the course from whence the effects of my sorrowful life are derived. But (alas) it may not be.

When I had answered her who first demanded of me the cause of my melancholy, another sitting *Beauty is* next unto me, seeing my tears almost dried *but a frail* up, said: "Gracious Fiammetta, whither *thing* is the shining beauty of thy fair face gone, and how is the lively colour of thy rosy cheeks extinct? What is the cause of thy pale and wan *The upper-* visage? Thy twinkling eyes, like to morn- *most attire* ing stars, are dimmed now with blue and *of Italian* *andSpanish* purple circles that compass them about, *Ladies and* and are so deeply sunk into thy brows that *Gentle-* *women is a* scarcely they may be discerned in thy fore- *fine black* head. Thy golden tresses, once so bravely *mantle of* *silk or saye* adorned with curious hand heretofore, *upon their* why now tied up diffusedly, and scarcely *other gar-* *ments,which* are they seen? Tell me, Fiammetta. For *covereth* thou makest me to marvel without end." *them from* *the head* And her I answered in few words thus: *to the feet* "It is a manifest thing that human beauty is but a fading flower, and that every day and hour it waxeth less and less, which (if it hath any trust

in itself) at length doth perceive itself to be but
nothing, and to lie miserably prostrate. He that
gave it me (submitting me the occasion of expelling
it again) with a dull pace hath taken it from me,
possibly (perhaps) to restore to me again, whensoever it shall please him." And this being said, not
able to withhold my tears, shrouded under my mantle
I shed them abundantly. And with these words I
lamented with myself, saying :

" O beauty, the uncertain Jewel of mortal men,
and the gift of a little time, which doth both come
and go sooner away than the pleasant Meadows
depainted with many flowers in the sweetest seasons
of gladsome springtide, and the verdure of high
Trees apparelled with sundry leaves, which are
no sooner for a little time adorned with the virtue
of Aries but immediately, with the hot exhalations
and vapours of parching Summer, are consumed
and taken away again. And if perhaps the burning
season doth leave any of them untouched, Autumn
doth not spare to leave them naked and bare. Even
so thou, beauty, most often in the midst of thy prime
and best years, injured by many accidents, dost
perish, which if perhaps they be pardoned thee in
youth, the riper age (though with all thy force and
means thou dost oppose to preserve the same) doth
take it quite away. O beauty, thou art but a flying
and inconstant thing, and not unlike to the waters,
which never return more to their first fountains :

214

and no hope in changing and brittle goods, and therefore less affiance, should be put.

" Alas, how did I once love thee, and how dear wert thou to me (miserable woman), and with what care wert thou nourished and kept of me ! But now (and deservedly) I curse thee, beauty. For thou art the first occasion of my lost liberty, the first entrapper of my dear Panphilus his soul; enjoying him, hast not sufficient force to keep him still. And he being now gone, hast not the power or virtue to call him back again. If thou hadst not been, I had not seemed pleasant to Panphilus his lovely eyes, and not having pleased them, he should have never sought to allure mine, and not enticing and pleasing them, as he did, I should not now sustain these pains of mind. Thou art therefore the only occasion and beginning of all my hurt. Oh, thrice happy are those Women who, without thee, suffer the rebukeful checks of rude and rustical behaviour, and are condemned for their foul and ill-favoured hue, because they (observing Diana's chaste and holy laws, and seldom troubled with pricking motions, as well devoid of peevish passions of their own parts as not fearing the forcible assaults of fond suitors) may live with their souls free from the cruel signory and tyranny of love. But thou, the only occasion of receiving continual molestation by them who never leave to gape on us, dost (by their importunacy) of force entice us to break that which we should most dearly observe. O happy Spurina, and worthy of eternal memory, who (knowing thy effects and unlawful affections) in the flower of her youth, with cruel hand did kill thee in her breast, rather choosing to be of the wiser beloved for her virtuous act than of wanton youths for her concupiscible beauty. Alas, if I had done so, all these griefs, all these thoughts, and these tears should have never thus molested my tender heart, and my now corrupted life should have yet remained within the compass of her first laudable bonds."

Hereat the Gentlewomen pulled me again, and blamed my superfluous tears, saying: "O Fiammetta, *None must* what misery is this ? Dost thou despair of *despair in* the mercy of the Gods ? Dost thou not *God's mercy* believe that they do pitifully forgive the greatest offences without shedding of so many tears ? This course which thou dost take in hand is rather the way to seek thy own death than pardon for thy faults. Rise up therefore and wipe thy face, and behold the sacrifice which the sacred Ministers of Jupiter are carrying to offer up to his mighty Godhead."

At these words (stopping my tears) I lifted up my head, which now I did not cast round about (as I was wont to do), assuredly knowing that my Panphilus was not there, nor to see if any other, or of whom I was beheld, or if the standers-by gazed on my apparel, and ornaments, as they were wont to

216

do, but rather wholly intent, and relying upon the favour of the supernal Gods, to pour forth some pitiful prayers for my Panphilus, and for his happy return, calling upon them with these words, I said : " O most gracious governors of high Heaven, and *The end of* general Judges of all the world, set now *one sorrow* some stint and measure to my grievous *is the* *beginning* pains, and prescribe an end to all my *of another* sorrows. You see I have not one merry hour, nor quiet day, since that in continued course the end of one sorrow is the beginning of another. But that sometimes I accounted myself happy, not knowing my miseries to ensue. First with vain labour to beautify my young and unripened years more than was requisite (sufficiently adorned of nature itself), having unwittingly offended you, for penance and satisfaction of such faults ye have of indissoluble and cruel love, which doth at this very instant torment me, made me a miserable thrall and captive. And you have afterwards filled my mind (not accustomed to troubles and sorrows) by means of it, with new avoiding cares. And lastly have divided him from me, whom I love more than myself : whereupon infinite perils are grown one after another in prejudice of my poor life. But if the prayers of miserable creatures sometimes penetrate your divine ears, then pitifully incline them to my petitions, and, not regarding the multitude of the faults which I have committed against you, let that little good (if ever I did any) be bountifully considered of you, and in guerdon of it favourably give ear to my jealous orisons, and grant my earnest requests, which as they are but easy for you to perform, so may you (by not denying me the same) give me most great content, and make me happy again. Alas, how well do I know that this prayer in the sight of you (most just Judges) is very unjust : but it must (needs) proceed from your justice that, of two evils, to wish the less and to prevent the greater is the safest and best counsel. To you therefore, from whom nothing is hid, it is manifest, that my beloved Panphilus by no means can slide out of my mind, nor those passed accidents out of my memory, the remembrance of whom, and of which, doth many times with griping griefs bring me to such a point that (to be rid of them) I have eftsoons desired a thousand manners, and sought as many means, of death, all which that little hope which remaineth for me in you hath forcibly taken out of my hands. If it be therefore a lesser evil to keep my Lover still, as I have done, than to destroy my wicked soul with my massacred body (as I believe it is), let him return, and be restored to me again. Let living sinners be dearer to you, and possible to return to you again, than the dead dying in their sin, and without hope of redemption. And vouchsafe rather to leese a part of your creature than the whole, which you have created. And if this be too great, and too much to be granted, let that which is the last end of all miseries, before *Miserable* that with deliberate and voluntary counsel *creatures* *require* (constrained with greater griefs) I take it *death* of myself, be granted to me. Let my words come before your sight, whom, if they cannot move to pity, then you other Gods dwelling in the celestial regions, if there be any of you there who, sometimes living here beneath, have had trial of that amorous fire which I feel, receive them, and offer them up to those higher powers, who will not take them uttered by my unworthy mouth, so that, obtaining grace for me, I may first live here joyfully, and after the end of my days enjoy part of your glorious fruition, and before time, to show sinners that it is a good and convenient thing for one sinner to pardon and help another."

These words having been spoken, I did put sweet odours and incense upon their Altars, with many other rich offerings, to make them more willing and ready to bend down their ears to my prayers and for Panphilus his help. Which ceremonies, after they were ended, departing from thence, with the rest of the Gentlewomen, I returned to my sorrowful lodging again.

THE
FIFTH BOOK OF BOCCACE
HIS FIAMMETTA

A S by those things which I have spoken of before, you may presume, even so (pitiful Ladies) hath my loathed life been assaulted in the cruel battles of Love, and yet is tossed every day upon more sharp and mortal pikes of jealousy. The which certes (considering my future estate) might justly be thought a pleasant peace and pastime. Myself also being stricken with fear (when it came to my remembrance), with fear (I say) of that, to the which point it did last of all transport me, and which doth yet almost possess me, to make the more delay to come to it, because I was ashamed of my own fury, and because in writing of it methought I re-entered into it again, deducting therefore my discourse in length, with a slow hand I have written and published those things unto you which were less grievous unto me : but being not able now to avoid these, nor to fly to them any more, the order of my narration drawing me on, I will (though fearfully) come unto it. But thou most holy pity, dwelling in the tender breasts of delicate young Gentlewomen, govern thy reins in them with a stronger hand than thou hast done hitherto, because in discurring this my doleful narration, and giving thee a great deal more scope than is precisely convenient, I might not (perhaps) turn thee into the contrary of that which I do seek and hope for, and so might take as it were, from the laps of these Ladies and Gentlewomen that read thee, their flowing and falling tears. The Sun was now turned another time into that part of the Heavens where the presumptuous Son was set on fire, when so rashly he guided his father's Chariot, after that Panphilus departed from me.   And I, miserable woman, had now by long use learned to

When Fortune doth begin to show herself contrary, then she goes increasing ever her spite suffer accustomed griefs, and I lamented more temperately with myself than I was wont to do, and believed that there were no more woes left for me to sustain than those which I had already endured, when envious Fortune, not content with my past miseries, did suddenly show me that she had yet more bitter poison to infect my afflicted soul withal.

It came therefore to pass that one of my dearest servants returned from Panphilus his country hither, who was of all that knew him, but especially of me, most joyfully welcomed. And telling of his own adventures and travels, and of those things which he had seen, intermingling better with worse, bechance he remembered himself at last to speak of Panphilus, of whose praises dilating very much (remembering the courtesies that he had sometimes done him), made me most contented, and plied my willing ears to his tale. And shamefast reason and womanly modesty did scarce bridle my eager will from running to embrace him, and to inquire of my Panphilus with an extraordinary kind of appassionate affection, as at that very present I felt. But yet staying myself, and he being also demanded of many concerning his estate, and having answered everyone well, I only asked him, with a merry countenance, how he employed himself and spent his time there, and if his mind was happily bent to return again. To which demands he answered thus :

" To what purpose (my good Lady) should Panphilus come again ? There is not a fairer Gentlewoman in all his country (which above all other Cities doth bring forth Goddesses for beauty) than she who most entirely loveth him, and by as much as I could understand of others (and as I verily believe) is dearly beloved of him again, otherwise I would account him but a fool, whereas heretofore I ever judged him to be wise."

My heart was so turned at these words as Œnone's was, sitting on the high hills of Ida, and seeing her lover come sailing homewards with the new Grecian Lady in the Trojan Ship : which thing I could scarce hide in my countenance, although very hardly I did the same : but yet with a dissembled and faint laughter I said unto him : " Certes, thou sayest even

true : for we could not imagine in this country any
one gentlewoman so different from his dainty liking,
whom we might deem worthy of his love, so high
was his inestimable virtue, so rare were his laudable
qualities, and so many his good graces. But if he
hath found out anyone there, he doth both well and
wisely in staying with her there. But tell me, with
what mind doth he brook his new wife ? " He then
answered : "He hath no wife; for she that came to
his house (as I told not long since) true it is that
she came, not to him but to his father." Whilst
Jealousy is he spake these bitter words, which so earn-
of all others estly I listened unto, passing out of one
the worst anguish into another anxiety a great deal
worse, pricked moreover with sudden anger and
grief of mind, my sorrowful heart began so to pant
and beat, as the swift wings of Procne, when she
begins to take her strongest flight, do beat against
the white Sea banks and shores.

And my fearful spirits began no otherwise to
tremble throughout every part of my body than
the superficial and uppermost part of the Sea, with
the gentle breathing of some calm wind descended
upon it, is commonly wont to do, or the bending
reeds scarcely shaken of some pleasant and soft
air, and I began to feel my strength by little and
little decay. Wherefore getting myself (as conveniently as I could) from thence, I went into my
Chamber, because none might perceive the violent

issue of my sudden grief. And being now gone out of the presence of everyone, I came no sooner into it but I began to pour out of mine eyes such plenty of tears as a swelling vein or fountain of water, bursting and gushing out, when it overfloweth the valleys, and I could scarce hold my troubled tongue from loud exclamations, and my hoarse voice from piteous lamentations, but casting myself (nay, rather falling) flat upon my miserable bed (the wicked witness of our loves) I would have cried out aloud, and said:

" O Panphilus, why hast thou betrayed me ? "

But my words were broken in the very midst, so suddenly were the vigour and forces taken from my tongue, and from the other parts of my body. And there I lay a good while, as one dead (nay, verily thought to be dead indeed) carefully watched, and giving no small wonder to everyone there, by this sudden trance (no skill of Physic, or secrecy of any art, being able to make my erring life return to her former place again).

But after that my sorrowful soul, which in lamenting had many times embraced the miserable spirits of my body to depart, did yet stay itself in the same, and recalling her forces again together, which were almost dissolved and fled away, my eyes received again their light, which for a good space they had lost.

And lifting up my head I saw many Gentlewomen

and others about me, who with their loving and pitiful services, bewailing my sudden swoon, had with most precious and sweet waters all bedewed me, and with many other instruments in their hands, and which I did see lying before me, labouring to regain my lost life. Whereupon, I marvelled no less at those waters, preserves and glasses that were about me than at the great lamentations of all the gentlewomen there.

And after that I had recovered my speech again, I demanded what was the cause of their assembly about me, and of all those things there. And one of them answered, and said :

" These things (good Lady) were brought hither (and for no other purpose we also came) to reduce thy fugitive soul into thy cold body again." Then after a great sigh, and faint spirit, I said : "Alas, good Gentlewoman, with what friendly office of pity (working rather a most cruel function, and repugnant to my will) do you think to have done me a thankful piece of service, whereas you have procured my great pain, and done me the worst turn as ever I had, in forcible retaining of my soul in me still, which was so well disposed, and so willing, to have left the most miserable body that liveth. Alas, it is enough that there was never anything which with like affection was desired of me, or of anybody else, which you have denied me. My soul, already dissolved from these pains and tribulations, had been nearly arrived to the wished haven of my desires, but you have hindered it her passage."

After these words, the Gentlewomen recomforted me with divers good speeches, but they spent both words and wind in vain. I feigned, *Miserable men desire to be alone to burst out their inward grief in lamentation* notwithstanding, to be of better cheer, and alleged new occasions of this miserable accident, because, when they were gone, I might have full scope to burst out my great and swelling grief. And after that some of them were departed, and the rest had taken their leave, myself beginning to show a merry countenance, and to dissemble my sorrow, I remained accompanied there only with my old Nurse and with my faithful maid, who had all this time been privy to my long plaints, and a procurer of my momentary pleasure, both which dutifully ministered comfortable salves to my unfeigned sores, possible enough to have healed them had they not been mortal. But I, thinking only of those unlucky tidings which I had heard, to one of you, Gentlewomen (to which I know not), I suddenly became an open enemy, and I began to revolve great and grievous matters in my perplexed mind. And that amassed lump of grief, which could not altogether contain itself in my breast, with a furious and despiteful voice I did in this sort partly drive out of me, saying:

"O wicked and false young man! O enemy to

227

pity, and pitiless wretch! O Panphilus, the worst of all those who without desert doth breathe this common air! Disloyal Panphilus, who having blotted me (most miserable woman) out of thy ungrateful memory dost now dwell and delight thyself with thy new deceitful dame! Accursed be that hapless day when first I saw thee, and that fatal hour, and very instant, in which thou didst please my simple eyes. Accursed be that Goddess which, appearing to me, with her allured promises flattered my wavering mind, and disturbed the same (though resisting with all her forces to the contrary) from the bounds of my right judgment, to like of thee (wicked wretch) and (ungrateful monster) to love thee.

"Certes, I think that she was not Venus, but rather some infernal fury in her shape, striking me with madness and filling me with frantic fury, as once she did miserable Atamas. O most cruel youth, whom amongst many other most noble, beautiful and valiant young Gentlemen I did fondly choose out for the best, where are now thy serious prayers, which for safety of thy life with tears thou didst oftentimes offer unto me, affirming that both that and thy death were in my hands? Where are now thy pitiful looks, and those two never-dried eyes, with the which (malicious man) thou didst never cease at thy pleasure to shed forth tears in my presence? Where is now the great love, that so

bravely thou didst feign to show me ? Where are
thy sweet words, and thy sore griefs, thy infinite
sorrows, thy pains and travails proffered and employed in my service ? Are all these fled out of thy
memory, or hast thou framed them anew to entrap
thy deceived and new lover ?

" Accursed be that pity of mine, which took that
life out of death his mouth, that (thereby making
herself then a joyful woman) should have rather
sent it to the darksome den of death. Now those
eyes, which whilom in my presence lamented, laugh
before their new Mistress, and that mutable heart
hath turned all his sweet words and fair offers to
her only, and now hast thou heretically dedicated
all thy services to her devotions.

" Alas, Panphilus, where are now those profaned
and perjured Godheads ? Where is thy promised
faith ? Where are thy infinite tears, of the which
(miserable woman) I drunk no small quantity,
believing them to be tempered then with as great
pity and love as now they are turned but to drops
of treacherous deceit ? All those placed in the
bosom of thy new Mistress thou hast with thyself
taken from me. Alas, how great a corsive was
it to my poor heart, when once before I heard
that by Juno's law thou wert combined to another
woman ! But perceiving that the covenants in
which thou didst bind thyself to me were not to
be preferred before them (although I did painfully

bear it), yet overcome with just grief, I did with
less anguish of mind endure it.   But now under-
It is a great standing that by the selfsame laws by the
grief that which thou wert bound to me thou hast
that which
doth justly (in casting me off) given thyself to another,
belong to it is an untolerable pain for me to sustain.
one should
unjustly be But now I know the cause of thy stay, and
another's openly perceive my own simplicity, with
the which I ever believed that thou wouldest (if
possible) have once returned again. Alas, Panphilus,
didst thou stand in need of so many guileful
arts and cunning fetches to delude me?   Why
didst thou so often, so solemnly and so highly
swear unto me, with continual asseveration of thy
most entire and sincere faith, if thou didst think
thus to deceive me?   Wherefore didst not thou
go away without taking thy leave, or without
making any promise of thy return?   I did (as thou
knowest) most fervently love thee, and thou wert
not then so much entangled in my love, and wert
not so straitly my prisoner, but at thy will (as to
my no small pain I now perceive thou hast done),
and without wasting such infinite and vain tears,
thou mightest have departed from me.   If thou
hadst done thus, then I should without doubt have
suddenly despaired of thy return, manifestly knowing thy deceit, and then with death ere this time,
or else with just oblivion, my torments should
have been concluded. But because they might be

230

the more prolonged in giving me a little vain hope, thou hast continuated and nourished them still. But I, poor soul, never deserved this at thy wicked hands. Alas, how sweet were thy false tears to me ; but now (knowing their vile effects) I feel them to be most bitter to my dying mind. Alas, if love did so strongly rule in thee, as he doth fiercely use his might and signory in me, tell me then, if it was not sufficient for thee to be once captivated, but that the second time thou must fall into his forces again ? But what do I talk of love ? For thou didst never love, but hast rather delighted to jest with young gentlewomen, and hast made it but a sport to deceive with thy subtlety their simplicity. If thou hadst loved (as I did believe thou didst) thou shouldest yet have been mine own. And whose couldest thou have been that had loved thee more than I ? Alas, what dame soever thou be that hast taken him from me, though thou art my mortal and only enemy, yet, feeling the great grief which his falsehood hath engendered in my breast, I must needs take pity on thee. Wherefore I warn thee to *He that de-* take heed of his deceits, because he that *ceiveth once* hath once deceived hath for ever after *deceiveth* *ever* lost his honesty and shame, and doth make it no matter of conscience to deceive everyone from thenceforth.

"Alas, wicked youth, how many orisons and sacrifices have I offered up to the Gods for thy safety, and now thou must fly from me, to go to another. O Gods, my prayers (I perceive) are heard but to the profit of another woman.

" I have the sorrow, and another sucks the sweet. I reap but dole and pain for my long devotions, and another delight and pleasure of him who in right and equity should be mine.

" Ah, wicked man, was not my beauty correspondent to thy bravery, my doings to thy desires, and my nobility to thy Gentility ? Alas, a great deal more ! Were my riches ever denied thee, or did I take any of thine ? Ah, never. Did I ever in deed or demonstration love any man besides thyself ? And (unless thy new love make thee digress too far from the truth) thou wilt confess and say no. What fault of mine therefore, what just occasion of thy part, what greater beauty, or more fervent love have taken thee from me, and given thee to another ? Truly none. And all the Gods be my records herein, that I never wrought anything against thee but that (beyond all terms of reason) I loved thee. And if this hath deserved such treachery as thou hast done, and workest against me, let thy own self (disloyal as thou art) be judge. O ye Gods, the just revengers of our unjust defects, I call upon you for cruel and due vengeance. I neither wish, nor go about to practise his death, who by his vile escape from me would have wrought mine. Nor do I pray that any other punishment may befall to his deserved guilt, but, if he love his new choice as I love him, that in casting him off, and giving herself to another (as he hath taken himself from me), she would leave him in that kind of life that (cruel as he is) he causeth me to lead." And so, with unseemly motions of my body, turning me now this way, now that way, like a frantic woman I tumbled and tossed up and down in my bed.

All that day was not spent in other speeches than in such of like tenour, and in most bitter wailings. But the night, worser than the day, and more apt for all kinds of sorrow (the melancholy darkness being more conformable to meditating miseries than the light), being now stolen on, it came to pass that, being indeed with my dear husband, and lying a great while silent to myself, and broad waking, yet warring within myself with hosts of dolorous thoughts, amongst which, calling to memory all my passed times, as well my pleasant occurrences as sorrowful passages, and especially that I had lost my Panphilus by means of a new love, my grief grew in such abundance that, unable to keep it any longer within, with great lamentations and doleful complaints I burst it out, albeit concealing the amorous occasion of it. And my sighs were so forcible, and my sobs so profound, that my Husband (being now a good while drowned in deep sleep) by the great noise and molestation of them was awaked, and turning himself to me, who was sponged in mine own tears, and taking me lovingly in his arms, with mild and pitiful words he said thus unto me:

"O my sweet soul, what sinister cause of so doleful a plaint in the quiet night, when thou *The love* shouldest take thy rest, doth trouble thee *of a good* thus? What thing is it that this long *husband* time hath made thee so melancholic and sad? Nothing must be concealed from me that may any way displease or discontent thee. Is there anything that thy heart doth desire, and that my wit and substance may compass for thee, or that in demanding of it thou mightest possibly have? Art not thou my only comfort, my joy and my good? And dost not thou know that I love thee above all worldly thoughts, yea, more than myself. Whereof not by show, nor one proof, but by daily experience, thou mayest live assured. Wherefore dost thou therefore lament in such sort? Wherefore dost thou afflict thyself in such extreme grief? Do I seem unpleasant, ill favoured or nothing gracious in thine eyes, or am I unworthy of thy beauty, or is not my birth, parentage and estate agreeable to thy nobility, or dost thou think me culpable in anything that I may amend? Speak, and tell me frankly, and discover to me the vale of thy desires. There shall be nothing left undone, or unattempted, for thy sake, if it may possible be. Thou dost (altered in visage and apparel, and ex-

234

tremely sorrowful in all thy actions) minister a doleful occasion and matter to me of an unquiet life. And though I have before seen thee continually sad and pensive, yet this day more than at any time. I thought of late that some bodily infirmity was the cause of thy paleness, but now I do manifestly know that it is grief of mind that hath brought thee to this pitiful case wherein I see thee, wherefore I pray thee disclose to me the root from whence all thy sorrows do grow."

Whom with a feminine and sudden wit, taking counsel of feigned tales and lies, which before had served me for a shift, I answered thus :

"O sweet Husband, dearer to me than all the world besides, I lack not anything wherein thy *Sometimes* forward help may avail me, and acknow- *the manner of one's death* ledge thee (without all doubt) more worthy *is more* than myself; but the death of my dear *lamented than the* Brother, of which thou art not ignorant, *death itself* hath long before, and now since, brought me to this extreme sorrow. Which, as often as I think of it, with bitter wailings doth rend my heart in pieces. And certes I bewail not so much his cruel death, a thing naturally incident to us all, but the strange and pitiful manner of the same : which thou didst know to be violent, infortunate and bloody. And besides this, the strange things, and ugly sights, that appeared to me after his death do kill my fearful soul to think of. I can never so little shut up mine eyelids, or give any slender sleep to my sorrowful eyes, but immediately, all pale, trembling, naked and full of gore, showing me his cruel wounds, he appeareth quaking before me. And even then, when thou didst perceive me to weep and lament, he came into the Chamber, standing and staring before me as I was asleep, in likeness of a horrible and fainting ghost, fearfully quaking with a breathless and panting breast, in such sort that he could scarce utter one word, but at the last, with extreme pain, said : ' O my dear Sister, wipe that blot of ignominy from me which, with an appalled and troubled face, looking ever for very grief and shame thereof on the ground, doth make my sorrowful ghost wander, with great disgrace and scorn, amongst other hapless sprites.' And although it was some comfort for me to see him, yet overcome with terror, which I had of his dreadful habit, and moved with just compassion of his words, with starting on a sudden, I awaked out of my feeble sleep, and thus my tears (the which thou dost now go about to comfort) fulfilling the duty of my conceived pity, did at hand follow. And so (as the Gods know), if weapons were fit for Women, I would ere this have revenged his miserable death, and with a fierce countenance and courageous heart sent the greedy glutton of his innocent blood amongst other damned souls. But alas, I can do no more than I am able. Therefore (dear Husband) not without great

236

occasion I am thus miserably tormented in mind."
Oh, with how many pitiful words did he then comfort
me, applying a salve to the wound which was healed
long enough before, and how did he endeavour to
mollify and diminish my plaints with those true
reasons, which for feigned tales he so carefully made.

But after he thought that he had comforted me
up a little he fell asleep again, and then I (thinking
Prayers of of the pitiful and tender love he bare me),
a desperate with more cruel grief secretly bewailing
lover my unjust requital of the same, began
again my interrupted and piecemeal lamentations,
saying: "O most cruel Dens inhabited of savage
and wild beasts, O hell, the eternal prison ordained
for wicked company, O any other exile whatsoever
deeper than those, open and swallow me up, and
with just pains torment my sinful and deserved
soul, and plague me, of all others the vilest Woman.

"O mighty Jupiter, most justly angry with me,
tumble down thy thunder, and with swift hand
throw down thy crushing bolts upon my hateful
head. O holy Juno, whose most holy laws (thrice
wicked Woman) I have infringed, take vengeance of
me now. O ye fierce Caspian Serpents, tear in pieces
this polluted body of mine. O ye hellish Ravens, infernal Harpies and cruel beasts, devour and entomb
me in your greedy maws. And you most fierce and
unruly Jades, the cruel quarterers of Hippolitus his
innocent members, rend me, impious and trothless

Woman, in a thousand pieces. And thou, most
pitiful Husband, sheathe thy revenging sword with
due anger in my culpable breast, and with plenteous
effusion of my blood send forth my wicked soul,
that hath so unworthily deceived thee. Use no remorse of pity, love nor moderate mercy towards me,
since that I have preferred the love of a stranger, and
of a perfidious Imp, before the bound faith and due
reverence which I owe to thy holy and unspotted
bed. O the worst of all womankind, most worthy
of great punishment for this and for many other
things, what fury appeared before thy chaste eyes
that day when Panphilus first pleased thee ? Where
didst thou abandon that love and piety which was
due to the holy Laws of matrimony ? Whither didst
thou banish thy reverend chastity (the chiefest
honour and ornament of women) when, for the blind
liking of disloyal Panphilus, thou didst forsake the
love of thy loving Husband ? Where is now the
pity that thy beloved youth doth show thee ? And
where are the comforts that he should now give
thee in thy perplexed miseries ? Lulled in the lap
of another Woman, he merrily passeth away the
weary time, and doth not care for thee, and yet in
truth he hath reason therefor. Wherefore it must
worthily fall so to thee as to all others which embrace licentious lust, neglecting lawful love. Thy
injured Husband, who with rigour should punish
thee, with great pity goeth about to comfort thee,

and he that should perform this just function careth
not (alas) wrongfully to torment thee. What, is not
he as fair as Panphilus ? And are not his virtues,
courage, nobility, and especially his love and con-
stancy, and all other good parts in him, are they
not far above all and everything that Panphilus
hath in him worthy of praise and commendation ?
Ah, there is no doubt thereof. Wherefore then didst
thou forsake him for another ? What blindness,
rashness, sin, and what iniquity, hath brought thee
to this ? Alas, poor soul, I know not.

" Only that those things which are frankly and
freely possessed are wont to be accounted of no
Things price and value, although they be (indeed)
freely pos- very dear and precious. And that those
sessed are
esteemed of which hardly, and with hazard, are gotten
slightly (be they never so vile) are esteemed and
embraced as most singular and sweet things.

" The daily fruition and glutting company of my
Husband, which should by great reason have been
most dear unto me, surfeited my queasy mind, and
so (satiating my changeable appetite) deceived me.
And I (mighty enough (perhaps) to have resisted)
do now miserably lament and bewail that which
I have left undone : nay rather I was without (perhaps) strong enough, if I would myself, if I had
called to mind those signs, and thought of that,
which the Gods, in sleeping and waking, had shown
me the night and day before my hapless fall. But

now not able to retire (though I would), but constrained by my appointed stars to combat still in these amorous conflicts, I knew too well what the Serpent was which stung me under my left side, and swelling with my sucked blood went away. And likewise I see the events that the prognosticating flower of my crown falling from my adorned head doth manifestly declare. But alas, this vain wisdom and aftersight cometh all too late.

"The Gods (perhaps) to purge themselves of some conceived wrath against me, and repenting that they had showed me any signs, took the knowledge of their future effects from me, not being able to restore them to me again, as Apollo from his beloved Cassandra, to whom, after he had granted a boon of a Prophetical spirit, did take the virtue and effect of it, in that she was not believed of any whensoever she divined. Whereupon placed in the midst of all miseries, not without great reason and just cause, I bewail and consume my life in woe."

And sorrowing thus with myself, and turning and tumbling myself in my weary bed almost all the night, I passed it away, without giving mine eyes leave once to shut up their lids. But if any sleep entered my sorrowful breast, it did so faintly remain there that the least stir or noise was able enough to have broken it. And yet, although it was but weak, it did not tarry with me without representing many fierce battles in his kind of

240

accustomary demonstrations to my affrighted mind.
And this did not happen to me that night only, of
which I spake of alone, but many times before, and
I was almost continually molested after with the
same accidents. Wherefore my soul, both waking
and sleeping, hath and doth feel equal and like tempestuous storms. The complaints which I poured
forth in the night time took not away their turn and
place in the day, but, as excused now for sorrowing again by reason of those lies which I told my
Husband, from that night forward I did many times
lament, and did begin to be extremely sad and
sorrowful in open and public company. But the day
being come on, my trusty Nurse (from whom the
least part of my griefs was not hid, because she was
the first that knew the amorous signs in my face,
and had also imagined divers future accidents in
the same) coming to visit me, when it was told her
Oh, how that Panphilus had chosen another Woman,
many times and doubting of me, and most careful for
simple
husbands my neglected weal, my Husband no sooner
are deceived went out of the Chamber, but she immediately entered in. And seeing me (through the great
anguish and grief of the last night) to lie as one half-
dead, with divers comfortable words she went about
to assuage my furious evils, and fervent passions,
and taking me in her arms, with trembling hands
she wiped my face all blubbered with tears, with
speaking these words:

Q   241

THE FIFTH BOOK

" Young Lady, and my dearest Mistress, thy sorrows make me beyond all measure sorrowful, and would afflict me more, had not I warned thee of them before. But thou (more wilful than wise), forsaking my willing counsels and precepts, hast headlong followed thy flattering conceits and pleasures, wherefore with sorrowful cheer I see thee unhappily overcome with these griefs, which must needs be due chastisements for thy rash and unreasonable follies. But because everyone may always as long as life doth last (so that he have a willing mind to perform it) decline from his wicked ways, and turn again into the right, I shall think it the dearest thing to me that may happen, if from henceforth thou wouldest shake off the dark cloud from the eyes of thy understanding, obscured by this wicked tyrant, and restore to them again the clear light of truth. What he is, the momentary delights and the prolonged griefs which thou hast passed and dost endure for him, may make thee *Youth fol-* apparently know. Thou hast, like a young *loweth will* and simple Woman, following more thy *more than* *reason* unbridled will than reined reason, fondly loved, and in loving, to that end which is not only expected, but commonly also desired in such passions, hast attained, and yet (as it is said) hast known it to be but a more short than sweet delight. And what thing else can there be desired or looked for hereafter, than that which thou hast already had.

242

" And yet, if happily it might come to pass that Panphilus should return again into thine arms, thou shouldest feel no other pleasure than thou wert wont to do. Fervent and hot desires are wont to be in new things, in the which many times putting a certain kind of hope of a false imaginative pleasure, and thinking that, that good is hidden in them (which perhaps is not), with great grief do make appassionate Lovers endure their force and heat. Whereas those things which are already known are wont to be more temperately and but meanly liked of, and not half so much in request. But overruled too much with the greediness of thy disordinate appetite, and disposing of thyself altogether to new and fanatical opinions, thou dost perform the contrary. Wise and discreet folks, perceiving themselves to be in troublesome places, and full of doubtful dangers, are wont to retire back again, rather content and willing to leese their labour and travail, which they have endured until that place, to the which they have arrived, and deeming it better to return safely again, than going on forward, to endanger themselves, and to get no other end of their rash attempt than sudden death. Follow thou therefore the like example, while thou mayest, and place now, with more modesty, advised reason before lawless will, and wisely hale and help thyself again out of thy pit of peril and sorrow, into the which thou hast suffered thyself foolishly to fall. Fortune, perhaps yet favourable unto thee (if with advice thou wilt take heed), hath not forestalled thy passage in returning back again, nor hath so covered and choked up the same, but that (discerning thy footsteps well) thou mayest by the selfsame come back again, from whence thou didst first move thy headlong feet, and be once again that Fiammetta which whilom thou wert wont to be.

" Thy good name, thine honour, and thy known virtues are yet unstained and whole, and whatsoever thou hast yet done is not in the minds of many secret, nor in the knowledge of any public person commaculated, which being once corrupted, hath been heretofore the only means, and yet is (as we daily see) an occasion, to make one fall into the uttermost and deepest place of all mischief. Proceed therefore no further, lest thou contemn and waste that which Fortune hath reserved for thee. Comfort thyself with this imagination, that thou didst never see Panphilus, or else that thy husband was the same man. Thy indifferent fantasy is apt to any conceit, and imaginations are easily suffered to be wrought like Ware. By this way only thou mayest make thyself merry again, which thing thou oughtest specially to desire, if anguish and sorrow afflict thee so much, as thy words do promise, and thy countenance doth protest."

That which doth principally help one from the bondage of love

These words and such like, not once, but many

times, with a sorrowful mind did I hear, without making any answers to them again. And though I was beyond all measure troubled in mind—notwithstanding I knew them to be most true, but yet the matter very ill-disposed—did receive them without any profit at all. But turning me now on one side, and now on another, sometimes it happened that, moved with raving anger, and not respecting the presence of my austere Nurse, with a voice enraged with womanly grief, and with a sorrowful kind of complaint, and greater than any of the rest, I said thus :

" O Megera, O Tesiphon, O Alecto, tormentors of wicked and woeful souls, let your horrible and ugly hair stand up, and incense the cruel and fierce Hydras with venomous anger, and kindle them to new kinds of quaking fears, and with flinging your crawling Snakes in her face, enter speedily into the wicked chamber of that damned adulteress. Inflame your miserable brands for her vile conjunctions that she enjoyeth now with her robbed lover, and beset their delicate bed about with them in sign of a dire presage to wicked lovers. O any else people of the black habitations of infernal Dis, O ye Gods of the immortal kingdoms of Styx, be present there, and with your luckless lamentations smite fear and horror into these faithless friends. O miserable Scritch Owl, sit and sing over their hapless house.

" And O you ominous Harpies, give them some

terrible sign of future woes. O eternal Chaos and darkness, enemy to all light, possess the adulterers' houses so, that their wicked eyes may not behold nor enjoy any comfortable light at all. And let your malice (O ye revengers of wicked things) enter into those minds which are so ready to change, and raise up cruel contention and tragical murders between them." After this, casting out a hot burning sigh, I added these words following : " O most wicked woman, whosoever thou art (unknown to me) thou dost now possess my lover, so long, and so often, wished for of me, and I (miserable woman) being far from him, do in the meantime languish in continual pain. Thou dost enjoy the guerdon of my travails and deserts, and I (deceived of the fruit) do remain still in sowing and pouring forth prayers, and consume myself in watering them with continual drops of tears.

" I have offered orisons and incense to the Gods for his prosperity (whom thou hast secretly embezzled from me) and they were heard only for thy profit. And now, behold with what art (I know not) nor how thou hast rooted him out of my loving heart, and engrafted him (false woman) in thine. And yet I know that it is so. But with such content, and so mayest thou love, and live (I wish) as thou hast made me to do. And if (perhaps) it be too hard for him to fall in love the third time, then let the Gods divide your loves, no otherwise than they did dissolve the Grecian Lady's and the Judge's of Ida,

246

or as they did dissever that of the young man of Abydos and of his vigilant and sorrowful Hero, or as they did break off those of the miserable Sons of Eolus—bending their sharp judgment only against thee, he himself remaining safe. O naughty woman, thou must needs have thought (viewing well his comely face) that he was not without some Lady, and loving Mistress.

"If thou didst therefore suppose this (which I know thou didst imagine), with what mind didst *Maledic-* thou practise to take that away which ap- *tions of an* pertained to another? With an envious *enamoured* *woman* and fraudulent mind I am sure. Wherefore I will, as my mortal enemy and wrongful occupier of my goods, pursue thee evermore, and as long as I live will nourish and preserve my life with hope of thy shameful and cruel death. The which I wish may not be so common and natural as to others it is, but that turned into a lump of massy lead, or Ixion's heavy stone tied about thy neck, thou mayest be cast into some deep and dark cave, amongst the midst of thy enemies' murdering hands, and that neither fire nor funeral be granted to burn and bury thy torn and massacred members, but being pulled in pieces, and scattered abroad, they may serve to glut the hungry maws of howling dogs and ravenous wolves. Which I pray (after they have devoured thy soft and tender flesh) may for thy naked bones fiercely jar and cruelly fight one with another, so that gradually gnawing, and breaking them in pieces with their whetted teeth, they may lively represent thy wicked prey and thee, delighted with thy gluttonous rapine, which in thy detested lifetime thou didst foully commit.

"There shall not escape one day, not one night, no, not one hour, but my ready mouth shall be full of endless curses. Sooner shall the Celestial Bear plump down into the ocean, and the raging waves of Sicilian Carybdis shall be quiet, and the barking Dogs of Scylla shall hold their peace, and ripe Corn shall grow in the waves of the Ionian sea, and the darkest night in her chiefest obscurity shall shine like Titan his beams, and water with fire, death with life, and the Sea with winds shall sooner with breachless faith be at truce and make concord together, before I will reconcile and establish a peace with thee (vile monster of womankind). But rather whilst golden Ganges shall be hot and Istrus cold, and while high hills shall bear sturdy Oaks, and the soft and watered meadows green grass, so long (foul brothel) will I be at continual war and defiance with thee, which neither mortal hatred nor death shall determine, but pursuing thee amongst the dead ghosts and fiends of Hell, with all those torments that are used there, I will continually plague, and eternally punish thy damned soul for thy condemned and hateful deed.

"But if perchance thou dost survive me, whatsoever the manner of my death shall be, and wheresoever my miserable Ghost shall wander, from *The virgins* thence, perforce, I will labour to take it, *—that is,* and, entering into thy loathsome body, will *the diviners* make thee as mad as the Virgins after they had received Apollo. Or else, coming in thy sight broad waking, thou shalt see me in a most horrible shape, and in thy fearful sleep oftentimes will I awake and affright thee in the uncomfortable silence of the dark night.

" And, briefly, in whatsoever thou goest about, or doest, I will continually be a horrible object to thy wicked eyes, and a griping corsive to thy hellish heart : and then (remembering this cruel injury) I will not suffer thee to be quiet in any place. And so long as thou livest, with such a hideous fury (myself the only worker of it) thou shalt be continually haunted.

" And when thou art dead I will minister occasions of more dire stratagems unto thy miserable ghost. Alas, poor wretched that I am, to what end are my bootless words prolonged ? I bark and threaten, and thou dost bite and hurt me, and, enfolding my beloved Panphilus between thy unworthy arms, dost care as much for my menacing and offensive words as high and mighty kings for their inferior and impotent vassals : and no more than conquering Captains for their confounded captives. Alas, would I had now Dedalus his art, or Medea's Coach, because making wings by the one for my

249

shoulders, and being carried in the air by the other, I might suddenly alight there, where thou dost basely hide and nestle thyself with thy stolen love. Oh, how many thundering words, and what threatening invectives, with bended brows would I cast out against that false youth, and against thee, unjust robber of another's felicity! Oh, with what villainous terms would I reprehend your detestable follies!

"And after that I had amazed, appalled and attainted your wicked faces with a shameful blush, with recital of these unshameful faults, I would then without delay proceed to sharp revenge, and taking thy hair (false enchantress) in my hands, with pulling and renting them, and drawing thee here and there by thy tresses before thy perfidious lover, I would glut my swelling anger, and tearing thy garments from thy disgraced body, with reproachful taunts I would triumph over thee, malapert and wicked traitoress. Nor this should not suffice me to fulfil my due anger, nor be half enough for thee to expiate thy odious crime, but with sharp nails I would disfigure that painted visard, which so much pleased his false eyes, leaving an eternal memorial of their characters and revenge in it. And thy miserable body with my greedy teeth piecemeal I should shiver, leaving the which afterwards unto him (that doth now flatter thee) to heal again, myself (joyful for part of so small vengeance) would hie me home again to my sorrowful habitacles."

250

Whilst I spake these words with fiery sparkling eyes, with closed teeth, and with bended fist, as though I had been at the very action itself, I remained a pretty while silent : and methought I had indeed played one Pageant of my greedy revenge. But the old Nurse, with mournful voice, lamenting, said thus unto me:

"O daughter, since thou dost not know the furious tyranny of this passion—which thou callest thy God —who doth thus molest thee, temperate thyself, and bridle thy piteous complaints.

"And if the due pity which thou shouldest take of thy own self doth not move thee hereunto, let *The care of* the regard of thy honour persuade thee *her honour* to it, which for an old error passed, may *must warn* *every wise* lightly be stained with a new shame : or *woman* at least withhold these complaints and *from vain* *thoughts* outcries, lest that thy loving husband per- *and deeds* ceive not the indirect causes of thy doleful plaints. And so for two causes he might worthily be sorry and aggrieved at thy senseless folly."

Then being put in mind of my husband, and thinking of the wrong and shame I had done him, moved with new pity, I lamented more sensibly than I did before, and discussing in my mind my corrupted faith, and the holy laws of wedlock violated, I said :

"O most faithful companion in my troubles, my husband may be sorry for little or nothing. For he, which was the occasion of my offence, hath been a severe purger of the same. I have long since received a guerdon, and am yet paid with so severe a reward for my demerits. My husband could not imagine to give me any greater punishment than that which my late lover hath afflicted me withal. Only death (if death be painful, as it is commonly said) my husband may annex to my other torments. Let him then therefore come and give it me quickly. It shall be no pain for me to die, but a wished pleasure, because I greatly desire the same.

" And it shall be more acceptable and welcome to me, performed by his own hands, whom so greatly I have offended, than perpetrated by any others, or by my own. If he do not give me it, or if it doth not voluntarily come unto me, my troubled wits shall find out some speedy passage to it, because by means of that I hope to conclude all my sorrow at once.

" Huge hell, the last and extremest punishment of damned miserable souls, in the most tormenting

Divers punishments of damned souls compared to the pains of a lover place of all, hath not any torture so forcible or equal with mine. Ancient authors allege and bring in Titius for an example of great punishment, saying that his increasing liver is continually beaked and devoured of a greedy vulture. And certes, though I account his pain not little, yet it is not like to mine. For if the hungry Vulture feed upon his liver, a hundred thousand thousand griping and stinging griefs continually gnaw my heart more than sharp bills of any preying Birds. They likewise affirm that Tantalus, placed between clear water and goodly fruit, doth evermore die for hunger and thirst.

" Myself (alas) put in the midst, and swimming in all mundane delights, with affectionate desire wishing my lover and not enjoying him, do sustain as much, nay, rather greater pain than he. Because, with never-ceasing hope, he thinks sometimes to taste of these fresh waters, and ruddy Apples, that hang on every side about him. But I (despairing now altogether of that which I once hoped would have been my comfort) do neither see nor can excogitate any ease for my grief; and loving him more than ever I did, by the alluring forces of another woman, and of his proper accord also, is so kept back that he hath not only cast me quite out of his remembrance, but that by means thereof I am debarred to entertain the smallest hope that may be of my welfare for ever after. And miserable Ixion also, turmoiling eternally at his unruly wheel, doth not feel such cruel pain, that it may be likened to mine. Because, myself shaken with continual motions of furious madness, by my adverse fates do suffer much more grief than ever he can do. And if the daughters of Danaus with lost labour do continually pour water into tubs full of holes, thinking to fill them, I strain forth greater plenty of tears

253

by the overflowing conduits of my eyes, drawn from the hollow cave and centre of my heart. Wherefore do I trouble myself to recite these infernal tortures by one and one since that there is heaped in me a greater Chaos of miseries than any there divided, or conjoined. And if I had no other kind of anguish to cruciate my miserable soul, that I must of necessity keep my dolours secret, or at the least conceal and hide their offspring, whereas they, with loud voices, careless speeches, public actions (conformable to their sorrows), might discover and manifest theirs, by so much the more should my pains be adjudged greater and more grievous than theirs. For (alas) how strong the restrained fire and how more violently doth it burn than that which hath full scope and no obstacle to exhalate and throw his flames abroad. And how grievous a thing it is not to be permitted to speak one word of extreme sorrow that doth sensibly torment one, and that it is not lawful to tell the annoyous occasion of it, but under the show of a merry countenance it is convenient to hide it in the secret closet of an impatient and painful heart. Wherefore, not extreme sorrow only, *Death a* but external death, shall be a lightening of *lightening* my grief. Let, therefore, my dear husband *of sorrow* come, and in one hour let him revenge himself, and rid me out of these pains. Let his unsheathed sword open my miserable and naked breast, and let him in one instant with plenty of my blood pull forth my sorrowing soul, and dissolve my infinite and heaped woes, and (as my vile wickedness doth deserve) let him tear this heart, the retainer of these vile injuries, the principal deceiver of his true affections, and the chiefest receiver of his feigned friend and secret enemy."

After that the Nurse did see me hold my peace, and begin to weep bitterly, with a mild and low voice she began to reply : " O dear daughter, what meaneth this, which so frantically thou speakest ? Thy words are as vain as thy conceits more foolish. I have seen (being now an old woman) many things which have passed in this world and have daily known the order and course of many ladies' and gentlewomen's loves. And (although I am not to be accounted myself amongst them) yet, nevertheless, have I once felt the secret poison of these amorous darts which are more grievous sometimes and much more troublesome to those of lower degree and of poor condition than to the nobler and higher personages, whenas all the means and passages to the attaining of their desires and pleasures are stopped and cut off from them that are needy and poor ; whereas they at their will, and with their wealth, may break an open way to heaven. And that, which thou sayest to be almost impossible, and so grievous unto thee, I never conceived, nor felt to be half so painful, and nothing so hard as thou dost make it. Which grief, although it be indeed very great, ought not, for all that, to work such effects in thee as to consume and waste thyself in such woes, and thereby to seek thy own death, which more rashly and furiously than by any good motion of wisdom or argument of reason thou dost wish for. I know well, that burning anger procured by fury is blinded, and careth not to cover itself, nor doth brook any bridle, and doth admit no reason, and is not afraid of death, but rather driven on headlong and urged of itself, it resisteth the mortal pricks of sharp swords. But if thou wouldest let this anger of itself wax somewhat colder, I doubt not but thy kindled folly should be made more manifest to that temperate and cooled part. And therefore, good daughter, with patience sustain his great force, and give place to his fury.

"Wherefore note my words a little, and settle thy mind upon the examples which I will propound *Weak* unto thee. Thou art with incessant anguish *comforts* of mind most sorrowful (if I have well perceived thy speeches) for the long absence of thy beloved youth gone from thee, and for his faithless fidelity, and for the second love of his new choice. And being aggrieved at these (perhaps) uncertain and unjust injuries reckonest no pain like unto thine. But (certes) if thou wouldest be so wise as I do wish thee, thou shalt for ease of all these painful accidents (pondering well my words) receive an easy and an effectual remedy. The young man whom thou lovest ought without all doubt (according to the laws and ordinances of love) to love thee again, as thou dost him, and if he doth not, he doth very ill—and yet there is no force to compel him thereunto, since everyone may use the benefit of his own liberty as it pleaseth him best. If thou dost love him greatly, and so much that thereby thou dost endure great pain, he is not therefore to be blamed; nor thou canst not justly be aggrieved with him therefore, considering that thou thyself art the chiefest cause of this. For mighty Love (although he be a great Lord, and his forces are inevitable) could not, for all that, against thy will place thy Lover in thy heart.

"Thy vagrant wit and idle thoughts were the first originals of thy love, which, if thou hadst effectually opposed with thy might, these sorrowful events had not happened unto thee, as now they have done, but, as one free from such uncouth passions, thou mightest have mocked him, and all others, as he, disporting himself with his new love (as thou sayest), doth now make but a jest of thee. It is therefore necessary, since that thou hast submitted thy liberty to his Law, to govern thy passions according to his pleasures, and since he thinks it best to be far from thee, that thou content thyself, and not repine thereat. If with tears he did vow entire faith unto thee, and promised thee to return, he did not use any new thing herein, but an old and common trick, practised out of memory, and

performed every day of most Lovers. And these are
the pranks, and many more such fashions of like consequence, which are daily taught and learned in thy
God his Court. But if he hath not kept with thee
that faith and promise, there was never any Judge
that, in deciding of this matter, could say any more
of it but that he did not well, and would so acquit
him, thinking also with thyself that he should do
the like (if any other strange love, or fortune, had
given thee over to such a breach of former faith)
as now thou shouldest, and I do wish thee to do.
He is not also the first that hath done so, nor thou
the first to whom like accidents have befallen. Jason
Divers departed from Lemnos from Hipsiphile,
examples of and returned into Thessaly to Medea, and
those that
forsook their from her afterwards to Creusa. Amorous
lovers Paris went from the woods of Ida from
Œnone, and returned to Troy with fair Helen.
Theseus went from Crete from Ariadne, and came
to Athens to Phedra. And yet for all this neither
Hipsiphile, Œnone nor Ariadne killed themselves,
but, rejecting all vain thoughts, buried their false
Lovers in dark oblivion. Love (as I said above)
doth thee no wrong at all, or hath done thee any
more than thou thyself wouldest take. He useth
his bow and arrows without any respect of persons,
as we may daily see by proof. And there are so many
and manifest examples, making so clear on his side,
and for his manner of inordinate dealings, that none

can worthily be aggrieved at any bad success which he giveth, and that can with reason (almost) bewail the ordinary grief, pains and care which by his means and molestations his followers have, but rather complain and lament their voluntary submission, and be sorrowful for their frank consent with which they yielded to him. For he, being but a wanton, naked and blind boy, doth fly and alight he knoweth not where himself. Wherefore, to be sorrowful for his accustomed and indirect usages, to bewail his unkind and froward abuses, to receive no comfort by him, or by no means to think to remove him, is rather a loss of words and wind.

" The new Woman, who hath taken thy beloved in her nets, or else whom he hath with his cunning guiles overcome, and whom with so many revenging words thou dost menace, with her own fault (perhaps) hath not made him hers, but he, with his important suits (it may be), and with his flattering and pitiful words, great gifts, and serviceable deeds, hath won her to be his. And as thou wert wont (not able to resist his enchanting prayers, and to behold his woeful tears), so she, perhaps, as flexible by prayers, promises and protestations as thyself, could not endure them without some great pity of his distressed and sorrowful cause. If he could so well, by amorous complaints, express his hot desires, and could so cunningly (as thou hast told), like a Crocodile, whensoever it pleased him, bewail and lament, then must thou clearly know that tears, joined with beauty, are of great force to obtain their request. And besides this. Say that the Gentlewoman, with her sugared speeches and gracious behaviour, hath overcome him; why, is it not a thing commonly used nowadays in the world, that everyone doth seek his own advantage, not having any regard or *Everyone* care to another his prejudice, but where and *seeketh* *his own* when he findeth, even there and then he *advantage* taketh as he best may. The good Woman, as expert as thyself in these affairs, knowing (perhaps) him to be a cunning Knight in Venus' Courtly battles, allured him therefore the more unto her. And who withholdeth thee, or what impediment hast thou to hinder thee, that thou mayest not do the like to some other? Which thing, albeit, I neither counsel nor command. But if there can be no more done than may be, and that of necessity thou art constrained to follow Love, whensoever thou wilt pull thy neck out of his servile yoke thou mayest quickly find a great number of young and lusty Gentlemen in this City, more valiant, noble, proper, more worthy and more loving, and a great deal more constant than he is. Who (as I certainly believe), to obtain but the smallest favour at thy hands that he hath had, would gladly kiss the very ground that thou treadest on. Whose sundry kinds of delightful services, and sweet pleasures, shall so by little and little drive him out of thy

260

remembrance, as he hath for love of his new Gentle-woman banished thee (perhaps) out of his memory.

" Jupiter laugheth at these promised faiths and solemn oaths when they are broken. And whoso-ever doth use one but according as he is used him-self. what can the world speak or think of any more than the deserts of such an one did require ? To keep faith with one that hath broken his is reputed nowadays but mere mockery, and to requite deceits with deceits is esteemed no small point of wisdom.

" Medea, forsaken of Jason, entertained Egeus. And Ariadne, forsaken of Theseus, got Bacchus for her Husband, and so were their mournings turned into mirth. Temperate therefore thy griefs, and suffer thy pains patiently, because thou hast not any occasion to be sorrowful more for another than to be pitiful towards thyself. And whensoever thou wilt thou shalt find opportunity enough to make them cease, considering that the same and greater griefs than thine were sometimes sustained and passed away by others, greater and more noble personages than thyself. For Deianira was forgot of Hercules for Iole, and Phillis of Demophoon, and Penelope of Ulysses for Circe. And all their tor-ments and passions were greater than thine, by how much the heat of their love was greater and more fervent than thine. And so much the more if their divine essence, immortal powers, and the haughty condition of those notable men and Women are

well considered, and yet they suffered them. In
these disgraces, therefore, thou art not alone, nor the
Grief is first. And those adversities in the which
less hurtful patients have company are not so grievous
when one
hath com- and painful to them, as thou thyself dost
pany in it say. Wherefore be merry again, and expel
these vain cares, admonishing thee to have before
thine eyes a continual doubt and fear of thy dear
Husband, and of his just anger, and yet uncon-
ceived jealousy, to whose ears, if perhaps these
follies (as needs they must at last) should come,
admit (as thou sayest), that he could give thee no
other, nor no less punishment than death, the very
same (forasmuch as one can die but once) ought
everyone (when his hour is come, and when he can)
to take it in the best sort and order he may. And
think, that if that kind of death, which in thy
rage and angry mood thou dost so quickly and so
wickedly desire, should follow and happen unto
thee, with what great infamy and everlasting shame
should thy living memory, thy dear honour, thy good
name, and thine honesty, survive and remain for ever
after blotted and ignominiously obscured.

" Worldly things should be used, not as troublesome substances, but as transitory shadows. Wherefore, from henceforth, let neither thyself, nor any
other, put any affiance in them, whether they have
a prosperous or preposterous issue, nor yet, thrown
down in adversity, let not any of the other side

despair of the best. Clotho mingleth these and those things together, and forbiddeth that Fortune be stable and constant, and changeth every fate. None had ever the Gods so favourable to their wills that they might presently bind them unto them, or could at any time have them tied to their affections. For they, provoked by the guilt of our sins, turn our affairs topsy-turvy, and Fortune again helpeth those that be valiant, courageous and stout-minded, rejecting those that are pusillanimous, fearful and doubtful in their enterprises. And now it is time to prove if virtue have any place in thee. Admitted that at all times it may never be removed, though oppressed with dark clouds of adversities and darkened with black tempests of misfortune it is oftentimes choked and lieth secret and hidden. Hope also hath this property annexed to it, that it is not a guide to afflictions, nor showeth any way to grief or sorrow. Wherefore, he that may hope in anything, let him despair of nothing. We are tossed with the fluctuant waves of our destinies, and those things (believe me) that they prepare for us cannot with so light care, with so small regard, or with so soon labour be changed. The greater part almost of that which we (mortal generation) either do, or suffer, cometh from the heavens above.

"Lachesis doth keep a decreed Law to her Distaff, and doth draw forth everything by a limited way. The first day she giveth thee is the last : neither is it lawful to wrest determined things, and wrought above with the influences of the Planets, to another course. It hath hurt many to be afraid of an immovable order, and many also in not fearing the same. Because while these are afearing their own destinies, the very same are already befallen to them unawares. Leave therefore thy griefs and sorrows, which voluntarily thou hast procured, and live joyfully, putting thy hope in the Gods, and endeavour to do well: because it hath oftentimes come to pass that when one doth think himself furthest from felicity, then with an inopinate step he is suddenly entered into it. Many Ships, securely sailing through the deep and wide Seas, have been oftentimes cast away in the mouth of the wished Haven. And some again, despairing altogether of succour, have in the selfsame day, and danger, yea suddenly, arrived to the desired end of their long voyage. And I have seen many trees smit with Jupiter's scorching lightnings, and in few days after again covered over with green leaves, and loaden with goodly fruit. And some, again, cherished with great care, by some secret and sudden accident withered quite away. Fickle Fortune doth yield sundry effects: for as she hath been the instrument of thy long grief, so (if by hope thou dost nourish thy life) she will likewise minister to thee many occasions and wholesome means of double joy again."

And now she held her peace.

But as many times as she perceived me distracted into these unwonted and extremest passions, so did the sage Nurse use these speeches towards me, thinking with herself to drive these irremovable griefs and obstinate anguish out of my mind, reserved only for the full consummation of my death. But none, or few, of her grave counsels did touch my troubled mind with effect, and the greatest part of them, spent in vain, vanished away in the air. And my sorrowful soul did every day more sensibly feel more green and grievous wounds. Wherefore, lying many times upright upon my rich bed, with my face covered between mine arms, I imagined divers great matters and strange things in my troubled mind. And now I will begin (pitiful Ladies) to tell of most cruel things, and not credible almost to be hatched in the breast of a simple Woman, if the sequel of these, or greater than these, were not seen afterwards to come to pass. My heart being therefore cleaved almost asunder with unspeakable grief, and perceiving my Lover to be far from me; like a desperate and frantic Woman I began thus to say to myself:

They that love unfor- tunately do often- times think to kill themselves

"Behold the very self and same occasion which Sidonian Eliza had to abandon this hateful world cruel Panphilus hath given me. And (alas) a great deal worse. It pleaseth him that, forsaking these, I seek out other regions. And since I am become his subject I will fulfil his hard behest and pitiless pleasure: and in one hour I will requite my hapless love, my committed wickedness, and my injured and dear husband with a tragical and unnatural death. And if oppressed souls, delivered out of this corporal prison, have any liberty in the new world, I will without delay conjoin mine with his. And where my body cannot be, my soul shall supply the place of it. Behold, therefore, I will die, and so rid me of all these pains. I think it most convenient, that with these hands I execute this last stratagem upon myself. Because there can be no other hand so cruel that can perfectly perform that which justly I have deserved. I will, therefore, without delay willingly take my death, the remembrance of which, although it be terrible to my weak fear, and to my womanly thoughts, yet shall it be as welcome unto me as this painful life is irksome unto my soul."

And after that I had resolved upon this last pretence, I began to devise with myself which was, of a thousand ways, the best to take my life from me. And first of all, cold and sharp irons came to my mind, the mortal means of many one his untimely death, considering that the said Eliza by their cruelty did forsake this common air: and then, after these, the deaths of Biblis and Amata were presented before mine eyes, the manner of which was offered to me to end my weary life. But more careful of my honour and good name than chary of myself, and fearing more the manner of dying than death itself —the one seeming unto me very infamous, and the other too extreme cruel in the mouths and minds of everyone—were occasions to make me refuse the one, and not to like of the other. Afterwards I imagined to do as the Sagontines, and as those of Abydos did, the first fearing Hannibal, of Carthage, and the other Philip of Macedon, committing themselves and all their goods to the fury of consuming flames. But knowing that this could be no small detriment to my dear Husband, unculpable and guiltless of my evils, I refused also this kind of death, as I did the rest before. After these I called to mind the venomous juices—which heretofore assigned to Socrates, to Sophonisba, to Hannibal, and to many other Princes more, their last days. And many of these, indeed, as they pleased my changeable fancy, so did I think them fit for the purpose. But, perceiving that in going about to seek them no little time was requisite, and doubting lest by inquiry of them my drifts should be called in question, and sifted out, and that my determined purpose also, in the meanwhile, might perhaps have been altered, I imagined to seek out some other kinds of death. Wherefore I bethought me (as many times I had done before) to yield up my feeble spirits between my knees, but doubting lest it should be known, and suspecting some other impediment incident to it, I passed to other headlong thoughts. And the very same occasion (and lest I should be also seen) made me forsake the burning, and swallowed coals of Portia. But the death of Ino and of Melicerta, and likewise the hunger-starved end of Erisichthone, occurring to my memory, the long time that I should have in executing the one and in staying for the other made me also to reject them, thinking that the pain of the last did a great while nourish the languishing body. But, besides all these ways, the precipitate death of Perdix, falling from the highest Tower of Crete, came also to my mind, which speedy kind of death only pleased me infallibly to follow, as one devoid of all ensuing infamy, saying to myself: " Casting myself down from the highest Turrets of my Palace, I shall crush my bones in a hundred pieces, and dash out my brains, and by all those several pieces will yield up my hapless soul, contaminated with prepared gore, and ready broken up to be offered up as a Sacrifice to the Gods. And few, or none, there are that will imagine and say that by mine own cruelty, fury or proper will this death befell unto me, but imputing it rather to some unlucky chance, with pouring out pitiful tears for me, will bewail my untimely death, and curse my froward Fortune."

This deliberation, therefore, took place in my mind, and it liked me especially to put the same in *Wicked* practice, thinking to have used great pity *thoughts* *ever war* towards me, if I had perhaps become piti- *with good* less and cruel against mine own self. This determination, therefore, had now taken sure root in my heart, and I did not attend for anything else but fit time, when a chilly cold, suddenly entering into all my bones, made me tremble for very fear, which brought these words with it, saying: "O miserable Woman, what dost thou intend to do? Wilt thou (overcome with mad anger) in a senseless rage and fury cast thyself away? If thou wert now constrained to die of some grievous infirmity wouldest not thou (alas) endeavour and seek to live, because at the length thou mightest see thy Panphilus once more before thy death? Dost not thou think that when thou art dead thou shall never see him again, and that no kind of pity that he may use in thy behalf may help thee anything at all? For what did the slack return of Demophoon profit unpatient and strangled Phillis? She, flourishing, without any delight felt his coming, which if she could have stayed for he might have found her still a Woman as he left her, and not a Tree. Live, therefore, Fiammetta, for he will yet for all this (returning as a friend or as an enemy at length) come to thee again. And with what disposed mind soever he return, thou canst not choose but love him still. And perhaps thou shalt see him, talk with him, and move his unconstant and hard heart to compassion of thy woeful plights. He is not made of sturdy Oak, nor of Flinty stone, nor born, bred, nor nourished in a hollow Cave amongst wild Beasts, and did never suck the milk of Tigers, nor drink any other savage and cruel beast's blood, neither is his heart made of Diamond, or of steel, and is not of so brutish and rustical inclination but that he will lend his ears and bend his heart to my pitiful plaints, passions and persuasions, and take some remorse of co-equal commiseration of my sustained sorrows. But if he will not be overcome with pity, then, wearied of thy loathsome life, it shall be more lawful for thee (driven on by manifest despair) to kill thyself. Thou hast passed away more than one whole year (without him) a pensive and painful life, and well mayest thou yet (though with redoubted grief) rub out another.

Any may have death whensoever they will Death doth not fail at any time, whensoever one doth either desire or procure it, which will be then as prest, and more ready to come, than now he is. And thou mayest then depart with hope, be he never so malicious and cruel, that being at thy present and hapless death he will shed some tears. Recall therefore again thy overrash and cruel advice. Because whosoever hasteneth too much to wicked counsel studieth afterwards to repent himself by leisure. And this

Who hasteneth to wicked counsel studieth to repent at leisure last part of thy tragical life, which thou dost mean to play, is not a thing that may afterwards be amended with vain repentance: which if it did follow could not, with all the force it had, recall it back again."

My mind being thus mollified with these arguments, with a sudden altered purpose, and inopinate advice, I kept a long time in an equal poise of moderate reason. But, dreadful Megera, lancing it with sharp and mortal wounds of grief, disturbed my settled senses, and disturbed my willing mind from following this good motion, and egged me on to prosecute and to practise my first unnatural and cruel resolution, which now I thought privily and earnestly to bring to effect. Wherefore (to cloak it) I always showed mine old Nurse a merry countenance, and did finely counterfeit my sad cheer with some pleasant kind of comfortable speeches, to whom, because I would have had her gone out of the Chamber, I said: "Behold (good Mother) how I have planted thy most true reasons and grave counsels with great profit in my breast, but, because this blind fury may depart out of my foolish mind, withdraw thyself from hence awhile, and leave me to my rest, that am now very desirous to sleep." But she, being as full of subtlety as myself, and as one that did divine of my secret intent, commended much the mind I had to sleep, and, as she was commanded, went a little way from me, into a dark corner hard by, but would by no means go out of the Chamber.

But, because I would not give her any occasion to suspect that which I went about, clean contrary to my mind and desire I seemed to like well of her staying still, thinking that after she had seen me sleep she would have gone away. With quiet rest, therefore, I feigned this imagined deceit, in the which, although nothing appeared outwardly, yet thinking of that hour which should have been my last in this pleasing world, full of bitter anguish, and environed round about with legions of stinging griefs, I muttered forth these words to myself, saying:

"O miserable Fiammetta, and of all Women that live in this world the most miserable, behold thy Glass is now run, thy latest day, hour and last period is come. And after that from the highest place of thy Palace thou shalt have thrown thyself headlong down, and that thy soul shall have forsaken thy bruised body, then let thy tears be dried up, let thy sighs then surcease, and thy sorrows and desires be determined, and then in one hour, with the dear price of thy spilled blood, and with the ransom of thy pale death, thou shalt redeem thyself from the bonds and captivity of love. And then shalt thou cancel the verbal Obligation of Panphilus his promised and unperformed faith. This day thou shalt have the deserved embracings of him. This day the Military Ensigns of love shall cover thy body with a dishonest and unseemly torture. This day thy wearied spirits shall see him. This day thou shalt know for whom thou hast forsaken thyself. This day of force thou shalt make him pitiful. This day thou shalt begin the vengeance of the young and wicked Sorceress, and thy malicious co-partner.

"But, O ye Gods, if any pity doth harbour in your divine breasts, be favourable to me in these my last prayers. Suffer not my death and the memory of my life to pass amongst the rude populare with blot of dishonour and stain of infamy. And if, in taking the same, there be any fault committed, behold there is a present satisfaction, since that I die with fear to publish the occasion thereof: the revealing of which should be, certes, no small comfort unto me, if I believed that in talking of it it might escape without ignominious blame. Make my dear Husband also (ye sacred Gods) suffer it with patience, whose true love, if I had duly observed and had rightly performed Juno's holy laws, I might have yet lived a happy and merry Woman, without troubling your divine Godheads with these earnest prayers. But, like an ignorant Woman of my thrice happy estate, and (as others of my condition are wont to do) following ever the worst, and *Women take ever the worst in hand* forsaking the best, am now worthily appaid with this unfortunate and due recompense. O fatal Atropos, by thy infallible blow to all the world, I humbly pray thee, that thou wouldest with thy power guide my falling body, and dissolve my soul not with too great pain from the thread of thy Sister Lachesis. And thee, O Minos, receiver of it, by that love that sometimes burned thee, and by this blood which now I offer unto thee, even by the same, and by what else may move thee (infernal Judge), I obtest thee favourably to conduct it to the places appointed by thy just judgment

S   273

for it, and that so cruel and sharp torments be not
prepared for it as to deem and repute the infinite
pains that it hath already passed but light in respect
of them to come."

After I had spoken these words to myself, incensed
Tesiphon appeared before mine eyes, and with a
senseless murmur, and contracted and menacing
forehead, made me afraid of a worser life to ensue
than that which was already past, but afterwards, with a kind of confused speech, saying that
nothing which was never tried could be hurtful, inflamed my troubled mind with a more eager desire
of my own ruin. Wherefore, perceiving that my old
Nurse was not yet gone, and doubting lest her long
tarrying might not mar my matters—being now
resolved to die—or that some other accident might
not take it quite away, with displayed arms upon
my bed, and embracing it, I said: "O bed, farewell,
praying the Gods that thou mayest be more fortunate and gracious to thy next Mistress whom thou
shalt receive than thou hast been to me." After
which words, my eyes rolling about the chamber,
the which I never thought to have seen any more,
surprised now with sudden grief, I was deprived of
the light of the Heavens, and grovelling up and
down, surseized (I know not) with what a shiver-
ing and trembling fear throughout all my body, I
would have risen up, but every part of the same,
overcome with quaking fear, did not suffer me, but

I fell suddenly down again, not once, but thrice, upon my face: in which occurrent I felt a fierce war between my angry soul and my timorous and vital spirits, which by main force did keep it still, that fain would have flown away. But my soul at last overcoming them, and driving away cold fear from me, suddenly kindled me with a hot and burning dolour, and so I recovered my wandered forces again. And, yet my face morphewed with the pale colour of death, I violently rose up, and as the sturdy Bull, having received some mortal prick, fiercely runneth up and down, beating and tormenting himself, even so, hellish Tesiphon, gadding madly up and down before mine eyes, made me (like a frantic and mad Woman, and not knowing mine own fancies) cast myself from the bed upon the ground, and led by this infernal fiend I did run towards the stairs that went up to the highest part of the house. And having in a trice leaped out of the Chamber, with most extreme lamentations and careless looks, viewing every part of the house, at last with a hollow and feeble voice I said : "O most unlucky lodging unto me, remain thou here for ever, and make my fall manifest to my Lover, if ever he return again. And thou, O dear Husband, comfort thyself, and from henceforward seek out a new wife, but a more wise, loving and more loyal mate than Fiammetta hath been unto thee. O my dear Sisters, Parents, and all the rest of my other companions and friends (with all ye my faithful Servants), live ye here with all the favour that the Gods may afford you."

Thus like a mad Woman, with sorrowful words I did hasten to my wicked end. But the old Nurse, as one by some sudden fear awaked out of a slumber, carelessly leaving off her work at the wheel, greatly amazed at the sight of this spectacle, lifted up her aged body, and, crying as loud as ever she could, made post haste to follow me, who with a hoarse voice, and scarcely understood of me, said: "O daughter, whither dost thou run ? What mad fury doth drive thee forward ? Is this the fruit that my words (as thou saidst), by the received comfort of them, did put in thy breast ? Whither goest thou ? Tarry for me (alas)." Afterwards with a louder voice she yet exclaimed: "O ye young men, and servants of the house, come, come quickly, and take away this fond Woman, and keep her back from her furious actions and desperate intent !" Her vociferations were of no force, and their haste less speedy. And methought I had Mercury his wings fastened to my shoulders, and that swifter than Atalanta, nay, than any wind, I did fly to my violent death. But of unexpected chances (appending as well to good as to wicked purposes) one (alas) was an occasion to make me still enjoy this loathsome life : because my long garments, waving and blown

The goodness of God oftentimes doth not suffer wicked determinations to come to effect

abroad with the force of my hasty flight, and friendly enemies to my furious pretence, myself also not able to restrain my course, were fastened (I know not how) to a shivered post by the wall as I was running, and interrupted my swift passage, which, for all the striving and pulling that I could do, did not suffer me to leave any piece of them behind me. Wherefore, whilst I was labouring to undo them, the sorrowful Nurse, breathless and panting, came upon me, to whom (I remember), with tainted cheeks, full of burning anger, and with outrageous outcries, I said: "O miserable old woman, pack from hence in an evil hour if thy life be dear unto thee. Thinking to help me thou dost hinder me, in not permitting me to execute this last and mortal duty, resolved thereunto, and spurred on *Who doth* with an eager desire to cut in sunder the *hinder one* web of all my woes. Because whosoever *that is dis-* *posed to die,* doth let one from dying that is disposed, *he himself* desirous and resolved to die, doth no less *doth kill* than kill him himself. Wherefore, thou *him* art now become my homicide, thinking to deliver me from death, and (like the greatest enemy to my quiet rest) dost endeavour with thy thankless office to prolong my sorrows."

My tongue exclaimed, and my heart burned with ire, and yet, thinking to have loosed my garments in haste, I did entangle them more and more, which, as soon as I had found out the way to undo, I was immediately held and stayed by the noise of the clamorous Nurse, so that, by her feeble forces and hanging upon me, I was greatly disturbed of my purpose. But, unwinding myself at last out of her hands, her strength had profited her nothing at all if the young Servants and Women at her continual exclamations had not come running from every part of the house and force, perforce, had not stayed me. Out of whose hands, with much struggling and divers frisks, and with greater forces also (the desire of death adding strength to my mighty will) I thought to have ungrappled myself, but breathless at the last, and overcome by them, I was carried back again to my Chamber, which once I thought never to have seen again. How many times (alas) with lamentable and bitter speeches did I chide them, saying:

" O vile and base Servants, what boldness is this, that makes you so malapert, and what precipitate presumption is this that moves you so rudely and so roughly to handle her whom you should rever-ence, and, contrary to your duty, thus violently to lay hands and grip your Mistress, to whom you should be most obsequious, and of whose welfare you should be most careful, and at whose will and pleasure you should be most diligent and ready? What kind of fury (mad wretches) hath inspired you to these rash dealings? And thou, wicked Nurse, the cruel example and mean of all my miserable griefs yet to come, why hast thou repugned my last designs ?

"Why, dost not thou know that in procuring and helping forward my death thou hadst done me a greater pleasure and a better turn than in withholding me from it ? Wherefore, let this miserable part be played, and let the end of my tragical life be duly accomplished by me, and (if thou lovest me, as I think thou dost) leave me to mine own will; leave me (I say) to mine own self to represent the last pageant of my doleful life. And (if thou art so pitiful and careful over me as thou showest) employ thy piety and study in saving my doubtful fame, and honour, which after my death shall still survive. Because in this piece of simple service, with which thou dost now hinder me, thy practice, pain and needless labour shall prove at length but vain. For dost thou think to take from me those sharp tools and cruel poniards with which I will at last broach this miserable heart of mine, and in whose points and edges consisteth the only hope of my desires ? Or else strangling cords, loathsome and swelling poisons, mortiferous herbs, choking rivers, burning coals and consuming flames ? What doth this vigilant care avail thee any more but to prolong a little this irksome life, and to reserve it to that kind of death (which even now, without touch or stain of infamy, might have set peace to my afflicted soul) which, by thy pitiless interruptions deferred, thou shalt doubtless, at one time or other, make most infamous unto all the world, and most shameful unto me. Because death is in every place, and consisteth in everything. Let me, therefore, now die, lest, growing to a more gracious condition of life, with a more inhuman mind and cruel hand, I prepare for myself the most miserable and cruel death that may be."

Whilst, wretched Woman, I spake these words, I could not keep my hands still, but sometimes falling on one servant, and sometimes on another, catching some by their locks, I pulled the hair from their head, and fastening my nails in the faces of other some, I made the blood to spin out of their cheeks, tearing from other some their poor garments from their backs.

But (alas) neither the old Nurse nor the mangled servants answered me one word again, but, lamenting my senseless actions, executed their piteous functions towards me, whom then, with gentle words and entreaties, I endeavoured to gain to my will, which served my turn nothing at all.

Wherefore, like a frantic Hecuba, making a great noise, and with outrageous speeches, I began to exclaim, saying: "O wicked hands, and prone to all mischief, you, the adorners of my hurtful beauties, were a great occasion to make me become such an one as to seem so fair and pleasing in his eyes that I was desired of him whom I love most of all. Since, therefore, these evils have sprung by your help, in guerdon of this, use now your wicked cruelty upon my accursed body. Rent it in pieces and open it, and, dived in my hot blood, pull out from my accursed body my miserable heart and inexpugnable soul. Tear out (I say) this false heart, wounded with blind love. And since that all means of mortal and murdering instruments are taken from thee, with these revenging fingers (the adorners of my baneful beauties) and with these sharp nails piecemeal dismember, and without remorse of pity, rent it out." Alas that my bootless speeches did menace and promise me desired evils, and commended them to the execution of willing hands, but the vigilant care of prying servants, being always ready to the hindrance of them, withheld them against my will. And the mournful and importunate Nurse, with doleful speeches after all this, began thus to say:

"O dearest daughter, by these miserable breasts which were the sources of thy aliments, I humbly *Affectionate* pray thee, that with a quiet and appeased *comforts* mind thou wouldest give ear to my words. By them I will labour to mitigate thy passions that thou shalt not sorrow any more, or to drive quite away (perhaps) from thee the blind anger that doth incend thee to this kind of fury, or else, with a more remiss and calm mind to make thee suffer the same: or else speedily to forsake it. Wishing thee to reduce that to thy erred memory that shall revive thee, and be no small health and great honour unto thee. It is therefore expedient for thee (good Lady), most famous for so rare virtues, as thou art endued with all the gifts of nature and fortune, not to be subject to pinching sorrow, nor (as a woman overcome) to turn thy back from daring dolours, from threatening mishaps and from pursuing woes.

"It is not a point of virtue to require death, and to call upon it, nor a part of magnanimity to *It is not* be afraid of life, as thou art, but rather, *virtuous to* to countermand pressing evils, and to fly *desire death* away before them, is not the part of a *and to be* *afraid of* courageous and resolute mind. Whoso *life* ever doth abate his destinies, and doth contemn, divide and cast from him the profits, pleasures, contents and goods of his life (as thou hast done), I know not what need he hath to seek death, and cannot tell why he feareth life, since that the one and the other is a will of a timorous person. Now if into the dark dungeon of extreme misery thou dost desire wilfully to cast thyself, seek not death, because this is the last expeller and extinguisher of it. Let this foolish fury fly out of thy mind, by the which (methinketh) thou dost seek both to have and to lose thy lover. Why, dost thou believe (by being dissolved into nothing) to get him again?" To whom I answered not a word. But there was such a rumour spread throughout the wide house, and throughout the City, and country

round about, that all my servants (no otherwise
than at the howling of some hungry wolf all the
nearest inhabitants are wont to meet together) came
running to me from every place, and all of them,
affrighted with sudden sorrow, demanded what the
matter was. But I had already forbidden them that
knew it to tell anything at all. Wherefore, covering the horrible accident with a cunning lie, they
rested all satisfied. My dear husband made haste
thither, and my loving sisters, my careful parents
and friends, with panting and fainting breasts, came
running to me. And every one of them, equally
deluded with a false tale, did (instead of a most
wicked woman) repute and praise me for a holy
Saint. And every one, after much weeping, first
reproved my life punished with so much sorrow,
labouring afterwards to comfort me up again. But
from thenceforth it fell out that some believed I
was haunted and stinged with some fury, and therefore like a mad woman continually watched me.
But some, more pitiful than the rest, marking my
mildness, and judging it (as it was indeed) but a
certain grief of mind, with taking great compassion
of me, laughed at that which the rest both did
and said. And visited thus of many, I remained
every day more amazed than other. And under
the discreet guard of the sage Nurse I was closely
kept. And as there is no anger so burning or so
extreme but by course of time is made cold again,

so remaining certain days in this case (as I have set down), I came to myself at last again, and did *All anger* manifestly know the Nurse's words to be *with time is* true. And with bitter tears, therefore, I be-*brought to* *nothing* wailed my past follies. But yet, although that the heat of my rage in time was spent, and became nothing, my love nevertheless did not one whit decrease, but tarried with me still by reason of the melancholy (used in other accidents before) which now continually I had, taking it grievously at the heart, to be forsaken for the unjust love of another woman. Wherefore I conferred with my Nurse oftentimes about this matter, and took counsel of her, desirous to find out some good means how to reclaim my old lover. And therefore sometimes I determined (by her advice) with pitiful letters to certify him of my sorrowful life and grievous misfortunes, and other sometimes we thought it more convenient, by some wise messenger, to let him understand of my daily woes, procured by his wilful absence. And truly although the Nurse was old, and the way very long and dangerous, yet she would for my sake have gone thither herself. But weighing everything well, we judged the letters, were they never so pitiful, were not of any efficacy to move him from these present new loves, so that we accounted those but lost labour. Admit that (for all this) I did sometimes write certain, which had the very same issue that we conjectured of before.

To send the Nurse thither, I thought it as far
from the purpose, because I did apparently perceive
that she could never come to him alive, and to put
my affiance and trust in another, I thought it too
prejudicial to my honour and honesty. So that these
first consultations were but frivolous. And there
was not left any way in my mind to have him
again but in my own person to go to him : to perform which enterprise there occurred divers things
in my mind : all which by good reason were at last
annihilated of my Nurse.

I thought sometimes to take the habit of a Pil-
grim, and with some faithful companion and secret
friend to seek him out in the very midst of his
countries. And although this did seem possible unto
me, notwithstanding, I did clearly see my honour to
be in great hazard thereby, having heard how fair
and wandering Pilgrims are oftentimes evilly abused
of wicked ruffians and thieves, by the ways and in
their travels. And besides this, knowing myself
obliged to my good husband, without whom, or his
leave, I could not conceive how to frame or how
to take in hand this long journey, which thing to
obtain in vain I might have hoped. Wherefore, I
gave no place to this bootless invention. And therefore I was suddenly transported into another device,
as inconvenient as the other was undecent for my
estate before, and I imagined indeed that it should
come to pass, and should verily have done it, if some

repugnant chance in the meantime had not happened, but hereafter (if I do but live) there shall not effectual practices be wanting to fulfil the drift of my pretences. I feigned in these my foresaid adversities, if the Gods had delivered me from them, to have made a vow, desiring to have performed the which, with just reason I might have travelled up and down in my lover his countries: passing through the which I had opportunity at will to see and to recall him back again: which I discovered to my dear husband, who willingly and lovingly offered to furnish me with necessaries in the same voyage, yet wishing me to attend a more convenient time. But the delays hereof being very grievous, and no less dangerous unto me, and fearing lest it might be suspected, and so detected a vicious and wicked journey and Pilgrimage, this (I say) caused me to enter into new imaginations, and into other counsels: all which seemed worser to me than the rest

By Hecate, which Proserpina denoteth, is understood art Magic
alleged before, except only the marvellous and supernatural effects of Hecate with the which, because I might most safely commit myself to the fearful spirits, I had much talk and conversation, and with those especially whom I had heard were most skilful, and who themselves did boast to excel in art Magic, promising to perform and bring to pass what I would.

And some of them swearing to carry me suddenly

thither, others to wean his mind from all other loves, and to ingraft it in mine again, others telling that they would restore me to my former liberty, and myself desiring that the least of these might come to pass, I found them as full of tattling words and vain promises as their unperformed and simple deeds did manifest. Whereupon my flattering hope remained many times confused, and in suspense by them; and therefore, thinking it best of all to shake off these wicked drifts, I attended convenient time, in the which my husband promised me to fulfil my feigned vow.

THE
SIXTH BOOK OF BOCCACE
HIS FIAMMETTA

MY sorrows (notwithstanding the hope of my future voyage) were continuated, and the sky, with continual motion carrying the Sun with it, did draw one day after another without any intermediate space of time. And vain hope held me in wavering doubts longer than I would, my great griefs and grievous love not any whit diminished. And now that Bull, *The description of the Springtide* which sometimes transported Europa, held Phœbus with his golden light, and the days borrowing light of the nights, of the shortest, became the longest. And flowery Zephirus (arrived with his calm and peaceful blasts) had set the boisterous wars of Boreas in peace. And the stormy and dark tempests banished away with the cold air, and the white snow, discovering the tops of high hills and the plashy meadows (washed with the abundance of falling rain), had made every flower fairer, all grass to wax green, and generally had renewed all herbage. And that hoary whiteness, which all the cold winter season hath covered every tree, was now changed into a lively and fresh verdure. And in every place that season of the year

T   289 did reign when joyful Ver abundantly enricheth the earth with his wished and welcome treasures. And the ground (starred, as it were, and wrought with violets, marigolds and sweet roses) did seem to countervail the eighth heaven in beauty, and Narcissus did now begin to grow on every meadow, and *By the* the mother of Bacchus also to show forth *mother of* sprouting and fructiferous signs of her *Bacchus is* *understood* fertile womb, and did with her green bur*the vine* geons (more than she was wont to do) overcharge her supporter and fellow Elm, himself also become now more heavy by his new garments. Driope, and the disastrous sisters of Phaeton, did also now show merry and cheerful countenances, having shaken off the miserable habit of hoary winter. The pretty birds, perching on every twig and bough, were heard to warble forth sweet and silver notes. And Proserpina her mother (that devout goddess of countrymen) joyfully waved up and down the fields with her goodly garments. And besides all these things my cruel Lord made every lusty, young and loving mind to feel the heat of his fiery darts hotter than before. Whereupon everyone, young Gentlewomen as well as gallant youths, adorning themselves (according to their degree) in the bravest manner and richest fashion of attire, endeavoured to please their best beloved. The merry feasts cheered up our Citizens, and filled all our City full of mirth, which were more magnificent and

copious than any that had been made in flourishing Rome of yore. And the Theatres, resounding
with sweet songs and melodious sounds, did invite
every lover to them. The Heroical young gentlemen sometimes mounted upon stately coursers, and
proud Genets did run at Tilt and Joust in rich and
complete Harness, and sometimes their pampered
and headstrong Horses, trapped all over with a
caparison of little silver and golden bells, did hotly
fight at Tourney. And sometimes, proudly pranc-
ing up and down on them, with skilful hand did
show how these foaming, fiery steeds with frothy
bit should be managed and ridden. The young
and wanton Ladies, with decked troops of beautiful
Gentlewomen following them (desiring to see these
sports), wearing fine garlands of new flowers about
their heads, did lend sweet and gracious aspects to
their gazing lovers, sometimes out of high windows,
and sometimes from beneath their doors. Of which
some with new gifts, others with a merry countenance, and some with sweet words, but generally all
with some favour or other, did friendly honour their
lovers and kindle greater flames in them. But I,
like a stranger and forlorn woman, sitting by myself
in a solitary place all alone, and comfortless for the
decayed hope of my joyful times, did not a little
sorrow with myself, but lament greatly and mourn.

Nothing pleaseth my melancholy fancies, no feast
could make my heart merry nor afford any comfort to

my grievous thoughts or ease my plaints. My hands
touched no green leaves, carried no sweet flowers
in them, and cared as little to handle any joyful
thing as my sorrowful eyes to behold them. And I
became so peevish an emulatress that I envied at
others' mirth, and with great desire did injuriously
wish that every woman might be so entreated with
love and served with such source of Fortune as I
was. For with what a willing ear and with what
great consolation do I remember that many times
I have heard the recounted miseries and miserable
mishaps that in times past and lately have befallen
Fortune to to unfortunate lovers. But while the angry
the afflicted Gods held me in this cursed condition of
more often- life, deceitful Fortune, with greater woes
times shows
a merry to afflict miserable men, changing, as it
countenance were, in the midst of their adversities,
showeth them sometimes a pleasant look, because,
abandoning themselves and trusting more to her
fawning smiles, they may fall into greater miseries
when their momentary mirth beginneth once, and
on a sudden to cease.

And so these ignorant fools, relying wholly upon
her, at last perceive themselves thrown headlong
down, as miserable Icarus in the midst of his flight,
trusting too much to his waxed wings, and, mounted
up to the highest skies, fell from thence into the
sea called yet after his own name.

This frowning Fortune, I say, perceiving me

amongst such silly souls, not to be content with these past evils that she had given me, preparing worser for me, with a false and dissembled joy began to smile upon me and to mollify somewhat her paused anger : because recoiling a good way back she might (no otherwise than the hot rams of Africa in rutting time to give a greater dub) assail and hurt me the more.

And in this sort, with a certain vain gladness, I made truce for a season with my sharp and still sorrows. But my faithless lover having now tarried a great many months more than those four promised past and unperformed, it fell out that, sitting on a certain day all alone in my sorrowful chamber, though wearied with the overcloying company of *Lovers are* doleful thoughts, and accustomed lamenta-*sometimes* tions, the old and feeble Nurse, with a more *comforted* *with one* hasty pace than her aged limbs could well *joy* endure, came rushing in, her furrowed face all bewet with trickling sweat, and, setting herself down by me, her breast panting up and down, and her eyes expressing a certain kind of joyfulness in them, she began many times to speak, but the precedent faintness of her wearied pulmon did ever break off her words in the midst. To whom (with a mind full of suspicious wonder and fearful doubt) I said : " O dear Nurse, what meaneth this great labour and pains that thou hast taken, thus tired thyself with ? What thing dost thou so earnestly desire to tell, and with such haste, that first thou wilt not suffer thy breathless spirits to rest them ? What, are they joyful or unlucky tidings ? Shall I prepare myself to fly, to die, or what shall I do ? Thy countenance (I know not how, nor wherefore) doth somewhat renew my drooping hope, but my affairs, hanging a long time in contrary suspense, persuade me to suspect more cruel mishaps, which are of common course and custom incident to miserable creatures. Tell me therefore quickly, and hold me no longer in doubt ; resolve me what the occasion of this thy haste may import. Tell me whether any happy God or haggish fury hath driven thee hither."

Then the old woman, having yet scarce recovered her wind, interrupting my words, and more joyful than before, said : "O sweet daughter, rejoice ; there is no cause of fear in my tidings. Shake off all grief and invest thy mourning mind again with thy shining robe of mirth ; thy beloved and loving lover is returned. And Panphilus (Fiammetta) is at hand."

These angelical words entered so deep into my amazed mind, and filled it with such sudden joy, as my eyes did presently show an evident testimony of the same ; but my pursuing grief and haunting miseries did incontinently bereave me of it and made me give no credit to them. Wherefore lamenting, I said : "O my dear Nurse, by those thy many years, and by thy aged body which long since hath desired eternal repose, I pray thee not to mock me (a most miserable and distressed soul), of whose cares and griefs thou oughtest also to be partaker. *Impossible* For first will the clear rivers (I think) re-*things* turn to their first fountains, and Hesperus will bring clear day : first will Phœbe with her brother's beams give light to the dark night, before my ungrateful lover will return. Who doth not know (alas) that, disporting himself with his new mistress, he is lulled asleep in the secure cradle of all delights, enjoying his merry times and loving her more than ever he did me. And think, more-over (Fiammetta), that wheresoever he were now, he would return to her again, and therefore not likely to come from her whom he loveth so extremely, to me whom he infinitely hateth." But presently she added : " O Fiammetta, as the gods shall receive the parting soul of this withered and old body, thy careful Nurse doth not lie in one word she hath told thee. Nor doth it become one of my age, with such or like tales, to mock distressed women, and thee especially, to whom I owe all the duty and love I may." Then I replied and said : " How came these blessed news to thy ears, and how dost thou know them to be true ? Ah, tell me quickly, because if they seem probable in my jealous and doubtful mind, I may rejoice myself with the happy utterance and sweet accents of them." And rising from the place where I was a little gladder than before and somewhat cheered in mind, I sat

nearer to the Nurse, and then she said : " Rising
this morning very early about my proper business,
which lay near to the Seashore, and earnestly musing
on them, I went with a soft and slow pace, with my
back turned towards the Sea, when a certain young
Gentleman leaping ashore out of a late arrived ship,
unadvised carried by the force of his skip, did boister-
ously and (as after I perceived) against his will fall
against me. Wherefore I conjuring the Gods and
with great choler turning towards him to blame
him for this received injury, with humble words he
meekly craved pardon at my hands.

" But earnestly looking on him, and marking
well his habit, I judged that he came from the
coasts and country of thy beloved Panphilus, and
therefore said to him : ' Gentleman (as the Gods
may be favourable unto you), of courtesy tell me
if you come from any foreign country.' ' Yes,
good woman, that I do,' said he again. Then said
I : ' Tell me from whence, good Sir, if it please
you.' And he said : ' From the coasts of Hetruria,
and from the most noble City in the same I lately
came, and of which I am.' As soon as I heard this
I then knew him to be Panphilus his countryman.
Wherefore I asked him if he knew Panphilus and
what was become of him.

" And he answered that he did know him very
well, and reported many good things to me in praise
and commendation of him, and besides this said

that he had now come with him, if a little business had not stayed him there, but that (without all doubt) in a few days after he would come thither.

"In the meanwhile, that we were thus talking, all his companions that came belike with him leaping on shore, and ready to depart, he went away with them. I leaving apart all other business, with the greatest haste I could (thinking that I should not have lived so long until I had told thee of it) came hither breathless and panting as thou seest. Wherefore live now merrily once again, and exile these sad thoughts." Which things, when she had spoken, with a most glad and joyful countenance I kissed her old forehead, and yet with a doubtful mind I many times afterwards conjured her, and did ask her again, if these news were true, wishing ever in mind that she should not tell the *The manner* contrary, and doubting lest she had de-*of those that* ceived me. But after that many times *doubt* with holy oaths she did swear that she had told me nothing more than truth, although that Ay and No went wavering up and down my suspicious head. Like a gladsome woman with these speeches I rendered immortal thanks to the Gods, saying:

"O supreme Jupiter, most royal rector and majestical sovereign of the high heavens. O luminate and radiant Apollo, from whom nothing is hid. O gracious Venus and most pitiful of thy subjects.

THE SIXTH BOOK

O sacred Boy carrying the golden and sweet darts, be ye all praised together and with equal honour magnified. Whosoever persevereth in your hope cannot perish in his long and doubtful travels. Behold by your favourable mercies, and not by my merits, my desired Panphilus doth return, whom I shall not so soon see, but that your altars (heretofore visited of me with most lamentable and pitiful prayers, and washed with bitter tears) shall now with my obsequious hands be perfumed with most sweet odours and precious incense. And to thee, Fortune, full of pity, turning now thy wrathful face away from my manifold evils, will I presently give, and erect, the promised image, with testimony of thy needful and imparted benefits.

"But most humbly obtesting you all with that humility and devotion which may make you most exorable, that you would deign to take away all unlucky occurrents possible to hinder my Panphilus in his determined journey, and to conduct him hither as safe and sound as ever he was heretofore." My prayers finished (no otherwise than an unhooded Falcon), rousing myself up together, and clapping my hands, I began thus to say : "O amorous breasts, weakened with long consuming sorrows, cast away from henceforth all pinching cares, since that my dear lover (remembering me again) doth now return according to his promise.

"Drive away sorrow, harbour no fear, and shake

off the great shame that doth abound in afflicted and despised things, nor (as Fortune hath heretofore guided you) presume not to entertain any more grievous thoughts, but dissolve now into nothing the dark clouds of cruel destinies, and let every semblance and thought of my miserable times depart now from me ; let my merry and pleasant countenance return again, and be made capable to rejoice at this present felicity, and let old Fiammetta with her ruinated soul be altogether blotted out of my memory." Whilst joyfully I spake these words with myself, my heart began yet to doubt (I know not what), and a sudden searching cold (being ignorant of the cause thereof) did overrun all my body, so that it counterchecked my will, ready to rejoice my mind.

Wherefore I remained a good while as one astonied in the very midst of my speech. Alas that *Miserable* this inconvenience and fault doth haunt *men never believe glad-* miserable and afflicted souls, that they can-*some things* not dispose and frame themselves to give credence to joyful things, apparent almost, and told them for their good and comfort. And admit that their happy fortune returned again, it is irksome nevertheless unto them to be merry at all, but believing it as a dream, they slenderly pass it away, as though it were not indeed. Wherefore, like one half amazed with myself, I began to say : "Who called me back again, or what forbade me from my new commenced joy? What, doth not Panphilus return? Truly yes.

"Who doth therefore command me to mourn again? There is no way now left, nor do I see any occasion to new make me fall into my old sadness. Who doth therefore forbid me to deck myself with new flowers, and to adorn my fine body with rich robes? Alas, I know not, and yet I am forbidden (I know) by some secret suggestion of sorrow, and relic of hidden grief, of which my soul is not yet clearly purged."

And standing on these doubtful points, and in this sort against my will, as though I had not been in myself, in the midst of all my doubtful errors great store of tears fell from my eyes, and in the chiefest of my new merry mood my accustomed lamentations abruptly disturbed it. And thus my long afflicted heart did by the ever-running conduits of my eyes send forth her wonted and wasteful tears.

And my unconstant mind (divining as it were of ensuing misery and of worse mishaps) did with great *Signs of a* grief and lamentations (like the Sicilian hill) *mind divin-* evaporate many scalding sighs and sobs, *ing things* *to come* most manifest signs, by the which I do now certainly know, that then there is some great and stormy tempest near at hand, when, without any blast of turbulent winds, the wary Seamen perceiveth the calm and quiet seas begin to swell. But

300

yet desirous to overcome that which my mind would not, I said : "O miserable woman, what ill news and what misfortunes to come needless dost thou feign in thy suspicious mind? Say that this which thou foretellest of may happen to thy doubting mind of consequent mishaps, thou fearest (alas) too late, and without any profit at all."

From these words (therefore) ever after I applied my mind wholly to a new kind of mirth, and I did (as well as I could) extinguish all melancholic thoughts. And warning my faithful Nurse to be diligent about Panphilus his return, I changed my mourning weeds into gorgeous and gallant vestments, and began to wax very curious, and careful of myself, because lest by my long affected countenance and disordered attire I might not at his return seem unlovely in his eyes.

My pale and lean cheeks began to recover their lost and lively colour, and recovering their forsaken plumpness, began to wax round again. And my tears now dried up, took away with them also those red and purple rainbows which encompassed my eyes round about : the which, being returned into their due places, received again their whole and perfect lights.

And my withered cheeks, being somewhat broken and worn by continual streams of tears that washed them, grew again to their old and former softness. And my neglected hair, although not suddenly they became not golden, they wanted not now their accustomed frizzlings and dainty deckings to make them look so passing fair as once they did. And my dear and costly apparel, having a long time lain unworn in sweet Indian presses, did now bravely set forth my seemly body. What more ? In brief, I turned *The effects* my pains to pleasures, my griefs to glad-*of them that* ness, my sighing to singing, my mourning *return to be* *joyful again* to mirth, and made a renovation of myself, and of all things else that belonged to me. And I made myself almost as beautiful as once I was, first, and brought myself wellnigh to my former estate and happiness of life, insomuch that the Gentlewomen my near neighbours, my dear kinsfolks, and my loving husband marvelled not a little at this sudden change, saying to themselves :

" What inspiration hath drawn her from so long sorrow, and mitigated thus her continual melancholy, which neither by sweet and effectual comforts, nor by friendly and loving requests, could heretofore be driven out of her obstinate mind. This is surely no less than a miracle." And as they wondered much at it, so were they also very glad of this sudden alteration. All my family, being very heavy a long time for my continual tribulation, began with me to rejoice now again, and as my errors were altered, even so it seemed that all things with the same were changed from sorrow into solace. The days, which erst I thought longer than they were wont to be, did (by reason of the hope which I had of Panphilus his return, seeming now longest of all unto me) pass away (methought) with the slowest course that might be. Nor the first were so well counted of me, but with greater care and diligence I marked these. In space of which time, sometimes sitting with myself all alone, and thinking of my past cares and careful thoughts, I did now chiefly condemn them, saying:

" Oh, how hardly of late have I thought of my dear lover, how rashly have I condemned his long staying, and how foolishly have I believed that he was wholly given over to the liking and love of another woman, induced thereunto but by the slender report of one of my lying servants. Accursed therefore be their buzzing tales. O Gods, how can men with such open and impudent countenances tell abroad false and shameless lies ? But everything (Fiammetta) should with more sound advice of thy own part have been considered, than so soon and so easily to have given belief unto them. I should (alas) have counterpoised the faith of my lover so many times sworn and promised to me, and as many times again with affectionate tears avowed, and should have weighed the love that he bare me, and yet doth, with their fabulous words, false rumours and base credits, in the equal balance of my right judgment, who (without any sacrament of urged oath, and myself not caring to inquire further, and not desirous to know any more than that they spake) told only the bare reports of others and with asseveration only of their first opinions and superficial knowledge, which do now manifestly appear to be erroneous and false.

" One alleging that he did see a young gentlewoman go into Panphilus his father's house, because he knew not any other young gentleman perhaps there but him, and not thinking of the unseemly and common wantons of old dotards, or else (ignorant (perhaps) of her alliance with them) believed by and by that she was his wife, and so without any more ado told it her who therefore did believe it, because she took but little heed and care of him that told it. Another, because he perceived him sometimes to eye some fair Gentlewoman, or else to dally with her, which (might be) was his Kinswoman, or someone with whom he was familiarly and honestly acquainted, did judge her to be his also, and affirming it again with simple words to me, I did, like a simple Woman, believe the same. Oh, that I had most duly pondered these things in my mind, how many tears, what infinite sighs, and what extreme grief had I never felt. But what thing can an enamoured and silly Woman advisedly ponderate in her mind, and directly do ? As sundry forces assail us, so do they toss and turn our minds to every change. And simple Lovers easily believe all things. Because love is a passion full of care and fear. For by continual use they addict themselves always to hurtful accidents, and desiring many things, believe most possibilities, contrary to their troubled fancies, so fixing their *Love is a* irremovable minds upon the first that to *thing full* the second reports, and things, they give *of care and* *fear* small belief, or none at all. But I am to be held excused; and therefore I always prayed the Gods that they would make me a liar in my fond imaginations and belief.

"But behold my prayers are heard, and he shall never understand these words which I have spoken against him, which, if he did know, he could say nothing else but that they proceeded from the fervent love I bare him. For how dear a thing should it be to him to hear of my torments and grief of mind, and to know of my past and prevented perils for his sake, because these are most true arguments of my undoubted love and faith; and I can scarce think otherwise but that he hath tarried so long, and to none other end, but only to prove if with a constant mind I could (without forgetting him) attend his coming again. Behold, therefore, and with what force of mind I have expected him. Wherefore from henceforth, when he shall perceive with what pain and tears, and with how many millions of martyring thoughts I have looked for him, love shall be born anew again in him, and no other God. Ah, when shall it come to pass that he (being once arrived) shall see me, and I him again?

"O ye Gods, which from your high thrones

contemplate all things here beneath, may I temper and moderate my eager desire, from embracing his *God seeth* body before all men as soon as I shall see *all things* him. Truly I believe I shall hardly do it. O bounteous Gods, when shall it be that, enfolding him straitly between mine arms, I shall render him treble again those kisses which at his departure he gave to my dying lips, without any exchange for them again! Certes, the presage which I noted, that I was not able to bid him farewell, is now true, and by that the Gods have very well declared to me his return. O ye gracious Gods, when will that time come when I may joyfully recount unto him the Seas of salt tears, and the worlds of woes, which I have passed, and worn out, and when shall I know the occasion of his long and sorrowful absence? Shall I live so long? Alas, I scarcely think it. Ah, let that day come quickly, because death (not long since so often called and procured of me) doth now terrify me, which (if possibly my prayers can enter into his ears) I humbly beseech, that flying far from me, he would let me spend the remainder of my young years in joy and pleasure with my beloved Panphilus." I was therefore very careful that no day should pass me wherein I did not employ my whole study and diligence to be very inquisitive of Panphilus his return, and to hear also of some true news of him. And my dear Nurse was not negligent in seeking out the young Gentleman, and bringer of these glad tidings, because she might with more sureness be ascertained of that which she had told me, which thing she did not only once, but as oftentimes as conveniently she could, and (as many times as she had done before) she did always bring me word, that his return was nigh at hand. Wherefore I did not only expect the promised time, but, proceeding a little further, I did imagine it possible that he was now come. And therefore a hundred times in the day I did run sometimes beneath to the door, and sometimes to the window, looking round about me a great way if I might perceive him come. And I saw not any man coming afar off that way that he should come but I did verily imagine that it was he, and with great desire did look on him so long until, coming nearer unto me, I might easily perceive that it was not he. Whereat being somewhat grieved in mind, I looked out to see if any other came, and sometimes one and now another passing by, and seeing that none of them was he, I remained (my greedy desire and hope deceived) full of confusion, and very angry with myself.

And if I was perhaps called into the house, or else by some other urgent occasion went from the window, a hundred thousand thoughts (as if a multitude of dogs grinding their teeth at me had bitten my soul) did sting and molest me, saying to myself: "Alas, even now (perhaps) he goeth by, or else is

already passed, whilst thou art here busied about
not so contented an office": and immediately I
went again to see if I could see him come,
making it but a short time between going
down to the door and running quickly
up to the window again. Ah, poor soul,
and wretched Woman, how much sorrow
and how many troubles didst thou sustain for him
whom, hourly looking for, thou couldest never perceive to come. But after that the day was come
in which my Nurse told me that he should arrive,
and of the which she had so often foretold me,
I adorned myself no otherwise than Alcmena did
when she heard that her Amphitryon was at hand,
and with my mastering hand left not anything
in me unbeautified, but set forth in the best and
bravest order, and in the finest fashion.

Read Ariosto of her that attended the return of her lover

And I could scarce keep myself in from going to
the Sea side because I might the sooner see him,
because (also) I heard certain news of the arrival
of those Galleys in the which my Nurse understood,
and certified me, that he should come. But thinking
with myself that the first Saint that he would visit
on shore was myself, I (therefore) bridled my earnest
and hot desire. But in fine (as I rightly guessed) he
came not at all: whereupon I began beyond all
measure to marvel, and in the midst of my late
joy arised in my mind divers kinds of doubts, which
were not so easily overthrown by superficial sup-

positions of his coming, or by any other shadows of gladsome thoughts. After a little while, therefore, I sent the old Woman to know what was become of him, and whether he was come or not : who went, as it seemed, with such an unwilling mind, and with as slow a pace, which did divine of some conse- quent and sorrowful tidings. Wherefore I accursed many times with myself, and with great anger blamed her crooked steps and aged paces. Who, staying but a little time abroad, came to me again with a sorrowful cheer and dull gait.

Alas, when I saw her come in this sort I could hardly contain my soul in my body, and therefore *Signs of* suddenly imagined that my Lover was dead *one that* by the way, or else that he was arrived *bringeth* *ill news* very sick. The colour of my face changed a thousand times in one instant, and going to meet the dreaming Nurse, I said unto her : "Tell me quickly what news dost thou bring. Doth my Lover live ?" She changed not her gait, nor an- swered me one word. And being now entered into my Chamber, and setting herself down, looked me very pitifully in the face. Wherefore every part of my body being shaken, like the tender Aspen leaves by some soft wind, I did being now to tremble, and hardly restraining my tears, I crossed mine arms, and did put my hands into my sorrowful bosom, saying :

"If thou dost not tell me quickly what this thy

309

sorrowful countenance doth mean, and what these sad signs which thou dost bring with thee do signify, there shall not any part of my garments remain whole to my body, nor hair untorn from my head. What secret occasion therefore may it be that moveth thee from telling it, but only that which I fear will prove ominous unto me. Conceal it no longer, but declare it, whilst I am attending for worse. What (tell me at a word), liveth my Panphilus?" She, pricked on by my angry words and threatenings, with a low voice, and looking down to the ground, said: "He liveth." Then said I again: "Wherefore dost. thou not tell me quickly? What envious accidents stay him from coming hither? Why dost thou hold me in suspense and wavering amidst a thousand fearful surmises? Is he sick with any malady? Or what froward occasion doth withhold him that, being come out of the Galley, he doth not come to see me?" Then she said: "I know not whether want of health or any other mischance doth detain him." Then said I again: "Hast thou not seen him, or is he not yet come?" "I have seen him," said she, "and he is come, but not the same whom we did expect." "How art thou sure," said I, "that he is not my Panphilus? Hast thou seen him at any other time, and didst thou now behold and mark him well?" "Truly," said she, "I did never see him that I wot of, but being even now brought unto him by that young Gentleman who told me the first news

of his return, and telling him that I had oftentimes in-
quired for him, he asked me what I would with him.
'His health and welfare,' said I. And I demanding
of him how his old Father did, and in what estate
the rest of his things stood, and what was the cause
of his long staying since his departure, he answered
that he never knew his Father, and that he was a
Posthumous posthumous-born, and that all his things
is he that were in good plight, and that he had never
is born after
his Father's been here before, and did mean to stay
death here but a small time. These things made
me to wonder, and doubting, lest I was deceived, I
asked him his name, which courteously and plainly
he told me; and I no sooner heard it but immediately I perceived, by the identity and likeness of it
with the name of thy beloved Panphilus, both thee
and myself to be greatly deceived."

When I heard these things (most pitiful Ladies)
mine eyes forsook their lights, and every sensitive
Effects of spirit, for fear of death, went their ways,
a sudden and falling down in the place where I sat,
passion there remained no more force in my body
than was scarce able to breathe forth one poor Alas.
Which, when the miserable old Woman perceived,
lamenting greatly, and calling the rest of my Women
about me, carried me like a dead woman to my bed,
and there labouring to reduce my wandering spirits
with cold water, believing a great while together to
recover life, and yet misdoubting also the same, they

311

watched me with diligent care. But after that my
forsaken forces came to me again, and after I had
poured forth many tears and sighs, I asked the
sorrowful Nurse another time if it were so as she
had said. And besides this, remembering with myself how wary and discreet Panphilus was wont to
be, and suspecting that he had wisely and of purpose
made himself unknown to the Nurse, with whom
he had never talked in his life before, I willed that
she should describe unto me the countenance, the
feature, the gesture, the personage and the fashions
of that Panphilus with whom she had talked. But
she, affirming first with an oath that it was no less
and no otherwise than she had told me, declared
to me afterwards in order his stature, the lineaments of his body and face, and, last of all, the
manner of his apparel. All which (alas) made me
give too great faith to that which the old woman
told me.

Wherefore, thrust off from all hope, I re-entered
into my former woes, and rising up like a frantic
Woman I pulled off my sumptuous garments of
joy, and laid aside my once dear but now unpleasant ornaments, and my frizzled shining hair,
with an envious Hecuba hand, I tore out of order,
and did carelessly ruffle them together, and despising all comfort, I began most bitterly to complain of
my incessant and miserable mishaps, and with cruel
words to condemn my failed hope, and to blame

the good thoughts and like concealed opinions of my untrue and wicked Lover.

And, in brief, I returned wholly to my old life of miseries, and had a more earnest and fervent desire

Hope doth still keep one in life of death than before, which I had not escaped (as yet I have), but that the hope of my intended voyage, with no little force, withheld me from performance of it.

THE
SEVENTH BOOK OF BOCCACE
HIS FIAMMETTA

N this kind of life, therefore (most piti-ful Ladies), I have remained, as by the recounted and passed accidents you may gather. And by how much my ungrate-ful Lord doth see my hope fly from me, by so much the more doth he work stranger effects in me than he was wont to do, and, blowing with more hot desires the glowing coals of love in my smothered breast, doth make them greater than before, which, as on the one side they do mightily increase, so are my pains and sorrows on the other by like proportion augmented, which, never being with due ointment assuaged of me, are by my own will and follies made more grievous and insupportable ; and being more sharp do more afflict my sorrowful and woeful mind. And I doubt not (but following their head-long course) they will at length, with some honest mean, open me the way of death, which heretofore I have so long and unfeignedly desired. But yet having my assured hope, as I have already said, in my pretended voyage to find and see him (ah, that ungrateful Panphilus, I mean) who is the original of all this, I did not seek to mitigate them, but was rather now resolved (as well as I could) constantly to endure them. For performance of which I found *To resemble one's pain with another's griefs is a lightening of sorrow* out one only possible way amongst many others, which was, to compare and measure my pains with theirs who had likewise passed such brunts as myself fighting under the amorous ensigns and in the dolorous battles of love: whereof I think to reap a double commodity.

First, in knowing myself not the first, nor to be alone afflicted with misery, as not long since my Nurse, in her alleged comforts, told me. Secondly, that every grief, pain and pang of their love being (in my judgment) sufficiently recompensed, I determined and resolved with myself to pass away ever after with my former, every other grief whatsoever; which I reckon no little glory to me, when I may say that I am only she that living hath sustained more grief and misery than any other woman. And with this kind of glory (forsaken yet of everyone as extreme misery indeed and of myself (alas) if I could otherwise do), in this sort, as you shall hear, I passed away my melancholy times. I say, therefore, that, martyred with these continual anguishes, and considering well of others who have not been exempted from the like, the painful loves of Inachus his daughter (who, being first a tender and delicate damsel, and passing lovely and beautiful, did seem lively to represent me) came to my mind, and after-

wards her great good hap and happy felicity, in
that she was not meanly beloved of mighty Jove.
Which thing doubtless could not be of her only,
but every woman also accounted a great glory and
praise. Afterwards considering how she was meta-
morphosed into a Cow, and how, by the severe
command of jealous Juno, she was kept of vigilant
Argus, I did judge her to be beyond all measure
tormented with great anxieties and grief of mind.
And certes, I am of opinion that her griefs did greatly
exceed mine, if that for her company and comfort
she had not had sometimes the assistance of her
loving God. And who doth doubt, if I had the
sweet company of my lover, who might any time
have helped me in these ruthful passions, or that he
had but sometimes taken any little pity of me, that
any woes whatsoever could have annoyed me so,
as they have continually done. Besides this, her end
made her passed and approved sorrows very light.
Because Argus being killed by her lover's messenger,
and she transported lightly with her heavy body
into Egypt, and returned there to her own shape
again and married to Osiris, she saw herself at last
installed in the Imperial diadem, and like a happy
Queen, to sway the regal sceptre of Egypt. If I
could but think, or hope, though in my old age to
see my Panphilus once again, I would say that my
griefs were not to be compared with the sorrows of
this Lady. But the Gods only know if this good

fortune shall ever hap to me or no, howsoever with false hope in the meantime I delude and flatter *The greater* myself. Next to her the unfortunate love *part of these fables are* of Biblis is represented unto my thoughts, *in Ovid* whom (methink) I see forsake all her wealth, joy and pleasure to follow unflexible Caunus. And with these I bethink myself also of wicked Mirrha, who, after the detested fruition of her odious loves, flying from her angry Father, who pursued her with menaces of just death, plunged also into that misery.

I behold also dolorous Canace, who, after the miserable birth of her incestuous conception, looked for nothing less but death. And thinking well with myself of their several sorrows, I did doubtless esteem them to be extreme, although their loves were but filthy and abominable lusts. But if I am not deceived I see them all ended, or else in short space to be terminated. Because Mirrha flying away, having the Gods pitiful of her pains, and answerable to her desires, was without delay transformed into a tree of her own name.

And she never after (although it doth continually distil Amber tears, as she did at the very instant when her form was changed) felt any of her former pains and plaints. And as the occasion of her sorrows did arise, so the cause of their privation was not also wanting. Biblis, likewise (as some say), without any longer delay, ended her doleful days with a cruel

halter: admit that others hold that by great favour
of the Nymphs (who did commiserate her hard
destinies) she was turned into a fountain of her
own name, till this day yet keeping the same.

And this befell to her when she knew that Caunus
denied her her desires, and scornfully rejected her
company, and with frowning brows reproved her
wicked suits. What shall I say in showing my own
pains, greater (alas) than those that molested Biblis,
and more grievous than those that Mirrha had, but
that the brevity of them hath had no small advantage over the length of mine. Those therefore well
considered, the pitiful loves of hapless Pyramus
and Thisbe were next objected to my remembrance,
of whom (I cannot but take great compassion),
imagining them both to be young, and with great
trouble and many sorrows, to have burned in each
other's love, and labouring with mutual presence
to have reaped the fruit of their fervent desires,
which with untimely death and in short time were
equally dissolved.

Oh, what a pitiful thing is it to think what grief
pierced poor Pyramus his heart when in the silent
time of night, finding his dear Thisbe's robes bloody
and torn of the wild beast at the foot of the Mulberry
tree, near unto the fountain and appointed meeting
place, by these dismal and unexpected tokens he
surely thought that she was devoured. The sheath-
ing, certes, of his own sword in his impatient breast

319

did show it manifestly enough. Afterwards discoursing in my mind the wounding thoughts of miserable Thisbe beholding her lover wallowing in his own gore, and panting yet with declining life, I think them to be so grievous, and imagine her tears also to be such burning drops, that I can hardly believe that there were ever any (mine own excepted) that did torment and scald more than hers. Wherefore these two (as it is now said) in the very beginning of their griefs and loves did end the very same. Oh, thrice happy souls if that in the other world, as in this, their perfect and firm love doth still remain inviolate. And so the pains, cares and infinite woes of all their former love could not be equivalent with the delights and content of their eternal company.

After these the grief of forsaken Dido entered with greater force and deeper consideration into my mind, because her condition did of all others most resemble mine. I imagined how she was building of Carthage, and studying with great Majesty to dictate laws in Juno's temple to her new people; and how she gave bountiful entertainment to Æneas, a stranger unto her by envious tempests of the Sea weatherbeaten and cast upon her Lybian shores; and how she was enamoured of his brave personage, and passing virtues; and at last how she committed both herself and all hers to the disposition and pleasure of that Trojan Duke, who, having used her royal Palaces at his pleasure, and soaked himself in all manner of delices in her country, she being every day more and more inflamed with his love, abandoning her at last, departed from thence. Oh, how much without compare did she seem miserable in my conceit, beholding her looking from her highest turrets towards the sea, covered with disanchored ships of her flying and unpitiful lover.

But I judge her more impatient than dolorous when I think of her cruel death. And, certes, at the first departure of my Panphilus I felt (in my opinion) the very selfsame grief as she did on the sudden endure at the sailing away of false Æneas. Oh, that it had so pleased the Gods that I, as unable to endure my grief as she was hers, had with some sudden death ended my loathed life, so that by these means I might have delivered myself from these pains and sorrows, as she did herself, which afterwards (by default thereof) did continually cleave in sunder my afflicted heart. After the miserable thoughts and the ruthful chances of unhappy Hero of Sesto came to my mind, whom (methought) I saw coming down from her highest Tower to the Sea banks and rocks, where she was wont sometimes to meet and receive her well-beloved and wearied Leander into her arms.

And even there again (methinks) I see her with what a pitiful and pale countenance she beheld her lover lying dead before her, driven first on shore by a friendly Dolphin, all naked, and soused in brinish

waters, and laid along upon the Sea sands, and
wiping with her garments the salt water from his
pale visage, and drowning him the second time with
the flowing streams of her swelling tears. Ah, what
great pity doth her cruel passages find in my sorrowful mind. More truly than any of those of the
foresaid ladies, and sometimes so much that, forgetting my own woes, I did weep and lament for hers.

And lastly, could I conceive no means for her
comfort but one of these two, either to die, or else
Sorrow to forget him, as other dead men have
ceaseth when been : in taking either of which her sorrows
hope is past (I think) might have easily been finished.
to regain the Considering that no lost thing, in recover-
thing which ing of which again there is no hope left,
is lost can grieve us any long time. But yet the Gods
forbid that this kind of comfort should happen to
me, which if it did come to pass, no counsel in such
a case should avail but that which persuaded me
once to a resolute and hasty death. For during the
time that my Panphilus liveth, whose life his happy
stars and predominant planets preserve as long as
he himself doth desire, that cannot (I hope) nor
shall not befall unto me. But seeing the intercourse
of mundane things in continual motion, this belief
is added to my hope, that in the end, or else (perhaps) before, he shall return, and be mine again, as
once he was. Which lingering hope not coming
to effect, doth hourly make my life grievous and

322

irksome unto me. And by thus much therefore I esteem myself oppressed with greater sorrow than *French* she was. I remember that in French *Rhymes* metres, to which if any credit may be lent, I have sometimes read that Sir Tristram and Lady Isotta have more than any other lovers mutually and fervently loved each other, and with their changing delights have had great misfortunes and adversities intermingled, even in the flourishing and bravest time of their youth, who, because, loving greatly together, they have tasted both of one end, it seems most credible that not without extreme sorrow and bitter grief on both sides they forsook their worldly delights.

Which may be easily granted if, in abandoning this world, they thought that in the other the same could not be found or had. But if they had this opinion, that they were as ample and common in the other (as they had indeed), then it is to be thought that death had rather afforded them some great content and joy than any sorrow and fear at all. For what certainty of grief may one give with testimony of a thing which he never proved ? None at all, truly. In Sir Tristram his arms wás his own death, and the death of his Lady also.

For if, in embracing her body so straitly and lovingly, it had grieved her at all, in opening his arms again, the pain (no doubt) had ceased. And yet for all this, let us admit and say, that it is by

323

great reason most fearful and grievous to taste of :
what grief can we say to be absolutely in a thing
that doth come to pass but only once, and which
doth occupy but a little space of time ? Certes, none.
Sir Tristram therefore and Isotta in one hour ended
their delights and dolours. The continued time of
my stretching grief and lasting sorrow hath without comparison greatly exceeded the brevity of
my enjoyed mirth and joys. But amongst the
number of these foresaid lovers my mind did think
of miserable Phedra, who, with her voluntary and
advised fury, was the occasion of his most cruel
death whom she loved more than herself. And I
know not truly what damage and great inconvenience did follow her of such a great fault, but I am
certain, if the like had ever happened to me, there
had been nothing but violent death that might
expiate the guilt thereof. But if she lived, she
buried him afterward in dark oblivion, as commonly
all things (as even now I said) are wont to be forgotten by death. And besides these sorrows which
Laodamia, Deiphyle, Argia, Evadne and Deianira,
and many others felt, followed hers in my scanning
thoughts : all which, either by violent death or by
necessary oblivion, received some comfort at last.

And who doubteth that burning fire, red-hot iron
and melted lead doth not grievously burn and scald
his finger who doth but suddenly dip it in and doth
quickly pull it out again ? Why, none I think.

And yet this is nothing to that extreme pain whose whole body is in either of these tormented and

Fire the longer it remaineth in anything the more it burneth plunged for a good space together : wherefore how many soever I have described above in woes, sorrows and pains, the same may be said to be but a momentary while in their superficial and counterfeit griefs, whereas I have really felt them, continually been in them, and am not yet free from them. Wherefore all these foresaid voes, in respect of mine, have been but amorous annoyances. But besides these miserable women, the no less sorrowful tears poured forth of those who with the unexpected brunts of cruel fortune have been confounded came before mine eyes.

And these are those of Jocasta, Hecuba, Sophonisba, Cornelia and Cleopatra. Oh, how much misery (considering well the miserable success of Jocasta's loves) do we see befallen unto her in all her lifetime, possible enough to have daunted and troubled the most stout and strongest mind. For she being very young was married to Layus, King of Thebes, who commanded that her first child should be thrown out to be devoured of wild Beasts, the miserable Father thinking by this to have prevented that which the heavens and his inevitable destinies with infallible course had prepared for him. Oh, what a grief (must I needs think) that this was to her soul, considering the degree of her that sent it, and that with her own hands she was constrained to deliver, and to send it to a cruel kind of death : and afterwards certified, by them that carried her unfortunate infant, of his mangled and devoured corpse, with what intolerable grief she believed that he was dead indeed. And to see her hapless Husband most miserably slain of him whom he had engendered in her own bowels, and that she herself afterwards, espoused to her unknown Son, had by him four children. And so how almost in one hour she saw herself mother and wife to this wicked Parricide : whom after she had perfectly known, when she saw him deprived first of his eyes, and last of his kingdom, and how his execrable fact and detested life was published to the whole world. In what miserable plight her soul was then, oppressed now with many years, which were rather desirous of repose than meet to be diminished with restless anguish, she may well think, and judge, who hath been tossed with the greatest or with like griefs of mind. But yet her dispiteous and cruel Fortune heaped upon her extreme misery greater and more bitter woes. For seeing the yearly intercourse and successive reign of her two Sons, with mutual composition divided between them, and afterwards the faithless brother pinned up in the City ; and seeing the greatest part of Greece under the regiment of seven kings : lastly, after many bloody battles, consuming fires, miserable spoil of Virgins, wives and goods : when she beheld one of

her prodigious Sons unnaturally to embrew his sword
in his own brother's blood, and when, her Husband's
Son driven out and exiled into another Kingdom,
she saw the ancient and old walls of her noble City,
builded first by the sweet harmony of Amphitryon
his Cythern, pitifully ruinated and beaten down:
and how her late, flourishing kingdom was miserably
divided and utterly dissolved: and having hanged
herself, left perhaps her Daughter in a most ignominious and shameless life. What could the
angry Gods, the world, froward Fortune, and the
malicious Hags of hell have conspired more against
her? Nothing, certes, in my opinion.

For let that ghastly place be surveyed, and every
torture therein duly considered, and yet I hardly
believe that there could not in the same such extreme
torments and pains be found. Wherefore I approve
and say that every and least particle of her anguish
and of her fault to be most grievous, and no less
impious. And as there is no woman that would
judge that my grief were not to be compared to
the greatness of this, so (truly) would I also say,
had not mine been amorous.

For who doubteth but that she knew (seeing the
abominable crimes of her wicked house, and of unnatural Husband (worthy of the condign anger of the
Gods), that duly scanned these adverse accidents)
these horrible accidents to be meritorious punishments for such heinous guilt and barbarous impiety?

None truly, that would judge her to be in her right wits. And if she were but a fool she felt her griefs the less, because (not fully knowing the weight of them) they could not so greatly grieve her. And whosoever knoweth herself worthy of such calamities and troubles that she endureth, with little grief, or none at all, she resolveth with herself more patiently to pass them away. But I never committed anything wherewith the Gods might justly be offended with me, having with continual offerings honoured them, and with holy victimy besought their divine graces, never despising their Godheads, as in times past the Thebans most wickedly did. But perhaps someone may well object and say : How canst thou affirm that thou hast not deserved punishment, or that thou hast not committed any fault ? Why, hast thou not violated the holy laws, and with an adulterous youth defiled thy marriage bed ? Yes, truly.

But if this matter be well propounded, as I have not myself only done this crime, so doth it not deserve (I think) so great punishment, and such grievous pains. Because she must think that I, being a tender young Gentlewoman, was not able to gainsay and resist that which the strongest men in the world, nay the Gods themselves, could not do.

And as I am not the first that hath committed such a friendly fault, so am I not alone, and shall not be the last, but having almost all Women in the world my companions in this excusable error, I am

not so greatly to be condemned for the same. And
those laws which I have infringed are of common
course wont favourably to pardon a multitude.

My fault, moreover, as it was most secret, so it
should not therefore be so severely and thoroughly
A secret punished. And besides all this, say that
fault is half the Gods were justly stirred up to wrath
pardoned against me, and did seek to give me sharp
corrections for my great offences, were it not a greater
part of justice, and more reason, to punish him
who was the occasion of my fall ? Now, whether
He that is burning and lawless love, or Panphilus his
the occasion rare beauty, brave personage and qualities
of sin ought
worthily to induced me to corrupt the sacred laws of
be punished wedlock, I know not, but knowing too too
well that both the one and the other were of most
great force to torment me most strangely. So that
this now did not happen by the sin committed, but
is rather a new grief and sequestered from the rest,
more cruelly cruciating the patient and sustainer of
it than any other.

The which, moreover, if the Gods for my committed offence had given me, they should do contrary to their right judgment and accustomed
manner, in that they should not with the sin recompense the punishment, which being compared to the
due pains of Jocasta, and to her deserved defaults,
and considering mine own errors, and the severe
punishment which I do suffer for the same, she must

needs be said to be but slightly punished, and myself with too rigorous chastisement, and unmeasurable pain, to be corrected. Nor let not any take hold of this, that she was bereaved of her Kingdom, deprived of her Sons, despoiled of her Husband and, last of all, of her own life, and I but only of my Lover. All which truly I confess.

But spiteful Fortune carried away with this Lover all my felicity, though that (which perhaps in other men's sight and judgment was accounted happiness) hath still remained with me, and which is clean contrary to my desires. Because my Husband, my parents, my riches, and all things else besides are a most grievous burden unto me, and nothing congruent with my wished content. Which things if she had taken from me, as she did my Lover, there had then remained a most open way for me to have fulfilled my desires, which undoubtedly I would have followed. By which if I could not have brought to pass my will, then were there a thousand kinds of deaths ready for me, to have rid me from all my woes and miseries. Wherefore I justly think that my pains are much more greater than any of the foresaid.

Methinks that next after these I see Hecuba coming to my mind, passing sorrowful in her counten-
Hecuba ance, who escaped from that general ruin, and surviving only to behold the doleful and destroyed Relics of so goodly a kingdom, the subversion of such an admirable City, the cruel

death of so Princely a Husband, of so many renowned Sons, and most fair daughters, to see the
destruction of so many magnanimous Nephews,
valiant Cousins and Allies, the rapine of so great
riches, the havoc of infinite treasure, the spoil of so
many Virgins, the ravishment of wives, and of all
sorts of Women, the extinction of such excellency,
the loss of so many Kings hewed and slain right
down, such bloody massacres and pitiful stratagems,
of the dismayed and betrayed Trojans, the impiety
perpetrated in the Temples—polluted, battered and
made plane with the ground—and the indignity and
irreverence done to their dishonoured and chased
Gods. And seeing herself to be old, and sorrowfully
recalling to her wounded mind what mighty Hector
was, what valiant Troilus, what doughty Deiphobus,
and what her youngest darling, Polydorus, and the
shining virtues of many noblemen more, and how
unfortunately she saw them all die ; remembering
also how the generous blood of her late mighty
and majestical Husband was cruelly shed in her
own lap before the holy Altars, and how she saw
fatal Troy, whilom reared up to the skies with
stately Towers, famous for magnificent buildings,
full of princely Palaces, and very populous with
noble and worthy Citizens, consumed with devouring
flames and wholly razed from the earth.

And besides all this, the pitiful sacrifice of her fair
Daughter Polyxena, offered up by unpitiful Pyrrhus,

to the shadow of Achilles. Oh, with what excessive grief and anguish of mind (must we needs think) that she beheld all these things. But short was the sorrow which her old and feeble mind, not able to endure the same, wandering out of her right course, made her mad, as her barking complaints amidst the fields and woods did plainly show. But I, with a more firm and perfect memory than is needful for such woes, to my great grief do continually remain in my sorrowful and sound wits, and do discern more and more the preposterous occasions of my present woes, and of my future sorrows. Because my manifold harms, enduring longer than hers, I think them (be they never so light) to be more grievous (as I have many times said) than the greatest and most sensible pains which is ended in a short time.

Sophonisba (equally participating the adversities in her Widowhood, and the joy of her marriage in one and selfsame moment almost of time),
Sophonisba jocund and sad, an honourable and glad spouse, and a poor prisoner, invested and despoiled of a Kingdom, and finally in these short alterations of tottering Fortune drinking her fatal poison (full of anguish and deadly grief), appeareth next unto my thoughts. Behold her sometimes a most high and famous Queen of the Numidians, afterwards the martial affairs of her Parents and friends having but an adverse and luckless issue, her Husband Siphax taken from her, and become prisoner to

AMOROUS FIAMMETTA

Masinissa King of Marsilia (warring under the Roman Ensigns) and herself in one hour deprived of her Kingdom, and prisoned also in the midst of her enemy's Camp, Masinissa afterwards making her his wife, and she restored to the same again.

Oh, with what despite, grief and bitter anguish of mind do I believe that she saw these things succeed abruptly one after another. Nor yet secure of her voluble and flattering Fortune, with how heavy a heart did she celebrate her new espousals, which griefs and extreme miseries, with a tragical end at last, and with a stout enterprise, she did fully finish. Because not one natural day after the nuptial rites being yet spent, and scarcely thinking with herself that she remained in the regiment and that she did bear the former sway of Sceptre, and warring thus within herself, and thinking of the new love of Masinissa, not framed well to her mind—the old love of Siphax being not yet extinct—with no trembling heart, but with a bold hand, received the mortiferous poison, which her new Husband sent her by her own Servant (the fearful messenger of her untimely death), and with certain despiteful and premised speeches, without any sign and token of fear in her resolute face, drunk of the same, immediately after yielding up her ghost.

Oh, how bitter may one imagine that her life was if she had had any longer time to meditate and think of her death that did follow. Who therefore is not to be placed but amongst those Women who have been but meanly and not much afflicted with *To think of* sorrow, considering that her speedy death *grief maketh* did prevent her beginning woes, whereas *it greater* mine have continued with me a long time together, and yet do accompany me against my will, and are sworn to remain still with me to make themselves more mighty thereby, and with their united forces to infest more their usurped habitation. After her, doleful Cornelia, oppressed with infinite sorrow, was objected to my musing *Cornelia* thoughts, whom smiling Fortune had exalted so high to make her the first wife of Crassus, and afterwards great Pompey his spouse, whose worthy valour had almost gotten him the chiefest principality in Rome, and attained to the sole government of all the Empire annexed unto it. Who, notwithstanding after that frowning Fortune changed her copy, in manner of a fugitive fled miserably out of Rome, and afterwards out of all Italy, herself also with her husband being fiercely pursued of conquering Cæsar. And leaving her in Lesbos, after many turmoils of inconstant fortune, overcoming his puissant competitor in Thessaly, by whose discomfiture and overthrow he recovered his force and might again, which not long since by his valiant enemy was greatly abated. And besides all this, with hope to reintegrate, and to renew his power in the conquered East, floating upon the

334

surging Seas, and arrived in the kingdoms of Egypt, offering himself voluntarily to the defence and trusty tuition of young King Ptolemy : being there cruelly done to death, she saw his embrued and headless trunk tossed and beaten up and down the raging waves. Which things if every one by itself, or altogether, be duly considered, we must needs say that without all compare they afflicted most grievously her dying soul.

But the sound and comfortable counsel of the sage Utica Cato, and the lost hope in these instabilities of Fortune to regain her Pompey again, in a little time mitigated, nay, rather annihilated her former sorrows, whereas I, still nourished with vain hope, not able by any counsel or comfort to drive away the same, but by the simple advice of my old Nurse (equally knowing of my sorrows from the beginning, in whose heart I knew goodwill more rife than wisdom ripe in her head, because believing oftentimes to remedy my griefs she hath redoubled them), do evermore remain and live consuming myself in bitter plaints and confounded in a thousand doubts and anxieties of mind. There are also many who (I think) do believe that Cleopatra, Queen *Cleopatra* of Egypt, did suffer intolerable grief, and that her pains did greatly exceed mine. Because first, seeing herself conjoined with her brother in the Kingdom, and living in all manner of pleasure and delights, and afterwards cast by him

335

into prison, was thought beyond all measure to be charged with insupportable dolour.

But the present hope of that which after happened made her to pass it over more lightly. For she, being delivered out of prison, became Cæsar his loving and beloved Lady. But afterwards forsaken of him, there are who think that for grief of these crossing cares her tender heartstrings did wellnigh break asunder, not regarding that there was a certain touch of unconstancy and breach of love, as well in her as in him, which at both their pleasures they did forsake, and take from one another, and bestow it elsewhere, as oftentimes she plainly showed how fitly she could do the same. But the Gods forbid that such consolation befall to my comfortless and afflicted soul. For he was never yet, or ever shall be, besides him to whom by many deserts I have avowed the whole term and travail of my life, that could affirm, or yet can say, that I was ever his, but in heart affianced only to Panphilus, and whose I will for ever remain.

Nor let him hope, whosoever he be, that any other love shall never be of such force as to drive his out of my faithful breast. Besides this, if she had been at Cæsar his departure left altogether comfortless by him, there would be some again who, ignorant of the truth, would believe that this was very grievous unto her: but yet it was not so. Because if she were on the one side aggrieved at his departure, the joy on the other, and the comfort, that she

received of her little Son Cæsarionem which she had
by him, and of her kingdom restored to her again,
countervailing her grief, nay, exceeding all her
former sorrows whatsoever, did yield her treble consolation. This joy hath force and strength enough
to overcome greater anguish and more extreme cares
of mind than those of them who love but a little,
and that but coldly too, as even now I said that
she did. But that which for the accomplishment
of her greatest grief was annexed to the rest was
that she was the wife of Mark Antony, whom she
had, with her libidinous enticements, stirred up to
civil, nay uncivil, wars against her own brother,
aspiring thereby and hoping (by the victory of them)
to have been crowned Empress of the Roman
monarchy. But double loss arising to her by this
in one hour, which was the death of her slain
husband and of her frustrate hope, of all other
women made her (as it is commonly thought) the
most unfortunate and most sorrowful Lady, and beyond all conceit to be confounded with the greatest
cares and griefs that might be. And considering
truly so high a mind and so proud a conceit, which
to be, first in imagination and afterwards indeed,
sole and sovereign Lady and Queen of the whole
circuit of the earth, by one infortunate battle to be
dashed and cast down (our sex also being naturally
given to aspire and domination), besides the foil of
the conquered, and the triumph of the victor, and

Y   337

besides this the loss also of so dear and brave a husband, it cannot be otherwise apprehended but that it was a wonderful corsive to her noble heart and an extreme torment of her dismayed soul.

But suddenly she found out a wholesome medicine, which did speedily help and heal this mortal malady, and that was a strange kind of death. Which, although for the time it was very cruel and sharp, was not for all that in execution any long time adoing; because in one little hour two venomous vipers may at the paps of a young and tender woman suck out both blood and life, as they did out of miserable Cleopatra's breast.

Oh, how many times would I have done the like, although for a lesser occasion according to the opinion of many, if I had been peremptorily forsaken, or if for fear also of ensuing infamy thereof I had not withdrawn myself.

With this and the aforesaid Ladies the excellency of Cyrus, killed of Tomyris and drowned in a bowl of his own blood, the fire and water of *Cyrus,* *Crœsus,* Crœsus, the rich kingdoms of the Persians, *Persians,* *Pyrrhus,* the magnificency of Pyrrhus, the power *Darius,* of Darius, the cruelty of Jugurtha, the *Jugurtha,* *Dionysius,* tyranny of Dionysius, the highness of Aga- *Agamem-* memnon, and the sudden changes of many *non* other more occurred to my thoughts. All which were stinged with these griefs, and spurned at the feet of scornful Fortune, as the foresaid women, or else, altogether comfortless, left to worse mishaps. Who also with sudden arguments of their better fare were aided, nor remaining any long time in them, did not feel the greatness and grief of them so entirely as I do. Whilst I went recount-

Company, as it is abovesaid, doth lessen the grief. Theistes, Tereus

ing the ancient sorrows in this sort, as you have heard, and seeking in my mind to find out some tears and sorrows in most respects like unto mine own, because, having company, I might not so greatly lament, and might suffer my grief with more patience, those of Theistes and of Tereus, both which were the miserable Sepultures of their own Sons, were objected to my memory. And I marvel what unnatural and forced patience (fearing their inward bitings) and what pitiless restraint did moderate those savage Sires from launching their sides, and with slicing knives to make way for their Sons struggling in their paternal bowels, and striving to come forth, abominating that wretched place into which they were so ravenously gulfed. But these also burst out, and (with that they could) choked at once their hatred and grief together, and so took in a manner a certain comfort in their harms, perceiving that without fault they were accounted miserable men but of their people—that which happened not to me.

For I have compassion borne me of that which did never grieve me, and dare not discover that which doth most of all afflict me, which thing if I

339

durst do, I doubt not; but as others in my miserable case have found out some remedy for their pains, *Lycurgus* so might I (perhaps) find out some ease and help as well as they. The pitiful tears of Lycurgus, and of his house (justly poured forth for dead Archemorus killed of the Serpent), come also sometimes to my mind, and accompanied with *Atalanta* the continual sighs of sorrowful Atalanta, mother of Parthenopæus, killed in the Theban Camps, which came so properly and so nearly to me with their effects that I could scarce conceive any greater than them in my mind, if I had not proved them myself, I say, that they were full of such great sorrow that they could not be more.

But every one of them are with so high glory eternished that they might be esteemed in a manner merry accidents than mournful stratagems—the sorrowful tears (of Lycurgus, I mean), with the mortal exequies, honoured of the seven kings, and infinite sports and spectacles made by them in solemnization of that glorious funeral, and those of Atalanta made notable and beautified also with the laudable life and victorious death of her young Son.

But I have not anything, nor any such cause, to make my tears scarce well employed, much less excellent, and myself content; because if it were so, whereas I now esteem myself more doleful and unfortunate than any other, perhaps I should be persuaded to aver the contrary. The long travels of

Ulysses, his mortal and imminent perils, his wandering and weary peregrinations, and all his deeds

Ulysses whatsoever, are next of all showed unto me, who never tasted them but seasoned with most bitter and extreme anguish of mind, and redoubled many times in my imaginations, they make me think mine to be far greater and much more grievous, and harken why. Because first, and principally, he was a man, and therefore of nature more strong and better able to endure them than I, being a tender and young woman; and he, being moreover continually armed with a stout, courageous and fierce mind, and beaten to daily dangers as one ripened amongst them when he travailed and turmoiled, did seem to have but his ordinary repose, nay, his greatest ease and pleasure in them.

But I being continually in my Chamber, and tenderly served with dainty and delicate things, passing my times away in pleasures, and daily accustomed to dalliances of wanton love, every little pain and fear thereof is most grievous unto me.

He driven and pricked on by Neptune, and transported into divers parts of the world, and of Æolus likewise received his troubles.

But with careful love I am infected, and with such a lord infested, that troubled and conquered them, that molested and tossed Ulysses. And if dangerous casualties and daily fears did seem to threaten him, of his proper accord he wandered

continually in seeking of them out. And who can
with just cause complain or be aggrieved for finding
None can of that which he doth so earnestly seek
be sorrowful for ? But I (silly wretch) would fain live
for finding
that they in quiet if I could, and would willingly fly
seek from woes and griefs, if that so rigorously
they did not rush upon me, and if I were not myself
so forcibly driven upon them.

Besides this, he was not afraid of death, and
therefore without fear did commit himself to her
force and might. But I live in continual dread of it,
though, compelled by extreme sorrow, I have some-
time (not without fear of greater grief) run willingly
unto it. He also by his long travels and jeopardies
of Fortune did hope to get eternal glory and never-
dying fame. But I am afraid of my escandalized
name, and infamous memory hereafter, if it should
come to pass that these secret loves should at any
time come to light.

So that now his pains are not greater and more
than mine, but are rather in number and quality far
less than mine, and by so much the more as they
are fabulated to be greater than ever they were indeed. But mine (alas) are, too true, so many and
more greater than I am able myself to recount.
But after all these, I see (methinks) the sorrows,
sobs and heavy sighs, the infinite woes and piteous
plaints, that Hipsiphile, Medea and Œnone had,
and the pitiful tears of Ariadne, which were more

copious than all the rest : all which I judge most like unto mine. Because every one of these (like myself), deceived of their lovers, watered the ground with tears, cleaved the heavens with continual sighs, and sustained without any fruit, or hope of future content, most bitter torments of mind. And admit (as it is granted) that these dolours were cast upon them by their ungrateful lovers, and by their injurious and undeserved ingratitude, yet with just revenge of their wrongs done unto them they saw the end of their tears : which comforts (although I wish it not) my sorrows also have not. Hipsiphile, *Hipsiphile* admit that she had greatly honoured Jason, and had by due deserts obliged him unto her, perceiving him to be taken away of Medea, had with as great reason as myself just occasion of complaint and sorrow.

But such was the providence of the Gods that, with righteous eyes beholding everything (but only my harms), they restored to her a great portion of her desired toy, because she saw Medea, who had taken away Jason from her (Jason forsaking Medea for the love of Creusa), quite dispossessed of her once enjoyed prey. Certes, I do not say that my grief should finish if I should see the same befall to her who hath deceived me of my Panphilus, unless I were that she that should allure him from her again, but will frankly confess that a great part of my sorrow would for a time cease.

Medea did also rejoice for revenge that she had (although she was no less cruel towards herself than *Medea* malicious against her ungrateful lover) in killing their common children in his own presence, and consuming the royal palaces of King Creon and the new Lady with merciless *Œnone* flames. Œnone, also sorrowing a long time, in fine knew that her disloyal lover suffered due punishment for breaking and corrupting the sacred laws of love, and saw his country, for the wicked rape and exchange of herself for his new adulteress, miserably wasted, and his own City, some-times the seat of demi-Gods and semi-Goddesses, but now an uncouth habitacle and a poor village of Shepherd swains, overthrown and razed clean from the ground. But truly I love my griefs a great deal more than I would either with tongue or heart wish so sharp a revenge of my wrongful Panphilus.

Ariadne Ariadne also, being Bacchus his wife, saw from heaven furious Phedra, who was the cause that Theseus, abandoning her, and leaving her desolate in the Island (being newly enamoured of Phedra) miserably bewitched with the incestuous love of Hippolitus her husband his son. So that, every-thing duly scanned, I find myself amongst the number of miserable and disastrous women to be tormented with more woes, griefs and with greater sorrow than any of the rest, and to have the sole principality and only name of all other distressed women whatsoever.

AMOROUS FIAMMETTA

And I can do no more. But if, perhaps (good Ladies), you accompt my framed arguments but frivolous assertions, and repute all these former examples but weak proofs, as forged in the simple conceit of an appassionated woman; and if you imagine them (because proceeding from a blind mind) to be but blind also, and of no conclusion, esteeming the tears, sighs and sorrows of others more extreme than mine, and thinking them to be more unfortunate than myself, let this only and last proposition therefore supply the defect (if any there be) of all the rest before. If he that beareth envy is more miserable and more wretched than he to whom he doth bear it, then of all the forenamed persons I am the most miserable and unhappy woman. Because I do greatly emulate and not a little envy their ordinary accidents, accounting them not so grievous nor so full of such great misery as mine are.

Behold, therefore (gentle Ladies), how by the old deceits of injurious Fortune I breathe a most wretched woman. And besides this, she hath done by me no otherwise than a candle burned to the snuff do cast up flashes of greater light, since that (in appearance only), making truce with my griefs and giving some pause to my daily woes and a little ease to my tormented mind, but by her cruel despite again returning afterwards to my former tears and to my sorrowful task, of all the wretched women

345

that live, she hath made me the most miserable, and the only receptacle of all despair and dole. And because, all other comparisons laid aside, with only one I may endeavour to make you more assured of my new evils, I affirm (gentle Ladies) and tell you with that gravity, that other miserable women my compeers may affirm greater, that my pains are at this present so much the more greater than they were before their vain and frustrate joy, by how *The second* much the second fevers assailing the sick *fevers hurt* patients with equal cold and heat are wont *more than* *the first* to annoy them (recovered once and now fallen down again) more than the first. And because I may rather heap pity in your minds with the imagination of the rest of my pains than fill your dainty ears full of new words tendering your wearied spirits with pity that I have of your patience, minding now not to be more tedious unto you, and not to draw forth your tears any further in length—if there be any of you at the least that in reading of it have (perhaps) shed or yet do pour forth any— and not to spend the time any longer in words, which calleth me back to tears, I am determined to hold my peace, making it manifest unto you that there is no more comparison of my shadowed discourse to those substantial dolours, which I feel indeed, than there is of painted fire, to that which doth burn indeed : the which I pray all the Gods that, either by your meritorious prayers or else by my earnest and effectual orisons, they would with some liquor of comfort extinguish, or with speedy death quite abolish ; or else with the joyful return of my Panphilus assuage and moderate the same.

FIAMMETTA SPEAKETH TO HER BOOK

AND thou, my little Book, drawn out (as it were) from the sepulture of thy Lady, art now (as it hath pleased me) come to an end, with a most careful, troublesome and tired foot, even such as thou art now, written by mine own hands, and with my falling tears in most places defaced, before the enamoured Ladies and wanton Gentlewomen, present and offer thyself. And if (pity being thy guide, as I do most assuredly hope it will be) they shall willingly look on thee ; and if Love hath not changed his Laws since I became a miserable Lover, let it be no shame for thee in so vile a habit (as I send thee) to go to every Lady, and Gentlewoman, of what honour and degree soever she be, so that they deign to give thee friendly entertainment. Thou needest not any other habit, since I thought this most fitting thy effects : considering that thou must be content to figurate my life, myself and my times (which being most unfortunate) make thee apparelled with misery as me appalled with mishap. Wherefore take thou no care for that which other books (whose subjects are contrary to thine) are wont to have, which are, sumptuous coverings garnished with curious and

costly works, depainted and beautified with sundry
fair colours, polished with fine shavings, laid on with
embroidered knots of Gold and silver, or else bearing high styles and glorious titles. These (I say) are
not beseeming the sad and heavy plaints which thou
dost carry in thy forehead. Leave these aside (my
woeful Book), and the great margins also, and ruled
spaces, the brave kinds of coloured inks, and the
great characters, placed in the beginning of happy
Books, which only sing of mirth, glory, joy and
bliss. It doth become thee best, with torn and
ruffled leaves, and tached full of blots and blurs,
to go thither; and to those to whom I send thee,
with ringing my distressed mishaps into the ears
of them that shall read thee, to awake and stir up
their hearts to holy pity and due compassion of
them. Of which piety, if (by thy suggestions) they
express and show forth any outward signs in their
fair and beautiful visages, then be not thou slack
to render them (as well as thou canst) immediate
and immortal thanks for their pitiful duties towards
thee. Why, thou and I are not reduced to such a
miserable condition, nor are not so heavily disgraced
of cruel Fortune, that these requitals should seem so
great but that we may, and can, well afford them.
Nor can she take this privilege from any wretched
Woman—that is, to set herself forth as a president
of mishap, and to give approved examples of misery
to those which live in happiness, because they may,

in their golden felicities and in their prosperities, use
a moderate mean, and so temperate their pleasures
It availeth that they fall not into that confused
much to labyrinth of love and into that miserable
take heed estate of life, as I have done. Which kind
by others' of life, both led and loathed of me, so
examples plainly (as I know thou canst well do) and so
particularly lay open before them that (if in their
wily loves they are but anything wary and but
meanly wise), by fear of our sustained harms, they
may be well advised, and forewarned in obviating
the secret and subtle deceits of young Men. Go,
therefore. But whether a hasty or slow pace is
fittest for thee I know not, nor what piece of thee
shall be first sought out, nor how nor of whom thou
shalt be received. But as Fortune doth guide thee,
so go thou on. Thy course cannot be much inordinate. Thy cloudy times do hide thy shining star,
which, if it did yet appear, furious Fortune hath so
eclipsed that she hath left no hope of thy better hap,
nor argument of thy health. And therefore thrown
abroad here and there (as a Ship without helm and
sails tossed up and down the surging waves), carelessly abandon thyself, and as the places require, use
likewise divers and congruent counsels. And if perhaps thou dost come to the hands of some one woman
who doth with so great content and happiness enjoy her loves, as we are most unfortunately molested
with ours, that will laugh and flout at mine, and

351

reprehend them (perhaps) and condemn them for foolish and yeld toys, with an humble and patient mind bear thou nevertheless their scorns, and digest their taunts which are but the least part of our great griefs, and which seem nothing at all to those that we have already passed. And put her in mind that Fortune is evermore unconstant and wavering; by which Caveat she may know that by the ordinary course of her mutability she may make us glad again, and may bring her to that kind of painful life as she hath now driven us unto, and that then, with like mocks and flouts, we will requite and pay hers home again. But if thou shalt find anyone that in reading of thee cannot keep the tears from her eyes, but that (condolent and pitiful of our cares and pains) doth with the same multiply thy blots, receive and gather them, as most precious and holy drops in thy bosom, and mingle them with mine; and then showing thyself more pitiful and afflicted, request her humbly that she would pray for me to him who doth with golden feathers in a moment visit all the world, so that, entreated by a more religious mouth, and by more meritorious prayers than mine, and therefore more pliable to the petitions of others than to my plaints, he may lighten my heavy sorrows, and take away my oppressing anguish of mind. And whosoever she be, even with the form of words which to miserable wretches is granted most exaudible, I pray, and

352

do with those prayers most heartily obtest, which
are in the ears of the hearers of them most effectual,
that she may never taste of such bitter miseries,
and that the placable Gods may be ever favourable
unto her, and that she may happily and perpetually
enjoy her love according to her own desires. But
if among the amorous company of wanton young
Gentlewomen posting thee from one hand to another thou dost (by chance) come to the fingering
of mine enemy, and to the wrongful usurpress of
my felicity, fly incontinently from thence as from
an infectious and naughty place, and discover not
one of thy leaves, lines or letters to her robbing
and bewitching eyes, lest that, understanding the
second time of our woes and pains, she might have
more occasion to boast and brag again that she
hath wounded and confounded me. But yet if it
chance that by force she keep thee, and (maugre
thy teeth) will see and read thee, then offer thyself in such sort to her that she may not laugh,
but lament in reading of my hard mishaps, and,
pricked with the sting of her guilty conscience,
she may be in mind persuaded to restore to me
again my unjustly detained Lover. Oh, what happy
pity and holy piety should this be, and then how
would the sour fruit of this harsh pain seem sweet
to my distempered taste. Shun the eyes of men,
of whom, if thou canst not choose but be seen,
speak unto them, saying: "O ungrateful generation,

deriders and deceivers of simple women, it is not meet for you (considering your demerits) to look into holy things, and fraught full of such pity as this is, and (knowing your remorse of pity to be so small, as your impiety and cruelty is great) unfit to meddle with distressed and pitiful things." But if to him who is the origin of all our harms thou dost chance to come, with this exclamation afar off greet him from me, saying :

"O thou which art more rigorous and harder than any Oak, fly from hence, and do not violate me with thy unworthy and polluted hands. Thy corrupted faith is an occasion of all this which I bring with me. But yet if with a courteous, gentle and indifferent mind thou wilt read me, recognizing thy former faults and present injuries unjustly done against her whose messenger of sorrow I am, and that returning to her again thou desiredst to be pardoned of her, then boldly see, touch and spare not to read me. But if thou wilt not perform this last requisite duty, it is not then so decent and honest a thing for thee to see the pitiful tears which thou hast unpitifully caused; and then would it be again but small for thy credit to increase them more and more if (in reading me) thou dost (as I think thou canst not) persist in thy first and froward will."

And if perhaps any curious and dainty Gentlewoman doth dislike of thy words so rudely composed and so disorderly couched together, tell her that that which is unpolished and unpleasant for her fine conceit she may (if she please) overslip and let pass, because brave and filed speeches require clear minds and free from all hurtful passions, and are best beseeming merry and calm times. And therefore thou shalt say unto her, that she may a great deal sooner fall in admiration, how my troubled wit, my tired pen, and pains did last out but for that little which thou dost tell out of order, considering that fervent love on the one side, and burning jealousy on the other, with divers conflicts, held my sorrowful soul in continual battles, thy obscure and cloudy times feeding the one, and contrary Fortune favouring the other. Thou mayest go safely away (as I believe) and securely escape from all awaits laid to entrap thee, and needest not care for the cavils of captious heads, because thou mayest be assured that Envy, with her venomous teeth or infectious tongue, shall neither bite nor sting thee.

But if perchance thou shalt find any (which I think thou never canst) that, being more miserable than thyself, might emulate thee (as one more happy and not so wretched as herself), then patiently suffer thyself to be bitten. But I do not well know what part of thee shall receive any new offence, since that with the cruel blows of angry Fortune I see thee torn and broken in every place. Thou canst not be injured now any more by her than already thou art, nor

FIAMMETTA SPEAKETH

from any high and happy seat is she able to make thee fall down to a more vile and base place, for so low as none may be lower is that where now thou dost remain. And admit that she hath not thought it meet to conjoin us with the superficial part of the earth, and doth still seek and suppeditate stranger occasions to inter us under it, we are so beaten, and so inured to adversities, that with those shoulders with which we have sustained and do yet bear the greatest and most heavy burdens of woes and sorrow, we shall with less pain and not with so great grief bear lighter and endure lesser than those. And therefore let her assail us when and where she will. Live, therefore. For nothing may deprive thee of this. And remain an eternal example and perpetual president of bitter anguish and grief of thy woeful Mistress to those who live in happy mirth and heavy misery.

Bueno fin haze, el qual bien amando muera

www.ingramcontent.com/pod-product-compliance
Lightning Source LLC
Chambersburg PA
CBHW032143010726
47494CB00002B/340